Cambridge Studies in Biological and Evolutionary Anthropology

Consulting editors

C. G. Nicholas Mascie-Taylor, *University of Cambridge*

Robert A. Foley, *University of Cambridge*

Series editors

Agustín Fuentes, *University of Notre Dame*

Nina G. Jablonski, *Pennsylvania State University*

Clark Spencer Larsen, *The Ohio State University*

Michael P. Muehlenbein, *The University of Texas at San Antonio*

Dennis H. O'Rourke, *The University of Utah*

Karen B. Strier, *University of Wisconsin*

David P. Watts, *Yale University*

Evaluating Evidence in Biological Anthropology

The Strange and the Familiar

Edited by

CATHY WILLERMET
Central Michigan University

SANG-HEE LEE
University of California at Riverside

CAMBRIDGE
UNIVERSITY PRESS

CAMBRIDGE
UNIVERSITY PRESS

University Printing House, Cambridge CB2 8BS, United Kingdom

One Liberty Plaza, 20th Floor, New York, NY 10006, USA

477 Williamstown Road, Port Melbourne, VIC 3207, Australia

314–321, 3rd Floor, Plot 3, Splendor Forum, Jasola District Centre, New Delhi – 110025, India

79 Anson Road, #06–04/06, Singapore 079906

Cambridge University Press is part of the University of Cambridge.

It furthers the University's mission by disseminating knowledge in the pursuit of education, learning, and research at the highest international levels of excellence.

www.cambridge.org
Information on this title: www.cambridge.org/9781108476843
DOI: 10.1017/9781108569125

First published 2020

Printed in the United Kingdom by TJ International Ltd, Padstow Cornwall

A catalogue record for this publication is available from the British Library.

ISBN 978-1-108-47684-3 Hardback

Contents

Contributors

Melanie M. Beasley
Department of Anthropology, Purdue University, West Lafayette, IN, USA

Jennifer F. Byrnes
Department of Anthropology, University of Nevada, Las Vegas, Las Vegas, NV, USA

John Daniels
Department of Statistics, Actuarial and Data Sciences, Central Michigan University, Mount Pleasant, MI, USA

Sharon N. DeWitte
Department of Anthropology, University of South Carolina, Columbia, SC, USA

Heather J. H. Edgar
Department of Anthropology, University of New Mexico, Albuquerque, NM, USA

Michelle M. Glantz
Department of Anthropology, Colorado State University, Fort Collins, CO, USA

Dänae G. Khorasani
Department of Anthropology, University of California at Riverside, Riverside, CA, USA

Marc Kissel
Department of Anthropology, Appalachian State University, Boone, NC, USA

Sang-Hee Lee
Department of Anthropology, University of California at Riverside, Riverside, CA, USA

Julie J. Lesnik
Department of Anthropology, Wayne State University, Detroit, MI, USA

Joseph McKean
Department of Statistics, Western Michigan University, Kalamazoo, MI, USA

Robin G. Nelson
Department of Anthropology, Santa Clara University, Santa Clara, CA, USA

Margaret J. Schoeninger
Department of Anthropology, University of California San Diego, San Diego, CA, USA

Ann L. W. Stodder
Office of Archaeological Studies, Center for New Mexico Archaeology, Museum of New Mexico, Santa Fe, NM, USA
Department of Anthropology, University of New Mexico, Albuquerque, NM, USA

Adam P. Van Arsdale
Department of Anthropology, Wellesley College, Wellesley, MA, USA

Cathy Willermet
Department of Sociology, Anthropology, and Social Work, Central Michigan University, Mount Pleasant, MI, USA
Maxwell Museum of Anthropology, University of New Mexico, Albuquerque, NM, USA

Introduction

(Re)Discovery of the Strange and the Familiar: Theory and Methods for a Twenty-First-Century Biological Anthropology

Sang-Hee Lee and Cathy Willermet

Disciplines have intellectual histories that must be worked through, and each has its own responsibility to assess its contributions to the modernist project.

(Fowles, in Alberti et al. 2011:898)

Why a Critical Reflection on Biological Anthropology?

In this unfortunate era of anti-intellectualism and fake news, it is essential that biological anthropologists engage with each other, the academy, the media, and the public about the nature of humans, how we got here, and how (and why) we vary. One of the strengths of anthropology is that we can be self-reflective. We can re-examine our questions, our theory, our methods, our data, and deal skeptically with all of them. What is a species? How do we identify groups? How do we recognize agency, or identity, or frailty, in the past? The colonial history of western science affects our interpretation of evidence (Roy 2018); now formerly colonized peoples have opportunities to produce knowledge of their own histories, so they can shift the narrative, making what was once a familiar story, strange (Rottenburg 2009; Véran 2012).

"Making the familiar strange" is a practice commonly found in ethnography and cultural anthropology (Rosaldo 1993; Thomson 2013; Véran 2012). It is seen as critical to denaturalize one's beliefs in order to open oneself to new beliefs and analytical frames (Alberti et al. 2011). Although cultural anthropologists often perform the defamiliarizing activity reflexively in their work, we biological anthropologists often consider the scientific approach as antithetical to reflexive, thick descriptive research. We are, however, not immune from the trap of reconstructing past and current peoples as timeless and stable (Rosaldo 1993), or considering our evidence as objective when it is not. Thomson (2013) writes:

I'm of the view that the notion of making the familiar strange is actually first of all about the researcher's state of being. It's about how we actually ARE as researchers in the world. (In other words it's as much ontological as it is epistemological and methodological.) It's about not taking anything for granted, being prepared to question everything, and certainly putting the things we think we know out for interrogation. But then it's about that shift, that disruption, being made apparent, being represented, so that the reader understands things anew as well.

In the philosophy of science, evidence (whether an object, experience, mental state, or physiological event) must inform knowledge. We do have evidence biases in biological anthropology, some of our own making, some not. The position of evidence in biological anthropology varies, from the objective absolute position with unassailable power ("data speak for themselves"), through the position of conceding the relative, qualitative value ("we need better, more data"), to the critical approach ("data are inherently biased"). Véran (2012:S252) argues "the power of biological anthropology relies on its capacity to provide hard evidence in key contemporary political issues such as origins, ancestry, anteriority, restitution claims, objective biological differentiations, or the impact of racism on human growth. This power is all the stronger in that it is reversible." The sense of objectivity of this evidence can work as much for, say, colonial groups as for the colonized – new discoveries can legitimize a native myth or challenge the African claim to the homeland of humanity.

Background on this Volume

Both of us have a long history of interest in exploring the nature of evidence, epistemology, and methodological approaches. Sang-Hee Lee questioned the parametric assumptions in statistical methods and explored alternative approaches including bootstrapping (Lee 2001; Lee and Wolpoff 2003), now a widely used approach. With Rachel Caspari, she redefined longevity, moving away from age-at-death estimations, which cannot be done accurately for older individuals (Caspari and Lee 2004, 2006). In an extensive literature review, Cathy Willermet (1993) documented that only 11 percent of the reported data used by modern human origins researchers was shared in tests of replacement or continuity models (Willermet and Clark 1995). She also questioned the boundaries of the sacred species concept, suggesting that species be better modeled using a fuzzy set approach (Willermet 2012; Willermet and Hill 1997).

So when we saw that the 2015 theme for the American Anthropological Association (AAA) meetings was "Familiar/Strange," we proposed a session that focused on examining our field, entitled "Scientific Approaches to Biological Anthropology: The Strange and Familiar." We undertook the process of "defamiliarization" to apply it to our own practice (noting that to describe our scholarly activity as "practice" already can be contentious) in biological anthropology. Besides ourselves, our presenters were Sharon DeWitte, Michelle Glantz, Robin Nelson, and Adam Van Arsdale. Rachel Caspari served as discussant for the papers.

In this session, we took a critical approach to models and methods that we practitioners take for granted as "familiar" and made them "strange." We asked our speakers to reflect on these three questions to address in their papers: What happened as a result of making the familiar strange? What new insights resulted? How did this change the process and practice of your research? (Adapted from Thomson 2013.) Papers in this session covered topics such as dealing with the inherent fuzziness of past human social behavior through biological distance modeling; using established methods, such as "body counts," in human biology research; the longstanding Osteological Paradox – acute deaths by disease leave no skeletal mark, yet lingering debilitation may, through frailty, an unfamiliar approach; how the familiar thinking on markers (cultural or anatomical) and chronology (Upper or late Paleolithic) bias our views; the balance between the incorporation of statistically rigorous methodologies in paleoanthropology and the limits imposed by a fragmentary and limited fossil record; the different intellectual traditions and center and edge modeling in the Central Asia late Pleistocene. Both ethnocentric views and unquestioned assumptions of research traditions can affect paleoanthropological model formation, and shape expectations of what we will (or should) find in the fossil record.

As it happened, the 2016 AAA theme was "Evidence, Accident, Discovery," which fit nicely as a continuation of the discussion we had started in the previous year. We proposed a second set of papers in a session entitled "(Re)Discovery of Evidence in Biological Anthropology: A Critical View." In this session, we explored what constitutes "evidence" in biological anthropology. What does constitute "evidence" in biological anthropology? Is it a physical object that can be placed in a bag and sent to the lab? Is it a part of a logical argument? In epistemology, evidence is required for factual, justified belief. Our session explored discovery, and sometimes rediscovery, of evidence and interpretations in biological anthropology. Our participants (Melanie Beasley, Virginia Estabrook, Julie Lesnik, Katherine C. MacKinnon, Ann Stodder, and Caroline VanSickle) took a critical look at the nature of our evidence, and how it is "discovered," collected, and interpreted. Ann Kakaliouras served as our discussant. Here we asked these questions: How do we reconstruct diet in the past, when large sections of the diet might be invisible in the archaeological record? What new evidence and insights can we obtain from "rediscovering" familiar nonhuman primate species? How can we integrate socially and politically contextualized interpretations of health, the bioarchaeology of care, and structural violence in the past? How can we integrate faunal evidence from paleoenvironments to reconstruct seasonality, and its impact on fossil hominins? How does a discovery of a new hominin species lead to a rediscovery of the lumper/splitter debate? How does a pelvis lead us to rediscover sex and gender?

Contributions in this Volume

The papers presented in the two sessions form the core of this volume, organized into two parts. Part I ("The Strange and the Familiar: New Landscapes and Theoretical Approaches") groups papers that critically evaluate some of our theoretical and methodological approaches, women in human evolution, the role of Central Asia in modern human origins models, the (mis)education of the public by noncritical dissemination of evolutionary studies, the concepts of insects as (not) the food of choice, and the reification of body counts.

In Chapter 1, Khorasani and Lee evaluate the incorporation (or lack of incorporation) of feminist perspectives in biological anthropology. Beginning with the presumption of a natural sexual division of labor by Darwin, they trace over time the pendulum of gender bias in scientific hypotheses about human origins. In a survey of public domain images of prehistoric humans, they document gender bias in the presentation of male and female tasks that reflect mid-twentieth-century western ideas about gender roles.

In Chapter 2, Glantz examines how the Central Asian Paleolithic record is characterized as secondary to Europe, Africa, or the Middle East. Glantz argues that the Out of Africa model of modern human origins acts as a transhistorical metanarrative that marginalizes the evidence from many regions. The evidence from Central Asian sites indicates highly locally variable micro-niches whose utilization depended upon population pressure, niche productivity, climatic and geographic constraints, and decisions by individual actors. She argues that treating Central Asia as a marginal periphery mischaracterizes its value as a refugia. Neighboring regions would also influence hominin groups, and modeling the interactions between these would help us better understand the interrelationships between Neandertals, Denisovans, and anatomically modern humans.

In Chapter 3, Kissel evaluates how scholars, public intellectuals, and popular authors currently frame narratives about human origins within the context of evolution. Public misunderstandings about the nature of genetic ancestry tests, for example, illustrate how the human ancestry narrative is highly personal and political. He critically assesses so-called anthropological hypotheses in the popular media about the nature of ancestry, violence, and progress. Kissel urges biological anthropologists to prioritize activities that connect students and the public to new narratives that infuse anthropological data with just and accurate representations of human nature.

In Chapter 4, Lesnik explores why westerners do not generally eat insects, which are a predictable and valuable source of food in many parts of the world. She expands on her research on the strong link between latitude and insect consumption by incorporating western cultural effects such as colonialism. The centuries-old western bias of insect consumption as bestial, primitive, and unsavory underlies more recent anthropological interpretations of insects as fallback foods, which nutritionally they are not. Her study of global data regarding insect consumption indicates that the strongest predictor of insect consumption is latitude – tropical areas have an abundance of species, increased numbers of insects, and increased consumption. European colonial intrusions into these areas brought colonizers in contact with insect-consuming indigenous populations, reinforcing the western bias against insect eating. Decolonizing this bias, Lesnik says, will increase inclusivity for indigenous peoples.

In Chapter 5, Nelson argues that the scientific racism infused throughout our discipline's origins biased the field toward more quantitative research. She traces this bias through biological anthropology's continued emphasis on measuring bodies. Nelson advocates for a mixed-method approach, a more balanced approach to human biological research that integrates quantitative research with, rather than at the expense of, ethnography and long-term qualitative research that provide both vital contextual information and a postcolonial research participation of the study subjects.

Part II of this volume ("[Re]Discovery of Evidence: New Thinking About Data, Methods, and Fields") groups chapters that explore the new ways to think about concepts of disability, frailty, and health, nonmetric data, bias toward complete specimens, and reconstruction of *Australopithecus anamensis* paleoenvironments. In Chapter 6, Stodder and Byrnes discuss ways paleopathology and bioarchaeology are reintegrating. In the past, as bioarchaeology has trended away from studies of individuals toward population studies, descriptions of pathological lesions indicative of chronic conditions were not included in many studies. Stodder and Byrnes track the increasing popularity of several approaches that link paleopathology to biocultural adaptations applied in bioarchaeology: the evolving stress model, which looks at the effects of cultural stress factors like structural violence on the skeleton; the life course approach, which links individual frailty to population health measures; and osteobiography, which studies an individual's remains in great detail to tell a phenomenological story. Finally, they call for more focused research on disability and care as cultural factors influencing health and stress in past populations.

In Chapter 7, DeWitte revisits the familiar bioarchaeological approach of viewing skeletal stress markers as evidence of frailty and poor health. She engages in a deeper, more fine-grained analysis of skeletal lesion patterning to uncover the relationship between higher socioeconomic status and stress as presented by healed lesions. This test of the Osteological Paradox reflects the increased survivability of higher-status individuals despite this group's higher proportion of lesions overall.

In Chapter 8, Willermet, Daniels, Edgar, and McKean explore a new statistical technique to analyze ordinal nonmetric data. Dental morphological trait data are recorded as degrees of expression of a particular genetic trait. Generally, these categorical data are dichotomized to create a frequency of presence, which is then used in biological distance statistical techniques. However, dichotomization causes loss of important measures of trait expression diversity. They propose a new technique, rank estimator of grade differences (RED), that does not require dichotomizing. They perform two tests on simulated and orthodontic data to test the RED method against mean measure of divergence (MMD) and pseudo-Mahananobis D^2 (pD^2). The RED technique performs as well or better; they discuss the advantages and limits of this new technique and encourage its addition to our statistical toolkits.

Van Arsdale examines the paleoanthropological application of the concept of analytical "rigor" in Chapter 9. If a "rigorous" test means restricting our analysis to larger and more complete samples, this could bias our study samples. Van Arsdale categorized 102 hominin fossils by degree of presentation and counted the frequency with which each was mentioned in published journals over a 28-year period, documenting a significant bias in the reliance on well-preserved fossils. This is a troubling result, as these fossils are not evenly distributed across time and space. He considers what effect this can have on our understanding about the past.

Beasley and Schoeninger, in Chapter 10, examine the link between climate, the environment, and hominin adaptations. Climate evidence is often not sufficiently localized to provide the evidence needed to link specific environmental reconstructions to the period when hominins shifted toward bipedalism. *Australopithecus anamensis* habitat and diet has been reconstructed using $\delta^{13}C$ to be a mixed mosaic habitat, but less certain is whether they utilized a particular niche within that habitat (dense woodland, open savanna, or fringe ecotone). Studies on chimpanzees, who also live in a mixed mosaic habitat, indicate $\delta^{13}C$ ratios are inaccurate predictors of niche utilizations when individuals are living in low-rainfall regions. Beasley and Schoeninger use $\delta^{13}C$ ratios from chimpanzees to compare their relationship to rainfall data. Results highlight the importance of relying on multiple types of data to reconstruct paleoenvironments and illuminates the paleoenvironments likely to be utilized by *Australopithecus anamensis*.

The contributions in this volume interweave different areas of growth in the field. Through this process of self-reflection, we point to where we see the future of biological anthropology is heading. This future, we believe, includes robust public advocacy for social justice.

Acknowledgments

We would like to thank the Executive Committee of the American Anthropological Association, who in 2015 and 2016 sponsored the sessions from which this volume derives. We would also like to thank those contributors to the original AAA sessions who, due to various conflicts, were unable to contribute to this volume: Virginia Estabrook, Ann Kakaliouras, Katherine C. MacKinnon, Rachel Caspari, and Caroline VanSickle. Many additional people helped to shape the ideas, including Agustín Fuentes and Milford Wolpoff. Dominic Lewis, Senior Commissioning Editor for Cambridge, and Editorial Assistants Aleksandra Serocka and Maeve Sinnott were helpful in all aspects of production. Last but not least, we are grateful to the reviewers who generously shared their time and insight to make this volume stronger.

References

Alberti B, Fowles S, Holbraad M, Marshall Y, and Witmore C (2011) "Worlds otherwise": archaeology, anthropology, and ontological difference. CA forum on theory in anthropology. *Current Anthropology* 52(6):896–912.

Caspari RE and Lee S-H (2004) Older age becomes common late in human evolution. *Proceedings of the National Academy of Sciences of the United States of America* 101(30):10895–10900.

Caspari R and Lee S-H (2006) Is human longevity a consequence of cultural change or modern biology? *American Journal of Physical Anthropology* 129(4):512–517.

Lee S-H (2001) Assigned resampling method: a new method to estimate size sexual dimorphism in samples of unknown sex. *Przeglad Antropologiczny – Anthropological Review* 64(1):21–39.

Lee S-H and Wolpoff MH (2003) The pattern of evolution in Pleistocene human brain size. *Paleobiology* 29(2):186–196.

Rosaldo R (1993) *Culture & Truth: The Remaking of Social Analysis*. Beacon Press.

Rottenburg R (2009) Social and public experiments and new figurations of science and politics in postcolonial Africa. *Postcolonial Studies* 12(4):423–440.

Roy RD (2018) Decolonise science – time to end another imperial era. *The Conversation* April 5. https://theconversation.com/decolonise-science-time-to-end-another-imperial-era-89189.

Thomson P (2013) Making the familiar strange: what's that about? https://patthomson.net/2013/02/14/making-the-familiar-strange-whats-that-about.

Véran J-F (2012) Old bones, new powers. *Current Anthropology* 53(5):S246–S255.

Willermet CM (1993) *The Debate over Modern Human Origins: A Scientific Tug-of-War* (MA Thesis). Arizona State University.

Willermet CM (2012) Species, characters, and fuzziness in taxonomy. *PaleoAnthropology Journal* 2012:70–86.

Willermet CM and Clark GA (1995) Paradigm crisis in modern human origins research. *Journal of Human Evolution* 29(5):487–490.

Willermet CM and Hill JB (1997) Fuzzy set theory and its implications for speciation models. In Clark GA and Willermet CM, editors. *Conceptual Issues in Modern Human Origins Research.* Aldine de Gruyter. Pp. 77–88.

Part I

The Strange and the Familiar

New Landscapes and Theoretical Approaches

1 Women in Human Evolution Redux

Dänae G. Khorasani and Sang-Hee Lee

In the history of paleoanthropology, generations of scholars have interpreted and imagined the role of women in shaping the evolution of humanity. Much of this literature about prehistoric women centers on the biologic differences between males and females, which in turn necessitated different evolutionary subsistence and reproductive strategies. When specialization in economic or subsistence production is differentiated by sex, it is typically referred to as a *sexual division of labor*. The idea that early humans divided their labor by sex is so influential that many believe the human lineage itself could be defined by the singular division between men hunting and women gathering.

Numerous scholars have addressed the naturalization of a division of labor that confined women to particular roles within human evolution based on their biology (see Conkey and Gero 1991; Hrdy 1999; Sørensen 2013). Challenges raised by feminist anthropologists in the 1970s and 1980s were mainly in response to the "Man the Hunter" model in anthropology from the decade prior, which argued for an essential division of labor where intellect, dominance, and hunting were framed as clear-cut male attributes (Lee and DeVore 1968; Watanabe 1968). Stereotypes central to definitions of gender had likely factored into how paleoanthropologists interpreted the prehistoric world and women's place within it (Gero and Scattolin 2002; Leibowitz 1983; Schiebinger 1999). Fundamental to this critique was the problematic conflation of gender and sex. Familiar hierarchical gender structures were presumed as innate biological predispositions, causing "female" subordination to be treated as part of the human condition, rather than a historical development (Leacock 1983). The conflation of gender with sex ultimately distorted the structure of foraging societies upon which paleoanthropologists had based their arguments about prehistoric society.

Anthropologists have frequently recognized the difficulty in developing a working definition of gender. This is not surprising, considering that until the early 1970s gender was more often associated with linguistic analysis and grammatical "genders," not people (Bielert and Geary 2017). In this chapter, we define *gender* as a cultural construct central to social categories of personhood, involving elements of physiological, performative, social, historic, and cultural aspects considered essential for the category (Kessler and McKenna 1978). *Sex* refers to the categorization of organisms based on their reproductive biology. From this perspective, sex and gender are not equivalent, although they overlap significantly in their perceived binary categories. As a result, sex and gender are often conflated in scientific discourse and even earlier feminist works.

In this chapter, we examine the role of women in human evolution in light of the influential model that suggests "men hunt" and "women gather" and ask if prehistoric humans truly practiced such rigid labor divisions in the way we imagine. The first section of this chapter addresses the origins of a sexual division of labor and the advent of "Man the Hunter" and "Woman the Gatherer" hypotheses. The Man the Hunter, or Hunting hypothesis, is arguably one of the most influential models in human evolution discourse in shaping our ideas about human evolution. This model was condensed from a series of original papers, presented at the "Origin of Man" symposium at the University of Chicago in 1966, and later published as an edited volume *Man the Hunter* (Lee and DeVore 1968). The connections drawn in this text between biology and social activities in human and non-human primates, especially by Sherwood L. Washburn, his student Irven DeVore, and colleague Richard B. Lee, would come to determine the trajectory of evolutionary studies in paleoanthropology for decades. The lasting contribution of this text is that it shifted the focus of human evolutionary studies away from simple technology milestones and toward more complex social labor divisions. Feminist critique beginning in the 1970s questioned the validity of these labor divisions presumed by the Man the Hunter model: Why a Paleolithic division of labor in the first place? Why was this division based on gender? And why was women's labor almost universally marginalized in these narratives?

The second section addresses the use of illustrative material and dioramic representations of women in human evolution. Diana Gifford-Gonzalez's 1993 study of women's roles in textual illustrations of Paleolithic life identified several motifs that framed women's work as primary domestic and "low-class" labor (1993:34). These gendered images were heavily reliant on western gender stereotypes and assumptions about appropriate roles for men and women. In order to better understand the current outlook of women in prehistory, we replicated Gifford-Gonzalez's study by searching related images through a Google image search. An important focus in our analysis of these images was the pictorial representation of women's labor and gendered activities within publicly accessed materials depicting prehistoric society.

The third section considers the very premise of a prehistoric sexual division of labor and explores the possibility of women who hunt. The deep associations between men and hunting in scientific discourse stems from historic transformations in the meanings of masculinity and increasing antipathy toward women's labor in the post-World War II era. Although feminist anthropologists have seriously questioned the Man the Hunter paradigm, "men and hunting" remains a familiar explanatory concept for the exclusion of women from certain aspects of evolution. Finally, the concluding section exhorts the field to further pursue evidentiary studies of women's roles in human evolution. Although a division of labor by gender is an especially salient feature of many human societies, there is no specific knowledge about when or how it came about. Formulating and testing hypotheses about women's roles and gender differentiation among early humans certainly merits our continued investigation.

Foundational Literature

The presumption of women's roles within a sexual division of labor has a much longer history than conceptualizations of "Man the Hunter." Charles Darwin, in his influential volume, *The Descent of Man, and Selection in Relation to Sex* (1871), presented a theory of sexual selection that argued for a package of four traits as the drivers of hominin evolution: enlarged brains (intellect), bipedalism, tool use, and reduced dentition. Darwin proposed *sexual selection* as a way to explain the more puzzling evolutionary traits in light of natural selection. His focus was on dimorphic features rather than behaviors; behavioral differences were implicated through his suggestion that weaponry could give males an advantage in male–male conflicts. Females were not involved due to their delicate nature. Clear differences between the sexes were highlighted in his texts, as he noted that "man is more courageous, pugnacious, and energetic than woman, and has a more inventive genius," in addition to an "absolutely larger" male brain (1871:317). For Darwin, these differences in physical and mental faculties translated to ascribed differences in labor. And while his characterization of male and female sexual natures was clearly laden with the sexism of the Victorian era, it passed into modern evolutionary theory largely unchallenged, though many paleoanthropologists still dispute the details (Hrdy 1999; Wiber 1997; Zihlman 1981).

The criteria established by Darwin that presumably made humans *human* was seized upon by Raymond Dart, who believed that early human tools and intellect were undoubtedly developed for killing and hunting. Dart had accrued fame for his discovery of the "Taung Child" in the 1920s and was a follower of Darwin at a time when Darwinism had fallen out of favor (Stange 1997). He proposed the Killer Ape hypothesis and "Osteodontokeratic" culture, in which he characterized early "ape-men" as hyperbolic carnivorous creatures who drank "the hot blood of their victims" (Dart 1953). Dart's ideas would later inspire playwright Robert Ardrey to compose a widely popular series of articles about "Man the Killer Ape" for *Life* magazine, starting in the 1960s, as well as a series of books on the topic (Ardrey 1961, 1966, 1970, 1971, 1976). At the same time, paleoanthropology was working out its own theory about innate male aggression and its relationship to hunting as an evolutionary driver.

Washburn was among the first to develop a hunting hypothesis to explain human behavior and evolution. He developed the sexual division model even further to argue that early man's hunting must have been the turning point in human evolution, going so far as to claim that human intellect, interest, and basic social structures were "[all] evolutionary products of the success of the hunting adaptation" (Washburn and Lancaster 1968:293; see also Washburn and DeVore 1961). Within this framing, adaptations and social selection for aggression and hunting acumen formed the foundation of human nature and a division of labor based on sex that was biologically fixed. In 1966, Washburn's student DeVore, and his colleague Richard B. Lee, organized a conference based on this hunting hypothesis, which would later result in an edited volume entitled *Man the Hunter* (Lee and DeVore 1968).

Inside the pages of *Man the Hunter*, a distinctive narrative supporting the primacy of hunting and male agency was solidified. Man was argued to be the hunter among hunters, and as the apex predator of the Paleolithic, early man had to adapt to fit the task. In their chapter on human evolution, Washburn and Lancaster (1968) argued that important human evolutionary traits were adapted to hunting, such as increased brain size, bipedalism, and greater technological advancement; but also contributed to undesirable traits, like a natural male propensity for aggression. Although the main focus was on male hunting behavior, it is also in this volume that the gathering woman was introduced. The model suggested a general archaic division of labor in which men hunted on behalf of their kin, and women gathered vegetation or else waited at home with the children (Dahlberg 1981; Epstein 1988; Woodburn 1968).

With the discovery of early hominin fossils in Ethiopia in the 1980s, Lovejoy presented his modified version of male hunting with the provisioning model (1981, 1993). His argument about early hominin behavior was generated from the idea that the different sexual adaptations he ascribed to males and females would enhance reproductive fitness. Lovejoy assumed that early hominin females, burdened by their young and ergonomic constraints, must have been bound to a home base in uncomplicated nuclear units. Males, unburdened by childcare, were free to provision by foraging for their mates, thus ensuring the survival of their offspring. Lovejoy had based this model on birds and primates, like Darwin before him, arguing that larger males played an important role as provisioner and protector. While the feminist perspective at the time was focused on establishing the importance of women's gathering activities, the provisioning model found theoretical support in sociobiology (Wilson 1975), where the concept of fitness was measured by reproductive success, and where male–male competition and activity was one of the primary behavioral aspects to be studied.

Primatologist Richard Wrangham and science-writer Dale Peterson presented an intellectual descendent of the hunting-provisioning model in their book *Demonic Males* (1996). Wrangham's modified version linked prehistoric male cooperative big-game hunting to men's propensity for violence, domination, and leadership. By contrast, women were thought to have evolved a predisposition for submission and caregiving, but were nevertheless attracted to the bloodthirsty "bad boys" of evolution. The evidence for such specific sexual specialization offered by Wrangham and Peterson was anecdotal and based on primatology studies (Nelson and Rosen-Ayalon 2002). However, despite the lack of evidentiary data, for many, the validity of evolutionary sex differences was well established by the 1990s and considered beyond question at the level of behavior and psychology. The sexual division of labor, Leakey and Lewin (1992) argued, is what gave rise to the near-universal social dominance of men over women in prehistory.

In the middle of the twentieth century, paleoanthropology was by no means the only anthropological discipline gendering the past based on apparent sex difference. The New Archaeology of the 1960s closely followed the work of archaeologist David Clarke, whose top-down analysis argued for a social model centered on the sexual division of labor as fundamental to human social organization and settlement (Clarke 1972). These mid-century archaeological studies were heavily reliant on stereotypical gender roles and classified women in the past as being inherently domestic and opposed to the "non-domestic" world of men (Edwards and Pope 2012:459). For example, Neolithic and Iron Age women were closely associated with material remains of the home, such as cooking pots and products for domestic consumption (Evans and Hodder 2006), while men were associated with stereotypically masculine, labor-intensive activities and "portable artefacts" associated with killing, "cutting-down," and of course, "hunting" (Hodder 1990:181).

At the same time as the hunting primacy was developed, primatology was establishing itself as a modern scientific discipline. Washburn and DeVore were involved in a funded study of African savanna baboons as a comparative model for early hominins thought to have originated in the African savanna, "from the viewpoint of man-the-hunter" (Haraway 1983:182). Primatology research provided the referential model primates, as first the baboons, then the common chimpanzees, became the evolutionary proxy for early hominins (Lasker 1999; Washburn and DeVore 1961). One of the earliest supporters of this view was zoologist Desmond Morris, who imagined in his book *The Naked Ape* (1967) early humans as a new kind of primate that hunted. By the end of the 1960s, primate studies of male-dominated hierarchies and mating privileges, combined with the Man the Hunter paradigm, made for a very powerful narrative of male supremacy and female subordination in human evolution.

Feminist pushback was almost immediate, beginning with Sally Slocum's paper "Woman the Gatherer" (1975) and the emergence of feminist empiricism in the 1970s (Gailey 2014; Tanner 1981). Slocum critiqued the direct association of males with active cultural reproduction and innovation (Slocum 1975). Committed to positivism, feminist empiricism at the time sought to expose male (Milton 1979; Ortner 1972) and western/white (Slocum 1975) bias within the sciences. Feminist researchers asked questions about what the women were doing, and about the "naturalness" of their sex differences and roles. Efforts were put forth to discover the women of prehistory, hitherto hidden, such as the anthology *Woman the Gatherer* (1981), edited by Frances Dahlberg. Within this text, the authors argued for the evolutionary importance of women's subsistence activities and collection of plant-based food-stuffs, while diminishing the emphasis on hunting as a primary means of survival. Instead, meat was argued to be a coveted food laden with privilege precisely because it was scarce (Hawkes and Bliege Bird 2002). Although meat probably occupied some portion of early hominin diet, food gathered by women was the primary means of provisioning.

The emergent Woman the Gatherer narrative is perhaps best represented by the early works of Adrienne Zihlman and Nancy Tanner, who challenged the basic assumptions of the Man the Hunter model as being vital to the development of human adaptations, arguing instead that women's activities were equally important to evolutionary advancement in a series of publications between the 1970s and 1990s (Tanner and Zihlman 1976; Zihlman 1985, 1997; Zihlman and Tanner 1978). This first wave of feminist critique was essential to bringing the dominance of male perspectives in anthropology under scrutiny. They and others argued that not only did women's gathering activity contribute a large proportion of the foods crucial to survival, but that it was women who often invented new technologies and transmitted this information through the generations (Gero 1991; Slocum 1975). In essence, female gatherers did not need male hunters to survive. This approach brought the pair-bonded monogamous Man the Hunter hypothesis into question and made the idea of aggressive males competing for available females much less plausible.

However, many had not appreciated the extent to which the struggle to define early hominin activities became a losing battle for feminists (Wiber 1997). Man the Hunter had emerged from this period of critique in the 1970s largely unscathed. This is especially clear when reading the almost concurrent publications by Richard Leakey and Owen Lovejoy in the 1980s, which still framed human development, intelligence, physicality, and complex social skills in terms of male activities. By reframing the narrative to emphasize the importance of gathering, the Woman the Gatherer model conceded the primary existence of a gendered division of labor between early man and early woman – feminists had inadvertently naturalized the very gendered division of labor they intended to challenge (Hager 1997; Haraway 1989; Zihlman 1985). Perhaps hunting did not make a reliable and dominant contribution in provisioning, but the point lay in the privilege and power associated with male hunting activities and meat.

Another example of an alternative hypothesis to Man the Hunter is Elaine Morgan's proposed Aquatic Ape hypothesis (Morgan 1972, 1982). Morgan enjoyed a career as a playwright and a writer in human evolution, paralleling Ardrey who was also a playwright and a writer in human evolution. The reception of the two writers in the realms of popular science and the professional field was dramatically different. The Aquatic Ape hypothesis was considered frivolous and dismissed as unworthy of scientific response (Richards 1991), while Ardrey's arguments about hunting men as killer apes were placed within the context of the mainstream ideas of the field; neither hypothesis was more strongly supported by empirical data than the other.

Remedial efforts to redefine and diversify women's roles in the prehistoric record were well underway by the 1980s in archaeology, starting with the household archaeology discourse with a critique that the gender narratives employed within archaeological discourse had ignored internal social dynamics and context (Conkey and Spector 1984). However, acceptance of gender theory within paleoanthropology was slow to take root, largely due to the struggle to navigate the problematic association of gender with biology. The problem was not simply methodological (Leacock 1983), because theorizing about gender and labor assumes gender roles could be determined in the past.

Thus, feminist paleoanthropologists set about revising the biological mandate of the ancestral females alongside concepts of gender. One of their aims was to dismantle Man the Hunter's excessive concern with female fidelity and male power. It was Sarah Blaffer Hrdy who introduced the sexually active female primate and the possibility that concealed ovulation evolved to decrease infanticide and confuse paternity, rather than to secure male investment, in her book *The Woman that Never*

Evolved (1999). At the same time as the usefulness of the male-primate models was questioned in the 1990s, the family unit also became a topic of debate, challenging the utility of the "nuclear" family concept in paleoanthropology. Instead of the provisioning model, Hawkes and colleagues (1997) argued for the importance of alloparenting and that intergenerational cooperation in caring for offspring came about with biologically adaptive postmenopausal lifespans in women, or the "Grandmother hypothesis" (Hawkes et al. 1997; O'Connell et al. 1999). Proponents of the Grandmother hypothesis contended that elder *Homo erectus* females provisioned their daughters' offspring, thereby enhancing the children's survival and allowing for development of several distinctive human traits, like longevity.

Man the Hunter conventions had associated the distinctive fossil record of *Homo erectus* with the co-adaptation of male-driven big-game hunting and paternal investment – a model that was later used to explain the emergence of *Homo sapiens*. However, feminist primatologists and paleoanthropologists of the 1980s and 1990s brought to light that hunting is known to be far more common among non-human primates than previously thought, but does not necessarily involve greater paternal investment. Grandmothers' participation in childcare would have freed women to forage for their families, without reliance on a provisioning sexual division of labor from males. This is turn suggests a more egalitarian structure with a greater capacity for food sharing and provisioning that would have allowed hominins to thrive in difficult habitats. The idea of intergenerational care was therefore a key feature that distinguished hominins from their primate cousins. And it was grandmothering, not hunting, that had brought about these important changes.

The movement toward revising both hominin models and the sciences was welcomed by second-wave paleoanthropologists. Lori Hager cast doubt on both the methods used to sex fossil australopithecines and arguments about the interpretation of sexual dimorphism (Hager 1991); nor was the relationship between sexual dimorphism and specialized sex roles as unidirectional as the hunting model had suggested (Leibowitz 1983). Zihlman continued to publish her research on female sexual selection, parental investment, and comparative ethnographic examples of modern-day foragers (1989, 1997). Nascent data on primates and archaeological bone assemblages were used to expand the possible roles for women, with an emphasis on the importance of gathering. Yet, despite clear efforts through the 1990s to revise the opinion of women in evolution, feminist scholars still ran into what Zihlman called "the Paleolithic glass ceiling" (1997).

Zihlman (1997) reflected on the November 1993 cover of *Discover* magazine, which featured a diorama from the new, permanent exhibit "Human Biology and Evolution" at the American Museum of Natural History, featuring an australopithecine male and female couple walking in the ash of an erupting volcano. Zihlman noted that the scene was not particularly sound in its science, but furthermore disturbing because of what the positioning of their bodies said about evolutionary gender relations. The taller individual (man) had his left arm protectively around the shorter woman's shoulder; the man was looking over his right shoulder toward the volcano, face toward the danger, while the woman was looking away from the danger, with a facial expression of fear and alarm. The man is depicted as the protector of the woman.

Despite the transformations that women in human evolution went through since the 1960s, the textbooks and museum displays through which anthropology reached the wider audience still assigned rigid roles to women in subsistence practices and sexuality. Dioramic displays of the period were like scientific versions of Adam and Eve, which presented a familiar narrative of our ancestors as necessarily pair-bonded reproductive units who practiced strict divisions where men hunted and women were dependents (Zihlman 1997). How far had the discipline really come in the last three decades if this was what paleoanthropology chose to communicate to the public? Diane Gifford-Gonzalez (1993), Marie Sørensen (1999), and Melanie Wiber (1997) also raised the issue of gender representation in publicly accessed dioramic displays. One of the great strengths of science is the power to correct bad science (Hrdy 1999), yet there exists a pervasive attitude in our models that functions to keep women in their place despite all efforts. Perhaps the true test of the strength of the women's movement in paleoanthropology will come when we cannot only dismantle our gendered theories of the past, but also the dioramic displays in the present.

Representations of Paleolithic Labor

Illustrated depictions of Paleolithic human life are perhaps as old as our knowledge of the subject. Many are familiar with the illustrations, paintings, and life-sized dioramas modeling early human evolution in both educational and public settings. These visual representations promise to reconstruct the past for us. The environment, behavioral patterns, labor activities, and social relationships are all on display. Rather than reconstructions of the actual past, these composed scenes of prehistoric life are dioramic representations of hypothetical or imagined scenes from daily life (Gifford-Gonzalez 1993). These illustrations fall somewhere between fact and fiction, realistic, but with a familiar narrative: men as fierce hunters, with a spear or weapon in hand to kill their prey and defend their kin. When not hunting, the men innovate and make the tools needed to solve their evolutionary problems. Life is hard and meager, but they face their hardships while standing proudly upright, always moving forward with determination. Meanwhile the women, if you can spot them, are in the background doing whatever it is women do.

The notion that gender in scientific illustrations is culturally reproduced with androcentric bias is also not new. There is a body of literature addressing the problematic naturalization of gender divisions in US high school and university curricula and science texts and museums (Rosse 1990; Schiebinger 1999). However, while overt forms of androcentric pronouns and male over-representation in educational texts appears on the decline, human evolution materials seem especially resistant to change (Wiber 1997). Even when male and female roles in human evolution are rewritten, the mainstream narrative remains untouched; stereotypical alpha-cavemen and subservient women continue to dominate the images in evolution textbooks and natural history museums.

In anthropology, the movement to acknowledge gender representations within evolutionary illustrations began in the 1980s with Adrienne Zihlman, who drew attention to the problematic assumptions underlying representations of prehistoric women and challenged the field to critically examine "how women have been depicted in evolutionary reconstructions" (Zihlman 1989:39) through numbers of females in comparison to males, placement of the two within the picture (i.e., foreground vs background), their labor activities, body posture, and asking whether a sexual division of labor was implied. Following Zihlman, other anthropologists have contributed comprehensive studies of visual gender representations in educational texts and museums (Ballard 2007; Moser 1998; Sørensen 1999; Wiber 1997).

However, the study of human evolution illustrations truly became broadcast across the field with Gifford-Gonzalez's pivotal paper on evolution dioramas in 1993. As a teacher, Gifford-Gonzalez questioned whether her intuitions about gender bias in dioramic displays held up against the evidence, leading her to analyze a set of illustrated reconstructions of Cro-Magnon hominin in widely accessible textbooks and print media. She surveyed a sample of 88 artist depictions of early human life created between the 1960s and 1980s, and found that of the 444 individuals surveyed (excluding gender-ambiguous adults), men constituted half of the individuals represented, while women were less than one-quarter, and children made up the rest of the sample. Moreover, a full 84 percent of the images featured men, but less than half contained women. With such striking numbers, Gifford-Gonzalez wondered why the available Paleolithic worlds seemed to be at odds with what she knew of prehistoric human societies.

It can be argued that depictions of prehistoric humans are themselves embodied narratives of a very specific evolutionary story. This is true for the images in Gifford-Gonzalez's survey, where she found a strong affinity toward representing Paleolithic life within classically "western" gender stereotypes and art genres. These gendered types included biased representations of women as natural caregivers, mothers, and domestic laborers, evoking imagery of an eighteenth-century scullery maid. These preconceptions about women's status, by both the artist and researcher, resulted in prehistoric women being placed in the background of dioramic representations, instead of the center foreground with the men. While in this setting, Gifford-Gonzalez observed that the women were commonly shown nursing children, preparing food, or performing menial domestic tasks such as hide-tanning. Body posture was another way to communicate their social position, as women's gender-specific activities were shown to be static and low to the ground, requiring them to crouch or hunch over. Gifford-Gonzalez argued that the resulting imagery coded prehistoric women as a primitive and tedious foil to the explicitly "masculine" technologies (i.e., spears, weapons) and evolutionary achievements of men. In contrast to the women, men were often shown standing or doing activities that involved moving their bodies, such as hunting or throwing spears; women, children, and elders were almost never found in these positions. The elderly and children, like women, were placed at the margins of artists' representations, as was characteristic of the genre.

The artistic conventions in human evolution as identified by Gifford-Gonzalez are now recognized as part of a larger pattern of gender bias in scientific illustrations (Wiber 1997). The results of her study embraced both human evolution illustrations and the entire process of naturalization by which these stereotypes of women's status were disseminated to the wider public. In this chapter, we ask, has anything changed since Gifford-Gonzalez's (1993) critique of early human representations? To investigate this, we tested the prevalence of androcentric gender bias in publicly accessible images of prehistoric hominins collected through an image search on the internet. Images depicting forms of labor were particularly interesting to us, because they reveal the social construction of gender that permeates paleoanthropological and archaeological discourse. We expected that after 50 years of efforts establishing the importance of women's labor in human evolution since the 1960s, women would be more equally represented, even while a clear delineation of labor by gender persists.

Materials and Methods

We took a survey of images in 2017, using the keywords "prehistoric humans" to focus on the most widely viewed images of prehistoric people in the context of human evolution easily accessed by the general public using Google's image search. Google's image search function is based on the PageRank algorithm, used by Google for rating web images based on measured human interest and highest number of links to those images (i.e., popularity) in relation to specific search terms (Page et al. 1999). We selected illustrated and dioramic representations of early human life, reflecting the criteria set by Gifford-Gonzalez (1993). Images in the form of illustrations, paintings, dioramas, and museum displays were kept in the dataset; particular attention was given to scenes showing labor and subsistence activities. Pictures showing human skeletal remains without context, pictures of real people, satirical cartoons, and video thumbnails (from YouTube) were considered irrelevant and were eliminated from the sample. Duplicates were also eliminated. The final dataset included 92 images, representing a total of 454 individuals. We collected data on the number of hominin individuals and types of activities depicted.

Although we recognize that sex and gender are not equivalent, the two are almost always conflated in these images, with no room made for queer or non-binary gender identities. Therefore, gender was assigned to individuals based on a combination of sex markers (presence of a beard or bare breasts), style of dress, and image context. Figures for which the biological sex was not clearly discernible were designated as "ambiguous." Children were not counted in the frequency count by sex/gender; they were included in the content analysis, as children's presence contextualizes childcare as a gendered activity when they are shown in proximity to women or men. Individuals were further grouped by body position and activity, with a focus on labor activities related to subsistence, material production, and parental investment as key features of gender-specific representations. We recorded the general positioning of their body and the labor activity being performed for each individual depicted.

Table 1.1 Gender distribution of individuals in image search results

Gender	N (%)
Men	299 (66)
Women	102 (22)
Other	53 (12)
Total	454

Note: The frequency difference between men and women is significant using a chi-square test ($p = 1.270 \times 10^{-22}$, $p < 0.05$).

Table 1.2 Body position of individuals in the search results

Body position	Men N (%)	Women N (%)	Chi-square p-value[a]
Standing	166 (56)	45 (44)	0.156
Crouching or sitting	94 (31)	51 (50)	**0.008**
Neither	39 (13)	6 (6)	0.083
Total	299	102	

[a] Items in bold are significant at the $p < 0.05$ level.

Labor activities that occurred more than once were assigned a category, with categories largely being determined by the content and context of the images themselves.

Results

The results of this study show gender bias in representations of early human life, as predicted in our hypothesis: men are depicted in higher frequency and are associated with a wider range of activities. The presence of men noticeably dominated the sample (Table 1.1). Of the 454 individuals surveyed, men constituted 66 percent of the sample: 299 were identified as men or male. Women numbered only 102, or less than one-quarter of the adult individuals (22 percent). There were 53 (12 percent of the total individuals) ambiguous adults. A chi-square test shows this difference to be significantly different ($p = 1.270 \times 10^{-22}$, $p < 0.05$). The numerical dominance of men is even more striking when considering that a full 99 percent of the images featured adult males or occasionally an ambiguous figure, but only one image featured a recognizably female hominin alone.

Body position and movement are key for communicating social status. In the sample, postures and standing positions differed between men and women (Table 1.2). Women's movements were depicted as more static and unaccented than those of men. Women were also more often shown in lowered postures, closer to the ground (bending over, squatting, kneeling, or sitting). Fifty percent of women were in a lowered position, compared to 31 percent of men. This difference is statistically significant ($p = 0.008$, $p < 0.05$). While 56 percent of men were depicted standing,

Table 1.3 Activities undertaken by gender, with a focus on subsistence practices

Activity	Men N (%)	Women N (%)	Chi-square p-value[a]
Hunting[b]	207 (69)	16 (16)	3.088×10^{-10}
Gathering	4 (1)	18 (18)	9.216×10^{-9}
Hard labor[c]	17 (6)	4[d] (4)	0.608
Holding or with a child	2 (1)	28 (27)	1.491×10^{-16}
Cultural activity[e]	23 (8)	3[f] (3)	0.077
Miscellaneous[g]	46 (15)	33 (32)	**0.001**
Total	299	102	

[a] Items in bold are significant at the $p < 0.05$ level.

[b] Hunting includes images of hunting and related activities, such as holding or throwing spears, rocks, or other weapons. The category also includes scenes of cannibalism and preparation of meat for food.

[c] Hard labor includes various labor activities, including cutting down trees, splitting rocks, building a structure, or carrying heavy objects.

[d] All four cases of women at hard labor show hide-tanning, close to the ground.

[e] Cultural activity includes practices of social importance that did not fit easily within the previous categories, such as ritualistic practice, storytelling, cave painting, and funerary activity.

[f] Of the three instances of women doing art, two are preparing pigment. No man is shown preparing pigment.

[g] Miscellaneous includes any ambiguous or one-off activities.

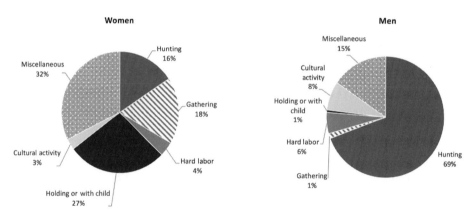

Figure 1.1 Activities undertaken by each gender.

compared to 44 percent of women, this difference is not statistically significant ($p = 0.156$). Men were also more frequently shown moving in a "dynamic" way or in mid-action poses.

Even more provocative patterns emerged when we examined specific activities enacted by men and women (Table 1.3; Figure 1.1). The activities associated with women coincided with those activities traditionally associated with American mid-century ideas about work appropriate for women: cooking, preparing food, cleaning, or other domestic activities. Only women are depicted with babies or children (27 percent of the adult women), except for two male examples. Only women are shown working on hides. The three activity categories that show statistical significance ($p < 0.05$) in the difference between men and women represented in proportion are hunting, gathering, and childcare. These are categories conventionally associated with a sexual division of labor.

Contrary to our expectations, however, there was not a high occurrence of women shown gathering in comparison to men. Interestingly, we found that while women occasionally held a weapon (7 percent holding a club or a rock), no image showed a woman holding or throwing a spear. Although there are a handful of famous images and reconstructed models of a Neandertal woman holding a spear, none of these images showed up in our search (38 pages of Google image search results). By contrast, 38 percent of men are shown holding or throwing spears. Men are also overwhelmingly depicted in association with a wide range of labor activities, such as hunting, carrying game, gathering, heavy labor, creating art, tool manufacture, or throwing spears. Depictions of men related to hunting and killing game were significantly high: most of the men (69 percent) were shown hunting and over half of the images in the entire sample displayed men engaging in hunting or hunting-related activities. Men were also strongly associated with social or cultural activity: only men were shown telling stories or participating in ritual burials of the dead.

Discussion

Results of our study are compatible with Gifford-Gonzalez's findings more than 25 years ago (1993). We found a high occurrence of images depicting prehistoric human evolution in ways that replicated archetypal gender and labor divisions identified by previous scholars. We found that women are still overwhelmingly imagined as performing tasks within a domestic setting. Rarely are women seen to exist in a world apart from men. Of all the images surveyed, only one image featured a recognizably female hominin on her own. The presence of women in most subsistence practices like hunting or gathering has likewise decreased, except for tasks related to meal preparation. Moreover, evolutionary images of women doing harder labor activities, like hide-tanning, also decreased. Gifford-Gonzalez's "drudge-on-the-hide" now appears to have been replaced with a "drudge-in-the-kitchen." We conclude that the most relative, publicly accessed images related to "prehistoric human" using Google's PageRank algorithm correspond to a clear gender bias and gendered division of labor in prehistory first critiqued many decades ago (Dahlberg 1981; Gifford-Gonzalez 1993; Slocum 1975; Wiber 1997).

Several motifs emerged from the images representing women and men that fit conventional western notions of appropriate gender roles. These images featured recognizable schemata involving women as mothers and cooks, and involving men as hunters and toolmakers. Men were most often depicted engaging in hunting or related activities. Some women were also shown engaging in hunting-related tasks, but in a lower frequency than men. One exception is childcare, an activity where women were overly represented in the illustrations. Such evocative symbols of womanhood in these images, reminiscent of the "Madonna-with-Child" trope, reinforce a pre-existing narrative involving women as idealized and static in history (Gifford-Gonzalez 1993:34). The comparative placement of men and women within these gendered motifs communicates a visual pattern that privileges men's labor over women's labor.

The androcentric narratives advanced by a variety of artists, scholars, and scientists are multifaceted and perforated by both patriarchal and classist undertones. Eleanor Leacock (1983) identified the close association of prehistoric women's work with lower-class activities as a result of the historic capitalist transformation of women's "domestic" labor into something unrecompensed and low-status, thus excluding them from access to networks of power and prestige. Benjamin Edwards and Rachel Pope (2012) noticed that a children's coloring book from the British Museum categorized men by their labor (as a carpenter or blacksmith) and left women uncategorized as anything other than "women." The inferred message is that women have no identity outside of their gender and their labor is inconsequential. Wiber (1997) explored gender difference in museum dioramas, noting that women were more often represented in lowered "undulating" postures (bending over, squatting, etc.) relative to men who mostly stood upright. The same observations can be made in the images of our study: Women were often depicted preparing food in a crouched position at ground level near the homebase, but seldom found in the landscape outside hunting or gathering.

The male dominance has also been noticed in natural history museum displays, in the number of male specimens in comparison to female specimens in terms of total numbers, postures, and the accompanying text. For example, Rebecca Machin's (2010) investigation of natural history galleries at the Manchester Museum showed that male animal specimens clearly dominated females in number and postures; she also noted that even the human evolutionary dioramas were dominated by men, since women or girls comprised only 13 percent of displays. Interpretive texts that accompanied these displays correspondingly took on the male point of view: for instance, stating that "males have harems," implying a male ownership of females.

Significantly, the frequency of men in the Google image search results exceeded our expectations for sex and gender distribution. Nearly every image (99 percent) featured at least one adult man (or ambiguous figure), but only one image depicted an adult woman on her own. This lone woman appeared to be semi-crouching in the middle of a meat-preparation task. This is comparable to Gifford-Gonzalez's findings in 1993, which found that 84 percent of the pictures she surveyed contained men and 50 percent of the images contained only men, while 7 percent of the images contained only women. She identified the numerical dominance of men as a "pattern of privileging" (1993:31), where the relative frequency and positioning of figures in the composition reflects choices regarding their importance. The privileging of men in illustrated depictions of prehistoric life conveys the idea that men are essential to human evolution, as their actions are worth viewing.

Scholarly drawings of early human life focus on men's actions and men's abilities to demonstrate an intimate and causal connection between masculinity and evolution. Women are mostly excluded from this narrative. When prehistoric women are represented, they are generally shown sitting down "at home" and doing domestic work. That not much has changed in these dioramic representations from the 1960s to the present suggests the existence of a strongly held androcentric bias in prehistoric narratives decades in the making. The resulting images naturalize a very specific division of human labor along sex and gender lines that lacks clear evidence. As modes of labor become emblematic of perceived gender differences, labor itself provides a means by which scientists naturalize their cultural constructions of gender, masking the scientific, evolutionary, and political questions at stake.

Do Women Hunt?

Turning our attention to the premise of a gendered division of labor, next we ask if hunting is indeed an activity exclusive to men. For paleoanthropologists, a concern with hominin labor was explaining the development of social relations in prehistoric societies that lacked economic specialization and concepts of private property. These queries looked to gender and perceived biological differences in sex to describe the formation of early human society. Many assumed that reproductive burden and physical weakness must have prevented women from participating in prehistoric hunting parties, initiating the first division of labor in human history (Watanabe 1968).

Ethnographic examples of hunter-gatherer societies in which men hunt are often used to support a theoretical division of labor in human evolution. Early studies, such as Murdock's ethnographic sampling of 224 societies in 1937, concluded that hunting was an exclusively male activity in 98.2 percent of hunter-gatherers, in no small part due to their physical superiority (Murdock 1937, 1949). Murdock argued that man, with "his superior physical strength," was more suited to wandering the world "to hunt, to fish, to herd, and to trade," while women were handicapped by the "physiological burdens of pregnancy and nursing" (Hayden 1981:403; Murdock 1949:7). Without evidence from the past to delineate social roles, anthropologists used early twentieth-century ethnography to formulate a general evolutionary model of social organization and human origins that posited that only men must have hunted (Bodenhorn 1990).

This assumption also formed the crux of the Man the Hunter model, which linked the origins of human evolution with the hunting practices of prehistoric men, framing hunting as one of "the most enduring characteristics of maleness" (Smalley 2005:184), or "one of the ecological characteristics of man" (Watanabe 1968:75). Watanabe noted that Ainu women hunted large game using rope and dogs (Watanabe 1968), but did not waver from the idea that "women did not hunt" (Goodman et al. 1985:1200). Sex differences in psychology and physiology, along with social taboos, were considered sufficient to explain the evolutionary division of labor, citing the non-existence of any society in which hunting game was the regular occupation of women (Watanabe 1968). Considering the primacy of hunting in human evolution, the exclusion of women from hunting was more than just an argument about labor – it was an exclusion from the story of human evolution itself.

Biology was looked at as the driving force behind sexual divisions of labor in prehistory. Women were considered a handicap on a prehistoric hunt due to their more sedentary and less aggressive nature, the demands of childcare, the handicapped biology and physicality, even the female body odors (Dobkin de Rios 1976; Hayden 1981; Tiger 1969). With so much going against women – their smell, their emotions, the weakness of their bodies, their parental responsibilities, etc. – it is no wonder that the woman who does not hunt seemed an evolutionary inevitability (Brightman 1996). Notably, these arguments cited little empirical evidence.

The biological approach continued in Lovejoy's provisioning model outlined in his paper entitled "The Origin of Man" (1981), fixing the origins of labor divisions and monogamy in the activities of our earliest known hominin ancestors, the australopithecines. Men maximized their reproductive fitness through provisioning, eventually creating the dominant and upright-walking, modern-day man. Shifting the focus from hunting to provisioning effectively expanded the activities undertaken by males.

Although Lovejoy did not explicitly assign hunting activities exclusively to males, his portrayal of hominin females as cavewives rendered their participation in prehistory mostly unremarkable, valued only for reproduction. Lovejoy noted that human females evolved to be "continually sexually receptive," citing "D.C. Johanson, personal communication" (1981). Frequent citation of Lovejoy's work in textbooks (recent examples include Foley and Lewin 2003; Larsen 2016; Workman and Reader 2004) indicates that these ideas have become orthodox explanations of human evolution (Fedigan 1986). Militaristic and androgenic terminology referring to male bodies as "fighting machines," naturally "aggressive" and sexually "ardent," or that men "dominate" and control public spaces, have created over time ideas about sex and gender in prehistory and the types of subsistence activities women might have participated in, or not (Fedigan and Fedigan 1989; Goodman et al. 1985; Hrdy 1999; Rosaldo 1974; Stange 1997).

Although supporters of the provisioning model focused on the biological limitations of the female body, critics pointed out that if men were truly concerned with familial provisioning their subsistence patterns would mirror those of women who gathered. If gathering actually yielded much higher, and more reliable, caloric intake than hunting (Dahlberg 1981), women gatherers were the providers. So, then, why hunt at all? To answer this question, Hawkes and Bliege Bird (2002) proposed the signaling theory, arguing that men hunted to signal their social status by sharing meat, a potentially rare commodity, publicly and widely across communities. Hunting became a cultural act, not a biological one. But if hunting was no longer the biological basis for human evolution, then what was hunting's role in human evolution? More importantly, why did women not hunt, if the question of biology was no longer an issue?

In reality, women do hunt, although systematic studies of women's hunting contributions have been few and far between. Fortunately, ethnographic evidence collected since the 1980s shows women's notable participation in hunting activities, suggesting that this is an area deserving of more scholarly attention. For example, Peruvian Matses women hunt alongside men to chase and kill animals (Romanoff 1983), while Hurtado and colleagues (1985) write about the Aché women trackers of Paraguay. Native American Cree women hunted for pelt-animals both alone or in groups, and other women, both married and single, hunted large game, such as moose, caribou, and bear (Brightman 1996). Noss and Hewlett (2001) write about the hunting activities of the Mossapoula Aka ("pygmies") women in Central Africa. Mbuti women of the Congo are recognized as hunters who assist hunting parties by driving game into nets and helping to carry the meat (Harako 1981). Highly skilled Ju'hoan women trackers locate large game and accompany men on expeditions, contributing substantially to hunting outcomes (Biesele and Barclay 2001). Australian Aboriginal women are known to provide meat for their kin from lizards and cats (Bird and Bliege Bird 2005). Comprehensive studies document the Agta women hunters of the Philippines (Estioko-Griffin 1985, 1986; Estioko-Griffin and Griffin 1981; Goodman et al. 1985) and Iñupiat women's contributions to hunting success in Alaska (Bodenhorn 1990; Guemple 1986).

Estioko-Griffin's research (1985, 1986; see also Estioko-Griffin and Griffin 1981) provides an important insight into how prehistoric woman may have hunted. Agta women hunt and many are considered master hunters. They are skilled in using bows and arrows, machetes, knives, traps, and dogs to hunt game (Goodman et al. 1985). Agta women hunters with children do not experience higher rates of child mortality or significant negative impact in hunting efficiency compared to women without children or women with children who do not hunt (Estioko-Griffin 1985). Agta women's hunting activity is reported to peak in their prime reproductive years (Noss and Hewlett 2001), and many Agta women are observed hunting during menstruation without reluctance and carrying nursing babies while on hunting ventures (Goodman et al. 1985). With no significant difference found between the average time spent hunting between women and men hunters, Goodman ultimately rejected the hypothesis that reproductive responsibilities affected women's ability to hunt (Goodman et al. 1985). Estioko-Griffin's research also favored the compatibility of women's roles as mothers with hunting activities.

Noss and Hewlett noted that while it was difficult to determine hunting yields by gender, since both Aka men and women often worked together, higher net-hunting return rates correlated to women hunters being in the majority (60 percent or more) of participants (Noss and Hewlett 2001). Likewise, Aka men do not easily fit into the stereotypical role of the hunter: They are known to gather honey and spend a great deal of their time caring for children.

Other human behavioral ecologists, such as Bailey and Aunger (1989), have pointed out that when women hunt, they often do so when hunting produces more calories per unit of time than other subsistence alternatives such as gathering. Their argument resonates with Hrdy's observation that female primates always seek to maximize their food intake (1999). Moreover, when "hunting" includes a range of behaviors that go beyond the killing of a live animal, it is clear that any gendered division of hunting labor quickly dissipates (Bodenhorn 1990). Ritual ceremonies to attract animals, spirit communication, specialized materials production, tracking, butchering, processing and preserving meat, familial land rights, etc. could all be considered important aspects of hunting. When ethnographers examine women's hunting practices within their social context, they often find that differentiated roles are not determined by sex, contradicting the widely held belief that only men engage in hunting historically (Estioko-Griffin and Griffin 1985).

With so much evidence supporting the efficacy and success of women hunters, it is important to consider the origins of the idea that labor divisions favor a men-only hunting scenario. Even in the earliest human evolutionary texts in which women's abilities were questioned, such as Darwin's *Descent of Man* (1871), women's ability to hunt was never explicitly denounced – it was not even a topic of conversation. So where did the idea that women do not hunt come from? Is *Man the Hunter* (1968) entirely to blame for our ideas about Paleolithic labor divisions? Or was this model the product of something else, such as transformations of our ideas about gender and hunting?

Prior to the 1950s in America, the public perception of hunting by both women and men was as a primarily recreational activity of the upper class, outside of any broader social context or gender politics. For example, in 1948 the sports magazine *Outdoor Life* published a rather spirited and bloodthirsty defense of hunting titled "I Just Like to Kill Things" (Smalley 2005:183). The author's image was splashed across the page: a young girl with cute pigtails. Her name was Kristin Sergel and her argument, outlining a case for recreational hunting, was not new. American sports and hunting magazines such as *Field and Stream*, *Forest and Stream*, and *Outdoor Life* had been defending the killing of wild game against animal rights activists since at least the late nineteenth century (Smalley 2005; Stange 1997). What was notable, according to historian Andrea L. Smalley, was the lack of gender content in Sergel's argument, where questions about women's participation in hunting (*Can women hunt? Should women hunt?*) had no place in her defense of hunting. In fact, Sergel was one of many women writing in hunting periodicals defending their recreational right to kill animals for sport. For these mid-century women hunters, the division in hunting was not between men and women, but between animal rights activists protecting the "dainty creatures of the field," and those who "just like to kill things" (Sergel 1948; Smalley 2005).

Indeed, women's participation in hunting was openly encouraged at the time and even said to enhance the sport and make it more "respectable" (Smalley 2005:189). At the time, women's sports hunting did not challenge post-war constructions of "femininity or domesticity," nor was it explicitly connected to any larger struggles for social or civil rights (Smalley 2005:183). It was only later, in the 1950s, when American post-World War II politics moved toward a more dominant, male-authored discourse that sought the removal of women from the workplace and factories. The aftermath of World War II coincided with the creation of a new, aggressive construction of masculinity that sought to include the previously excluded working-class man (Haraway 1989; Stange 1997). Hunting periodicals of the time reflected this shift as sports hunting became explicitly connected to post-war formulations of homosocial middle-class masculinity that "revolved around militarism and close, emotional bonds between men" (Smalley 2005:184). Writers for periodicals like *Field and Stream* suddenly started to defend hunting in gender-specific terms, proclaiming that women could not possibly comprehend the deeper cultural meanings and bonds men derived from hunting together. Authentic hunting quite literally overnight became a "masculine performance" for men alone.

Men's post-World War II antagonism toward women's hunting became entrenched in the very fabric of western society, and the post-war popular image of hunting as a quintessentially masculine activity prevails to this day (Smalley 2005; Stange 1997). Undoubtedly, hunting is one of those culturally defined activities upon which gender roles and male anxieties are projected. The deep association between men and hunting also became the primary component of the Man the Hunter model, which served as a single explanation for human evolutionary progress. It is not a coincidence that paleoanthropologists developed this model, built upon questionable ethnographic accounts and fantastic accusations about women's bodily functions, in the American post-war era of the 1950s and 1960s. In this sense, hunting is perhaps a unique lens through which we can see how male bias and historic context can work together to fabricate a past that is neither accurate nor desirable (Smalley 2005). Within an anthropological discourse, any discussion about our evolutionary past will eventually lead to the Man the Hunter model. But it is not just a model about men and hunting, it is a story that tells us a great deal about how we imagine and value the women of prehistory as well.

It is important to remember that we share an evolutionary history with real women who lived complex lives and performed multiple social roles. An alternative model may be put forward featuring an egalitarian society conferring a significant survival advantage for those groups practicing gender parity involving bi-parental investment, pervasive alloparental care of children, and greater cooperation to meet the higher offspring costs (Dyble et al. 2015). We need to expand our discourse to include variability of gender roles instead of a static view of the division of labor. We need to provide a more credible framework for understanding the possibilities of women in human evolution.

Conclusion

Since the 1970s, feminist scholars have consistently called for a need to recognize and dislodge the idea that women are not participants in human evolution to the same extent as men. Although advances in the discipline broadened our understanding of prehistoric women's roles and variability in the division of labor, many mainstream evolutionary studies continue to frame women in the past as being inherently domestic and opposed to the domain(s) of men. Public dioramic displays also continue to reflect these academic trends. In studies of prehistoric life imagery conducted in the 1980s to the 2000s, women are consistently represented as inertly domestic or caregiving. The visual devices observed in our survey of the most viewed Google images relating to "prehistoric humans" do not differ from studies in the previous decades. The resilience of these schematic forms indicates that they are more than clichéd arrangements of human bodies; they are cultural condensations of meaning that make it deceivingly easy to think of gender inequality as something that has always been part of our biology and evolution.

A sexual division of labor has traditionally been framed as a defining characteristic of human evolution, providing explanations for both male dominance and female diffidence. This division became a near-universal concept in paleoanthropological research cobbled together from ethnographic accounts and early primate studies of intensely aggressive baboon and ape societies. However, feminist research has challenged the utility of primate models in our understanding of prehistoric human behavior.

Equally critical is a focus on the evolutionary models that seem most obviously gendered, taking seriously the ways in which historic gender bias has constructed our understanding of prehistoric women's work, femininity, and their social status. Certainly, there is an abundance of examples in ethnographic accounts and historic texts that link gender to particular activities, such as men and hunting or women and mothering, but this link in and of itself tells us little about prehistoric transformations of either gender or labor. There are still arenas of paleoanthropology that fail to recognize or correct the historic distortion of women's roles in human evolution and prehistory. Explanatory structures like Man the Hunter will always fail to account for the true nature of how our ancestors lived because it does not consider women.

Some prehistoric women were certainly mothers, but they were also proficient hunters, warriors, toolmakers, leaders, and grandmothers. In endeavoring an evidence-driven study of women's roles throughout evolution from the ground up, rather than treating women's activities as unremarkable or fixed, we may avoid the uncritical use of gendered narratives that lack actual scientific merit.

Centering women in the analysis of what is more likely a story of profound social cooperation across categories of people and labor reveals much more about human evolution than the myth of Man the Hunter ever could. Future models of women's roles in relation to the sexual division of labor will need to be revisited using different explanatory structures if we are to engage in meaningful endeavors to reveal the importance of our maternal ancestors.

Acknowledgments

We thank Robin Nelson, Cathy Willermet, and anonymous reviewers for their helpful comments that strengthened this chapter.

References

Ardrey R (1961) *African Genesis: A Personal Investigation into the Animal Origins and Nature of Man*. Atheneum.

Ardrey R (1966) *The Territorial Imperative: A Personal Inquiry into the Animal Origins of Property and Nations*. Atheneum.

Ardrey R (1970) *The Social Contract: A Personal Inquiry into the Evolutionary Sources of Order and Disorder*. Atheneum.

Ardrey R (1971) *Aggression and Violence in Man: A Dialogue between Dr. L.S.B. Leakey and Robert Ardrey*. L.S.B. Leakey Foundation.

Ardrey R (1976) *The Hunting Hypothesis: A Personal Conclusion Concerning the Evolutionary Nature of Man*. Atheneum.

Bailey RC and Aunger Jr R (1989) Net hunters vs. archers: variation in women's subsistence strategies in the Ituri Forest. *Human Ecology* 17(3):273–297.

Ballard S (2007) Warriors and weavers: constructing Iron Age identities in museums. In Hamilton S, Whitehouse RD, and Wright KI, editors. *Archaeology and Women*. Left Coast. Pp. 167–182.

Bielert C and Geary DC (2017) Is sex a dirty word? *Quillette* September 19. https://quillette.com/2017/09/19/sex-dirty-word.

Biesele M and Barclay S (2001) Ju/'Hoan women's tracking knowledge and its contribution to their husbands' hunting success. *African Study Monographs* 26:67–84.

Bird DW and Bliege Bird RL (2005) Mardu children's hunting strategies in the Western Desert, Australia: foraging and the evolution of human life histories. In Hewlett BS and Lamb ME, editors. *Hunter-Gatherer Childhoods*. Aldine de Gruyter. Pp. 129–146.

Bodenhorn B (1990) "I'm not the great hunter, my wife is": Iñupiat and anthropological models of gender. *Études/Inuit/Studies* 14(1–2):55–74.

Brightman R (1996) The sexual division of foraging labor: biology, taboo, and gender politics. *Comparative Studies in Society and History* 38(4):687–729.

Clarke DL (1972) *A Provisional Model of an Iron Age Society and Its Settlement System*. Methuen.

Conkey MW and Gero JM (1991) Tensions, pluralities, and engendering archaeology: an introduction to women and prehistory. In Gero JM and Conkey MW, editors. *Engendering Archaeology: Women and Prehistory*. Blackwell. Pp. 3–30.

Conkey MW and Spector JD (1984) Archaeology and the study of gender. In Schiffer MB, editor. *Advances in Archaeological Method and Theory*. Academic Press. Pp. 1–38.

Dahlberg F, editor (1981) *Woman the Gatherer*. Yale University Press.

Dart RA (1953) *The Predatory Transition from Ape to Man*. Brill.

Darwin C (1981 [1871]) *The Descent of Man, and Selection in Relation to Sex*. Princeton University Press.

Dobkin de Rios M (1976) Female odors and the origin of the sexual division of labor in *Homo sapiens*. *Human Ecology* 4(3):261–262.

Dyble M, Salali GD, Chaudhary N, et al. (2015) Sex equality can explain the unique social structure of hunter-gatherer bands. *Science* 348(6236):796–798.

Edwards B and Pope R (2012) Gender in British prehistory. In Bolger D, editor. *A Companion to Gender Prehistory*. Wiley-Blackwell. Pp. 458–479.

Epstein CF (1988) *Deceptive Distinctions: Sex, Gender, and the Social Order*. Yale University Press.

Estioko-Griffin AA (1985) Women as hunters: the case of an eastern Cagayan Agta group. In Griffin PB and Estioko-Griffin AA, editors. *The Agta of Northeastern Luzon: Recent Studies*. University of San Carlos. Pp. 18–32.

Estioko-Griffin AA (1986) Daughters of the forest. *Natural History* 95:36–43.

Estioko-Griffin AA and Griffin PB (1981) Woman the hunter: the Agta. In Dahlberg F, editor. *Woman the Gatherer*. Yale University Press. Pp. 121–151.

Estioko-Griffin AA and Griffin PB (1985) Women hunters: The implications for Pleistocene prehistory and contemporary ethnography. In Goodman MJ, editor. *Women in Asia and the Pacific: Towards an East-West Dialogue*. University of Hawaii Press. Pp. 61–81.

Evans C and Hodder I (2006) *A Woodland Archaeology: Neolithic Sites at Haddenham*. McDonald Institute of Archaeological Research, Cambridge University.

Fedigan LM (1986) The changing role of women in models of human evolution. *Annual Review of Anthropology* 15:25–66.

Fedigan LM and Fedigan L (1989) Gender and the study of primates. In Morgan S, editor. *Gender and Anthropology Critical Reviews for Research and Teaching*. American Anthropological Association. Pp. 41–64.

Foley RA and Lewin R (2003) *Principles of Human Evolution*, 2nd edition. Wiley-Blackwell.

Gailey C (2014) Feminist methods. In Bernard HR and Gravlee CC, editors. *Handbook of Methods in Cultural Anthropology*, 2nd edition. Rowman and Littlefield. Pp. 151–184.

Gero JM (1991) Genderlithics: women's roles in stone tool production. In Gero JM and Conkey MW, editors. *Engendering Archaeology: Women and Prehistory*. Blackwell. Pp. 163–193.

Gero JM and Scattolin MC (2002) Beyond complementarity and hierarchy: new definitions for archaeological gender relations. In Nelson S and Rosen-Ayalon M, editors. *In Pursuit of Gender: Worldwide Archaeological Perspectives*. AltaMira Press. Pp. 155–171.

Gifford-Gonzalez D (1993) You can hide, but you can't run: representations of women's work in illustrations of Palaeolithic life. *Visual Anthropology Review* 9(1):23–41.

Goodman MJ, Griffin PB, Estioko-Griffin AA, and Grove JS (1985) The compatibility of hunting and mothering among the Agta hunter-gatherers of the Philippines. *Sex Roles* 12 (11–12):1199–1209.

Guemple L (1986) Men and women, husbands and wives: the role of gender in traditional Inuit society. *Études/Inuit/Studies* 10(1–2):9–24.

Hager LD (1991) The evidence for sex differences in the hominid fossil record. In Walde D and Willows N, editors. *The Archaeology of Gender*. Archaeological Association, University of Calgary. Pp. 46–49.

Hager LD, editor (1997) *Women in Human Evolution*. Routledge.

Harako R (1981) The cultural ecology of hunting behavior among the Mbuti pygmies in the Ituri Forest, Zaire. In Harding RSO and Teleki G, editors. *Omnivorous Primates: Gathering and Hunting in Human Evolution*. Columbia University Press. Pp. 499–555.

Haraway DJ (1983) Signs of dominance: from a physiology to a cybernetics of primate society. *Studies in History of Biology* 6:129–219.

Haraway DJ (1989) *Primate Visions: Gender, Race, and Nature in the World of Modern Science*. Routledge.

Hawkes K and Bliege Bird RL (2002) Showing off, handicap signaling, and the evolution of men's work. *Evolutionary Anthropology* 11(2):58–67.

Hawkes K, O'Connell JF, and Blurton Jones NG (1997) Hadza women's time allocation, offspring provisioning, and the evolution of long postmenopausal life spans. *Current Anthropology* 38 (4):551–577.

Hayden B (1981) Subsistence and ecological adaptations in modern hunter/gatherers. In Harding RSO and Teleki G, editors. *Omnivorous Primates: Gathering and Hunting in Human Evolution*. Columbia University Press. Pp. 191–214.

Hodder I (1990) *The Domestication of Europe*. Blackwell.

Hrdy SB (1999) *The Woman that Never Evolved*. Harvard University Press.

Hurtado AM, Hawkes K, Hill K, and Kaplan H (1985) Female subsistence strategies among Ache hunter-gatherers of eastern Paraguay. *Human Ecology* 13:1–28.

Kessler S and McKenna WM (1978) *Gender: An Ethnomethodological Approach*. Wiley.

Larsen CS (2016) *Essentials of Physical Anthropology: Discovering Our Origins*, 3rd edition. W.W. Norton & Company.

Lasker GW (1999) *Happenings and Hearsay: Reflections of a Biological Anthropologist.* Savoyard Books.

Leacock EB (1983) Interpreting the origins of gender inequality: conceptual and historical problems. *Dialectical Anthropology* 7(4):263–284.

Leakey RE and Lewin R (1992) *Origins Reconsidered.* Bantam Doubleday Dell.

Lee RB and DeVore I, editors (1968) *Man the Hunter.* Aldine de Gruyter.

Leibowitz L (1983) Origins of the sexual division of labor. In Lowe M and Hubbard R, editors. *Woman's Nature: Rationalizations of Inequality.* Pergamon Press. Pp. 123–147.

Lovejoy CO (1981) The origin of man. *Science* 211(4480):341–350.

Lovejoy CO (1993) Modeling human origins: are we sexy because we're smart, or smart because we're sexy? In Rasmussen DT, editor. *The Origin and Evolution of Humans and Humanness.* Jones and Bartlett. Pp. 1–28.

Machin R (2010) Gender representation in the natural history galleries at the Manchester Museum. In Levin AK, editor. *Gender, Sexuality and Museums.* Routledge. Pp. 187–200.

Milton K (1979) Male bias in anthropology. *Man* 14(1):40–54.

Morgan E (1972) *The Descent of Woman.* Stein and Day.

Morgan E (1982) *The Aquatic Ape.* Stein and Day.

Morris D (1967) *The Naked Ape: A Zoologist's Study of the Human Animal.* Jonathan Cape.

Moser S (1998) *Ancestral Images: The Iconography of Human Origins.* Cornell University Press.

Murdock GP (1937) Comparative data on the division of labor by sex. *Social Forces* 15(4):551–553.

Murdock GP (1949) *Social Structure.* Macmillan.

Nelson SM and Rosen-Ayalon M, editors (2002) *In Pursuit of Gender: Worldwide Archaeological Approaches.* AltaMira Press.

Noss AJ and Hewlett BS (2001) The contexts of female hunting in central Africa. *American Anthropologist* 103:1024–1040.

O'Connell JF, Hawkes K, and Blurton Jones NG (1999) Grandmothering and the evolution of *Homo erectus. Journal of Human Evolution* 36(5):461–485.

Ortner SB (1972) Is female to male as nature is to culture? *Feminist Studies* 1(2):5–31.

Page L, Brin S, Motwani R, and Winograd T (1999) *The Pagerank Citation Ranking: Bringing Order to the Web.* Stanford InfoLab.

Richards G (1991) The refutation that never was: the reception of the Aquatic Ape theory, 1972–1987. In Roede M, Wind J, Patrick J, and Reynolds V, editors. *The Aquatic Ape, Fact or Fiction? The First Scientific Evaluation of a Controversial Theory of Human Evolution.* Souvenir Press. Pp. 115–126.

Romanoff S (1983) Women as hunters among the Matses of the Peruvian Amazon. *Human Ecology* 11:339–343.

Rosaldo M (1974) Culture and society. In Rosaldo M and Lamphere L, editors. *Woman, Culture and Society.* Stanford University Press. Pp. 17–42.

Rosse SV (1990) *Female-Friendly Science: Applying Women's Studies Methods and Theories to Attract Students.* Pergamon.

Schiebinger LL (1999) *Has Feminism Changed Science?* Harvard University Press.

Sergel K (1948) "I just like to kill things". *Outdoor Life* 109:29.

Slocum S (1975) Woman the gatherer: male bias in anthropology. In Reiter RR, editor. *Toward an Anthropology of Women.* Monthly Review Press. Pp. 36–50.

Smalley AL (2005) "I just like to kill things": women, men and the gender of sport hunting in the United States, 1940–1973. *Gender & History* 17(1):183–209.

Sørensen MLS (1999) Archaeology, gender and the museum. In Merriman N, editor. *Making Early Histories in Museums.* Leicester University Press. Pp. 136–150.

Sørensen MLS (2013) *Gender Archaeology.* Wiley.

Stange MZ (1997) *Woman the Hunter.* Beacon Press.

Tanner N (1981) *On Becoming Human.* Cambridge University Press.

Tanner N and Zihlman A (1976) Women in evolution. Part I: innovation and selection in human origins. *Signs: Journal of Women in Culture and Society* 1(3, Part 1):585–608.

Tiger L (1969) *Men in Groups.* Random House.

Washburn SL and DeVore I (1961) Social behavior of baboons and early hominids. In Washburn SL, editor. *Social Life of Early Man.* Aldine de Gruyter. Pp. 91–105.

Washburn SL and Lancaster CS (1968) The evolution of hunting. In Lee RB and DeVore I, editors. *Man the Hunter.* Aldine de Gruyter. Pp. 293–303.

Watanabe H (1968) Subsistence and ecology of northern food gatherers with special reference to the Ainu. In Lee RB and DeVore I, editors. *Man the Hunter.* Aldine de Gruyter. Pp. 69–77.

Wiber MG (1997) *Erect Men/Undulating Women: The Visual Imagery of Gender, "Race" and Progress in Reconstructive Illustrations of Human Evolution.* Wilfrid Laurier University Press.

Wilson EO (1975) *Sociobiology: The New Synthesis.* Belknap Press.

Woodburn J (1968) Stability and flexibility in Hadza residential groupings. In Lee RB and DeVore I, editors. *Man the Hunter.* Aldine de Gruyter. Pp. 103–110.

Workman L and Reader W (2004) *Evolutionary Psychology: An Introduction.* Cambridge University Press.

Wrangham R and Peterson D (1996) *Demonic Males: Apes and the Origins of Human Violence.* Houghton Mifflin Harcourt.

Zihlman A (1981) Women as shapers of the human adaptation. In Dahlberg F, editor. *Woman the Gatherer.* Yale University Press. Pp. 75–120.

Zihlman AL (1985) *Australopithecus afarensis:* two sexes or two species? In Tobias PV, editor. *Hominid Evolution: Past, Present, and Future. Proceedings of the Taung Diamond Jubilee International Symposium.* Alan R. Liss. Pp. 213–220.

Zihlman AL (1989) Woman the gatherer: the role of women in early hominid evolution. In Morgan S, editor. *Gender and Anthropology: Critical Reviews for Research and Teaching.* American Anthropological Association. Pp. 21–40.

Zihlman AL (1997) The Paleolithic glass ceiling: women in human evolution. In Hager LD, editor. *Women in Human Evolution.* Routledge. Pp. 91–113.

Zihlman A and Tanner N (1978) Gathering and the hominid adaptation. In Tiger L and Fowler HT, editors. *Female Hierarchies.* Beresford Book Service. Pp. 163–194.

2 Hegemony and the Central Asian Paleolithic Record

Perspectives on Pleistocene Landscapes and Morphological Mosaicism

Michelle M. Glantz

With some notable exceptions (Trinkaus and Shipman 1993; Wolpoff and Caspari 1997), paleoanthropology is the least reflexive branch of its parent discipline, anthropology. In some ways, the dramatic post-World War II corrections embedded in the New Physical Anthropology of Sherry Washburn (see Mikels-Carrasco 2012) are responsible for the loss of this theoretical lens in paleoanthropology today. The reorientation of physical anthropology represented a singular moment in history, when disciplinary self-reflection was required to salvage the scholarly field from utter vilification, given its role in the architecture of Hitler's "Final Solution" (Proctor 1988), and to better align it with the natural sciences (Fuentes 2010; Marks 2011). With its focus on human evolution and adaptive processes, the New Physical Anthropology demanded the deconstruction of the damaging hierarchies of humans that a methodological focus on typology spurned. Washburn also sought a humanistic physical anthropology, producing scholarship that served to better society. Over the last 70 years, however, paleoanthropology has concerned itself primarily with increasing the precision of our methods and taking advantage of new technologies instead of examining the interplay between knowledge construction, power, and the validity of our interpretations. Perhaps because our focus of study is no longer alive, we have collectively forgotten about reflexivity, and this has left room for the creation of ideological hegemonies about human evolution that remain robust in the field today (Haraway 1988; Mikels-Carrasco 2012).

Here, the term hegemony serves as a heuristic device and fitting metaphor for an ideological hierarchy in which models about human evolution sit. The dominant ideologies, in turn, influence our scientific narratives at every scale, from localized site analyses to studies of *Homo erectus* craniofacial morphology. Moreover, the social fabric that created and subsequently supports these narratives is something that escapes our traditional empirical approaches to research, as we cannot readily see, touch, or measure it. Here, the social fabric is treated as an abstraction that acknowledges how multiple threads that make up a social order are interwoven. The relatively underdeveloped reflexive gaze in paleoanthropology is both the product of the salient hegemony as well as its protector.

Dominant ideologies have an impact on the perceived value of research focused on datasets not central to their core arguments. In the context of this chapter, the Out of Africa narrative of modern human origins (Stringer 1989) as well as the privileged position of the European paleoanthropological record (Villa and Roebroeks 2014) in our field has created subordinate datasets. The former is a product of the late 1980s – the result of new chronologies for the Levantine Middle Paleolithic sites of Qafzeh (Schwarcz et al. 1988) and then Skhul (Stringer et al. 1989), a novel type of genetic analysis focused on mtDNA (Cann et al. 1987), and hominin fossil discoveries from South and East Africa (see Smith et al. 1989; Stringer 1994). The perceived superiority of the European Upper Paleolithic and its association with modern humans has a much longer history in comparison (see Trinkaus and Shipman 1993). Subordinate datasets and their related interpretations do not possess the cultural capital to threaten the primacy of the dominant narrative. The Central Asian paleoanthropological record is one such subordinate dataset and the topic of this review.

A relative dearth of paleoanthropological data from Central Asia compared to that of Europe, Africa, and the Middle East frequently serves as justification for its secondary role in interpretations of human evolution. Yet, the relationship between power and knowledge production, specific to the formation of hegemonies, also can be invoked and requires critical examination. My goal here is to explore the consequences of the assimilation of this regional dataset into a single dominant interpretative paradigm. It seems that only those who work in peripheral areas (i.e., South Asia, Southeast Asia, North Asia, Oceania, and even West Africa) realize they are given short shrift in Old World scale interpretations of the processes that give rise to the origins of our species. Central Asia is one region among many that is too often characterized as reacting to or absorbing the results of evolutionary change that happens elsewhere. I argue that assimilation into the dominant narrative has obfuscated an understanding of the ways the region and its record are distinct from that of Western Europe and potentially disrupts the Out of Africa perspective.

This work addresses human evolution during the late Pleistocene, specifically the demise of the Neandertals and the role the landscapes of Central Asia played in this process. I will review three often overlooked aspects of the Central Asian record and integrate them into a conceptual model about the region that challenges the status quo. First, climatic variation in Central Asia during the late Pleistocene and its impact on landscapes and productive niche space is not the same as that experienced by Europe or East Asia. Second, variation in the archaeological record, particularly at the Middle to Upper Paleolithic transition, suggests the dominant interpretive paradigm is insufficient and simplistic. Finally, morphological variation was observed in the scant Central Asian hominin fossils before the publication of the ancient DNA datasets that suggest unique patterns of genetic diversity as well as admixture in the region (Glantz et al. 2008, 2009). In this regard, hominin morphological variation could be a result of this admixture, or the morphological pattern of Central Asian hominins, writ large. These three key observations, important in their own right, support a biogeographic model that suggests the Inner Asian Mountain Corridor (IAMC) of Central Asia acted as refugia for multiple hominin populations (Beeton et al. 2014; Glantz et al. 2018). Refugia are identified following Hewitt's (1996) definition of a refugium as an area in which a particular species persists for one entire glacial–interglacial transition. Rather than a "marginal periphery" of Europe and the Levant, language sometimes used as a proxy for "terra incognita," this region and its unique environments supported an evolutionary history of its own, with populations of hominins adapting to local circumstances.

A Little More About Reflexivity and Hegemony in Paleoanthropology

If we consider paleoanthropology as a cultural system, with shared symbols and language, it is somewhat unusual that this culture is seemingly devoid of practices that encourage self-reflection, or reflexivity (Babcock 1980), and then cultural critique and transformation. Marks (2002, 2009, 2011) has taken the field to task for our devotion to positivism and empiricism as we rush to embrace the mantle of "real" science to achieve legitimacy for our research. Testing hypotheses does not absolve us from the pitfalls of being a science dedicated to asking questions about ourselves and our evolutionary history. Although the New Physical Anthropology firmly rooted our theory and methods in evolutionary biology, and this is without question a good thing, the shift encouraged some theoretical blind spots.

Moving away from the theory and methods employed by the other subdisciplines and social sciences (see Mitchell 2002; Scott 1998 and references therein), paleoanthropology stopped considering those seminal contributions of anthropologists to reflexivity theory that produced a general critique of the social sciences (Asad 1973; Clifford and Marcus 1986; Flanagan 1981). These contributions link the researcher and the research process to relationships of knowledge production and power. Perspectives on reflexivity clearly outline how a failure to acknowledge these relationships can invalidate scholarly conclusions. It therefore follows that without reflexivity, power structures develop in the discipline that serve to support specific scientists with particular perspectives on the data they themselves collect and that these perspectives then transform into natural truths, and represent dominant ideologies.

Existing power structures in paleoanthropology are observable at multiple levels, including and perhaps most importantly, preferred and privileged types of anthropological training and the dominant theoretical models produced by those who are similarly trained (and usually from similar national, socioeconomic, linguistic, as well as gender and ethnic backgrounds). Relying on empiricism does not guarantee that all scholarly voices participate in the debate, nor does the scientific method require us to reflect back on the interpretive paradigm itself. The paradigm is taken as inevitable and natural, and resists dismantling even by those scholars who are privileged by the context that created the dominant perspective in the first place. The result of these myriad hegemonies is straightforward, although the power structures themselves are often relatively opaque because the process renders them normative. The consequence is that we highlight some datasets while ignoring others and this "favoritism" has an impact on our interpretations of human evolution.

Hegemony is a heavily used term in anthropology, and is often employed to describe the cultural structures that support the dominant worldview (that of the west and of white men) and the impact this dominance has on the colonized, women, minorities, the poor, etc. More applicable to the topic reviewed here, science and technology can be construed as a form of "consensual hegemony," one that the USA promoted post-World War II to maintain American leadership and make the world safe for democracy. Nandy (1988) explores issues related to science and technology and institutionalized violence. The author suggests that the culture of modern science extends an invitation to state power to use scientific knowledge outside the reaches of the democratic process and, alarmingly, to support the growth of institutionalized violence. Superficially, observations of science's participation in hegemonic structures that, in turn, dictate social hierarchies seemingly have little to do with paleoanthropology. However, paleoanthropology has fought hard to be counted as a science, and we have benefited from the same colonial structures – our narratives are reflections of this.

Part of the maintenance of this consensual hegemony is the complete primacy of English language in scientific publications. There is no question that this primacy is also true of scholarly work in anthropology; even for a discipline that elevates indigenous knowledge, describes it, and gives it voice, our academic business is conducted in English. Perera makes clear that in science, "the English language plays a dominant role, one could even call it a hegemony. As a consequence, minimal room or no room at all is allowed to communicators of other languages to participate in science in their own voice, they are compelled to translate their ideas into English" (quoted by Huttner-Koros 2015). As English speakers, it is important to consider what nuances are missed when paleoanthropological interpretations are translated into English. This is a critical type of reflexivity and also one of the reasons anthropology programs require functional fluency in a second and sometimes third language, although this expectation is more historical than current.

The Metanarrative

The metanarrative in which other paleoanthropological datasets are subsumed follows the arc of anatomically modern humans (AMH) migrating out of Africa, ultimately moving into Europe and across Eurasia with an Upper Paleolithic toolkit, displacing and then finally replacing the Neandertals (and other archaics in the east), normally associated with marginal Middle Paleolithic equipment. As a corollary to this, any evidence of archaic hominins associated with modern behavior, i.e., material culture, is somehow the byproduct of an interaction with AMH on the landscape. Complicating the dominant taxonomies, high-status genomic research has now forced paleoanthropologists to add the caveat that archaic hominin displacement occurred with some admixture. However, this admission does not change the trajectory of the metanarrative; the expectation that the superior (biologically and/or culturally) always vanquishes the inferior, a colonial narrative so normalized in paleoanthropology that it often disguises itself as neo-Darwinism.

Even scholars who work in both Europe and Africa suggest that what I refer to as a metanarrative no longer has the evidentiary basis to maintain its primacy in the conceptual models that depict late Pleistocene human evolution (Villa and Roebroeks 2014; Zilhão 2011). Villa and Roebroeks (2014:5) rigorously document that the contemporary archaeological record is robust enough to overturn a "long tradition of thinking in terms of Neandertal–AMH dichotomies, steered by overstressing developments within the Upper Paleolithic of Europe, the record of which has become almost like a yardstick for modern human behavior." Yet, the metanarrative persists.

In the humanities and social sciences, metanarratives are often described as transhistorical and deeply embedded in a particular culture. Insofar as paleoanthropology (consisting of its record depicted in a variety of media, its scholars, students, the interested public, and supporting institutions) can be referred to as a culture, it can be argued that the Out of Africa metanarrative is wholly integrated and has emerged as transhistorical; it defines contemporary social phenomena. In fact, critiques of the dominant Out of Africa narrative engage in what can only be described as postmodern skepticism about this "totalizing schema," one that offers unified explanations of all knowledge and experience (Bertens and Fokkema 1997:186). Reflecting on the metanarrative and its ability to subordinate datasets, rendering them incapable of altering perceptions about the dominant ideology, is necessary for the evaluation of the validity of our interpretations of human evolution.

Metanarratives require the strange to be made familiar. I argue that the strange must remain strange in order to resist assimilation so that the dominant narrative is disrupted and perhaps rewritten. It is not that empiricism has failed. Instead, specific "ideas" about empirical results, often only loosely tethered to those results, have disenfranchised research that produces conclusions at odds with the dominant narrative, even when similar methodological approaches are followed.

Comments on the Paleoanthropological Record of Pleistocene Central Asia

Figure 2.1 depicts the area of Eurasia typically regarded as Central Asia and includes the distribution of most of the Paleolithic sites in the region ($n = 66$). The areas most intensely studied are in the piedmonts of the southern Tien Shan and Altai mountains, respectively. While the Russian Altai is within western Siberia instead of Central Asia proper, its position at the northeastern extent of the IAMC necessitates its inclusion in the discussion. Excluding those from the Altai, only eight Central Asian Paleolithic sites have more than one associated radiometric determination and a dating regime that includes multiple methods. Although stratified sites in Central Asia mostly fall within Marine Isotope Stage (MIS) 3 (60,000–24,000 years ago), new uranium-series dates from Obi-Rakhmat Grotto in Uzbekistan bracket the roughly 10 meters of deposit from 109,000 ± 2000 years ago to 98,000 years ago (Asmerom et al. 2018). The 109,000 year date for the level that contained the OR-1 hominin pushes it back into the later phases of MIS 5

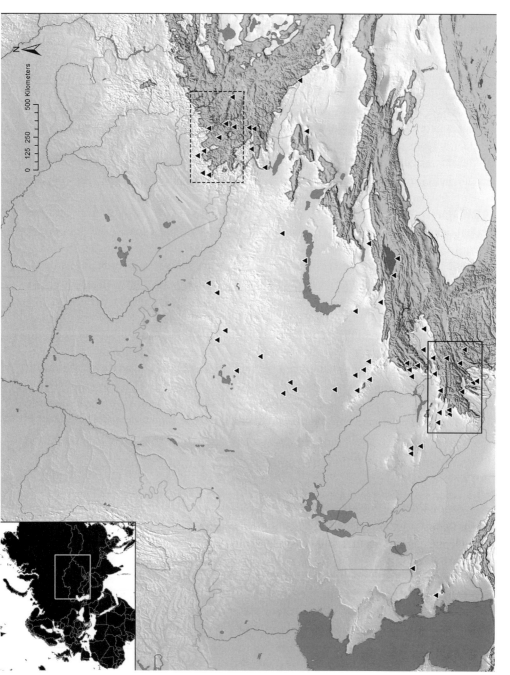

Figure 2.1 Map of Central Asia, including the Altai mountains of the Russian Federation. Triangles represent Paleolithic sites, with the solid lined box around the sites of the southern Tien Shan mountains, and the dashed lined box around those from the Altai. Figure was previously published in Glantz et al. (2018).

(130,000–71,000 years ago) instead of the conservative 90,000–60,000 years ago window given to stratum 16 in a previous study (Glantz et al. 2008). However, hominins occupied Central Asia well before MIS 5. In the loess formation of the Tajik depression, situated below the Brunhes/Matuyama boundary and above the Jaramillo subchron, the site of Kul'dara is roughly 900,000–800,000 years old. The stone tool accumulations from the localities of Karatau and Lakhuti recovered from younger paleosols of the Tajik depression represent additional evidence of pre-MIS 5 hominin occupation.

The paleoanthropological record of Lower Paleolithic hominin habitation of Central Asia is seemingly a set of discrete data points. Too few sites separated by too much time undermine any interpretations of hominins continuously exploiting Central Asian landscapes over the past million years. Continuous versus discrete evidence of occupation, however, depends on the spatiotemporal scale of analysis and the relative "value" of the region with regard to the metanarrative. We typically do not consider the European record to reflect spotty or non-continuous habitation after 1.2 million years ago, even though gaps of 100,000 years or more exist in some areas and the chronological associations of Middle Pleistocene fossils remain problematic.

Certainly, we can agree that hominins inhabited Eurasia in varying densities after Dmanisi at 1.7 million years ago. Because Eurasia is a large super-continent with juxtaposed niches of varying productivity, the spotty record of one region versus another does not mean all hominin groups returned to Africa or relegated themselves to a small corner of the Levant during periods of deteriorating conditions. These questions of scale are important because it is equally true that Eurasia was never totally abandoned after 1.7 million years ago and, at the same time, local extinctions of hominin groups occurred, small groups merged together, and population densities ebbed and flowed over space and time in response to local climate conditions and cultural decision-making.

Contemporary socioeconomic and political circumstances directly bear on the quality and quantity of the archaeological record in regions undergoing change. Political stability, either because of colonialism, or long independent national histories, supports the construction of dense archaeological records. The geopolitical conditions since the fall of the Soviet Union dramatically and negatively altered academic institutions that supported archaeological research across the former Soviet Republics. As academic priorities shifted in this new environment, and Soviet-trained archaeologists retired, Paleolithic research suffered from a lack of state-sponsored funding as well as a decrease in student interest. Graduate students overwhelmingly seek professional degrees they can leverage in the new economies of independent nations, as the proliferation of freshly minted private business schools across the republics attests. It is not surprising, in this context, that the Central Asian Paleolithic record is mostly the product of Soviet-era exploration from the 1930s to the late 1980s.

Although fleshing out the impact of these geopolitical factors on paleoanthropology in Central Asia is somewhat beyond the scope of this chapter, I offer this short review as a cautionary tale about interpreting the relative density of the archaeological record in the region as a literal reflection of alternating phases of hominin occupation and abandonment. Whether Central Asia was occupied continuously during the Pleistocene is an argument about the evidence of absence versus the absence of evidence, following Dennell (2003, 2011). This debate is important because characterizing landscapes as "abandoned," "vacated," and "marginal" implies that the intensity and severity of climate change in the region, the relative productivity of the niches, as well as the effectiveness of hominin adaptations (biological/cultural) are the only explanations for a sparse, non-continuous archaeological record. In addition, if Central Asian landscapes were periodically abandoned, as hypothesized by a number of researchers, then historical contingencies that may have shaped evolutionary processes on the local scale can be ignored because their impact on the metanarrative is interpreted as non-significant. Hominins are described as migrating into the "empty" region, following some preferred climate trend (e.g., Asmerom et al. 2018), and then associated archaeological records are overlain with the history important to the metanarrative, or perceived as unique or "new" to a single moment in history. Yet, it is more likely that population interactions were tethered to the long chronologies of local conditions and more dynamic than the archaeological or genetic records can resolve.

The factors that bias the archaeological record are multifaceted and have a differential impact on regions within national boundaries. For example, the variables that affect the quality of the North American Paleo-Indian record are different from those that have an impact on the representativeness of the Mesolithic record in the Levant. However, the notion that recent history and contemporary geopolitics manipulates the quality of our datasets is the type of reflexivity that researchers in our field implicitly understand but do not often put into practice with regard to methods of analysis and resulting interpretations.

Three Observations About Human Evolution in Central Asia

Climatic Variation

Fitzsimmons and colleagues (2017, 2018) and Beeton and colleagues (2014) provide relatively detailed reviews of the factors responsible for climatic fluctuation in Central Asia during the Pleistocene. The main question about Central Asian climatic regimes is the degree to which the chronology and intensity of fluctuations from glacial to interglacial conditions matched those of Europe and East Asia. The chronology of the maximum extent of the glaciers within Central Asian mountain systems is not only different from other areas in the Himalayan–Tibet orogen (Owen and Dortch 2014), but also asynchronous with the global Last Glacial Maximum at 26,500–20,000 years ago. In general, the mountainous areas that define the IAMC, the Altai, Tien Shan, and the Pamirs, experienced the high levels of precipitation that support the growth of mountain glaciers earlier than other parts of the Old World. However, Central Asian last glacial maxima are not monolithic; they occur at different times in different places along the IAMC. Chronologies derived from [10]Be methods suggest maximum glacial advance was achieved as early as MIS 5b (93,000 years ago) in some regions and not later than the early part of MIS 3 (60,000 years ago) in others. As Europe and East Asia experienced deteriorating temperatures and high levels of precipitation that culminated in the coldest phases of the Pleistocene period co-occurring with the maximum glacial advance at roughly 20,000 years ago, Central Asia was drying out.

While the juxtaposition of steppe, mountain steppe, and foothills occurs in other parts of the Old World, the climate of the Central Asian steppe is relatively unique. Its highly continental environment is extreme when compared to other steppes/plains because of its geographic position at the heart of Eurasia and the high elevations of the associated mountains. These factors insulate the area from moisture delivered by the Siberian and East Asia monsoons. In a study that built on a previously described ecological niche model (Beeton et al. 2014), Glantz et al. (2018) used the WorldClim dataset (Hijmans et al. 2005) and ocean–atmosphere simulations for past climate (Otto-Bliesner et al. 2006a, 2006b) to compare the range of four BioClim variables shown to be significantly correlated to hominin site distribution in Central Asia. Results indicated that aspects of the abiotic profiles of the foothills and adjacent steppe were significantly different during glacial and interglacial periods. The foothills experienced greater levels of annual precipitation during interglacial periods than the steppe, as well as a reduction in seasonal temperature extremes during glacial periods. Higher annual temperatures, less precipitation, and significant differences with regard to seasonal temperatures across both interglacial and glacial periods support the characterization of the steppe as a progressively extreme environment when compared to that of the foothills. Most importantly, while a trend toward aridification characterizes the entire region during MIS 3 and 2, the desert/steppe only expands during interglacial periods. Paleoanthropologists rely on dichotomies in their conceptual model construction – for example, glacial versus interglacial is also framed as cold versus warm, bad versus good, deteriorating climates versus improving conditions. Because of this, it is somewhat counterintuitive to think of an interglacial period creating challenging conditions for hominins in one area, but suitable conditions in another at a similar latitude. The differences in abiotic optima here are a consequence of the heterogenic conditions resulting from elevation variation (Fahrig 2003).

In addition, the growth and maintenance of mountain glaciers at high elevations during the terminal phases of MIS 5 and early MIS 4 (roughly 70,000 years ago) were a product of the same climatic conditions that preserved humidity in the valleys of adjacent foothills, similar to conditions present at Obi-Rakhmat Grotto roughly 100,000 years ago. Although the aridification of Central Asia must have negatively affected the habitability of the steppic zones adjacent to the IAMC, humid conditions characterize most foothill environments, even when the juxtaposed steppe expanded and the footprint of desert areas within the steppe increased during MIS 3. These climate dynamics coupled with the elevation variation specific to the region's topography likely encouraged the lower elevations of the IAMC to act as multiple refugia, southern and cryptic, respectively (see Hewitt 1996; Holderegger and Thiel-Egenter 2009; Stewart and Stringer 2012).

The foothills of the IAMC provided a more predictable set of abiotic circumstances for hominins (i.e., reliable water and a relatively consistent temperature regime) than the steppic areas. Landscapes with high levels of elevation variation typically support micro-niches that often are more stable and mild during climatic downturns than those from the immediate adjacent areas, like the steppe or juxtaposed high-elevation mountains (Fahrig 2003). At both a highly localized and a mid-range scale like the one defined in Figure 2.1, source–sink theory (Pulliam and Danielson 1991; Runge et al. 2006) allows the conception of the foothills as a source, and the deteriorating conditions of the steppe to act as a sink, that during some periods directed hominins into the foothills. During glacial periods, however, hominins expanded into the steppe while maintaining their core presence in the foothills.

Paleoclimatic reconstructions of Central Asia serve as a foundation for considering models of hominin population dynamics separate from the continent-scale perspectives on hominin migration out of Africa, the origin of AMH, and the demise of the Neandertals. Regional examinations of past climate in Central Asia call into question a typological model of marginal versus productive environments and the associated assumptions about when during the Pleistocene, and where on the Eurasian landscape, these good and bad niches existed. Instead, previous research shows that hominins in Central Asia faced specific and local ecological challenges within a dynamic and diverse landscape. During the late Pleistocene, hominin populations in the region leveraged the productive foothill micro-niches against the periodically diminishing returns of an increasingly desertified Central Asian steppe.

However, even this mid-scale approach to hominin mobility patterns is certainly a gross simplification of a process that should be characterized as resource and climate dependent; the complex interplay between population pressure, niche productivity, geographic constraints, and the product of decision-making among actors within their social networks. It is possible that during certain climatic periods, the populations residing in the northern and southern aspects of the IAMC, respectively, were connected and, at other times, separated by differential and asynchronous exploitation of the adjacent steppe or by their relatively small operating size as groups living in the foothills, a relatively limited geographic area.

The patterns of fragmentation and cohesion of hominin groups in Central Asia were influenced by the dynamics of neighboring regions, but also present a unique history that requires exploration so that hypotheses can be constructed that are independent from the dominant metanarrative. Characterizing the paleoclimate of Central Asia as either preventing or facilitating hominin migration from the west and southwest before mid-scale and regionally circumscribed hypotheses are tested positions this area as subordinate to the metanarrative. Until more archaeological surveys and excavations are carried out in Kyrgyzstan, the Xinjiang Uyghur Autonomous Region of China, Mongolia, and eastern Kazakhstan, mobility patterns will remain elusive. Moreover, resolution of these patterns relies on independence from the metanarrative gained by fighting our impulse to make the strange familiar.

Variation in the Central Asian Middle to Upper Paleolithic Record

Invoking the influence of migrating AMH out of Africa or the superiority of the European Upper Paleolithic record to explain aspects of that from Central Asia assumes the validity of the metanarrative before it is tested; this is the power afforded to it. Descriptions of the Central Asian Paleolithic record that appear in the English literature follow the basic outline of this narrative. For example, following Dibble (1987) and Rolland and Dibble (1990), Vishnyatsky (1999) effectively erased all evidence of lithic variability related to style by sweeping variants like the Mountain and Soan traditions of the foothills of Tajikistan and Uzbekistan under the carpet of generalized Middle Paleolithic techno-typology. Both Davis (1990) and then Vishnyatsky (1999) identified the Zagros as the source of the Middle Paleolithic tradition of Central Asia. Although this analysis may stand the test of time, it makes it difficult to employ granular hypotheses that are able to reveal how hominins in Central Asia adapted to those unique environments within the constraints of relatively poor raw material sources. Assuming all variation in the Central Asian Paleolithic was continuous, the result of a specific and singular technological approach, and originated outside the area, supports the characterization of Neandertal material culture as limited and the area as marginal and peripheral to a core in which innovation may have occurred.

As biological anthropologists look for the material evidence of the improvement in cognitive abilities assumed to co-occur with the appearance of modern humans, they often pressure archaeologists to hypothesize about the identity of the makers of the stone tools they study. A focus on identity, like in contemporary identity politics, may serve to marginalize further those groups whose differences tend to be exaggerated when compared to the dominant (superior) group (AMH). Because the Teshik-Tash 1 fossil from Uzbekistan was associated with a Middle Paleolithic tradition and described as a Neandertal, the flake-based toolkits of Central Asia were uniformly deemed as "archaic," awaiting replacement. Since the late 1970s, observations about the stone tool assemblages from the region offer further support of the narrative that the Neandertals were relegated to a periphery and eventually replaced. Although Ranov and Davis (1979; Davis and Ranov 1999) never explicitly invoke the metanarrative, their observations that the Middle Paleolithic persists chronologically well after the Upper Paleolithic takes root in adjacent areas west, southwest, and north of Central Asia is easily accommodated in it. The initial Upper Paleolithic and early Upper Paleolithic traditions that characterize the final phases of MIS 3 in Europe, the Middle East, and even a few of the Altai sites of Russia are absent from this time period in Central Asia proper. Evidence that complicates these observations has only recently been published.

Fitzsimmons and colleagues (2017) provide a robust chronological framework for two sites in southern Kazakhstan, Valikhanova and Maibulak, respectively, associated with the piedmont of the Tien Shan. This framework places both sites broadly within the temporal domain of the Middle to Upper Paleolithic transition or, alternatively and conservatively, entirely within the sequence of the Upper

Paleolithic – i.e., from 47,000 to 25,000 years ago. Serial blade production, typical of most Upper Paleolithic toolkits, is virtually unknown at these open-air sites. Where bladelets are preserved, enough discoidal and chopping tools are present that the industries can be characterized as mixed, showing both Middle and Upper Paleolithic features. Fitzsimmons and colleagues (2017) make the important point that assemblage analyses support multiple interpretations, none of which are mutually exclusive. For example, the persistence of discoidal technology at Valikhanova may be unrelated to the Middle Paleolithic but instead represent a continued preference for a flake-based toolkit within an Upper Paleolithic context. This mix of flake and bladelet production at the same site, however, is relatively unique. Bladelet production appears relatively early at a small number of Central Asian sites and may represent the historical and local antecedent to the technological mix present at Valikhanova and Maibulak.

An alternative hypothesis suggests a twist on the metanarrative in that Central Asian archaeological variability mirrors the multiple and multidirectional hominin migrations into the region and their impact on local population coalescence and fragmentation. In this regard, hominins from elsewhere bring bladelet technology into the region, but it does not replace wholesale other technologies (or populations affiliated with those technologies like Neandertals with the Middle Paleolithic), as the European Upper Paleolithic is interpreted as doing in Europe. And finally, Fitzsimmons and colleagues (2017) suggest that technologies used to mark cultural affiliations, i.e., "the Upper Paleolithic," are so useful to hominin resource exploitation and relatively easy to invent and reinvent that they should not be used as proxies for specific traditions at all. Importantly, these varied interpretations do not negate the original observations of Ranov and Davis (1979; Davis and Ranov 1999); they simply add to the cannon of archaeological diversity during MIS 3 and 2 the region supports. Although this new work is an example of the accretional quality of knowledge construction in paleoanthropology, the metanarrative and the hegemonic system that frames it certainly influence this process.

The Central Asian Hominin Record, Morphological Variation, and Genetics

While the resolution of Central Asian paleoenvironments has improved and the chronological framework of existing archaeological sites has grown, the quality of the hominin fossil record is still shabby. Only new discoveries will alter the fact that this record is small in individual number, highly fragmentary, not representative in terms of anatomy, and disproportionate of juveniles. Still, some published descriptions of the hominins comment on their lack of strict morphological conformity to the existing late Pleistocene record of Europe and Africa (see Glantz et al. 2008, 2009 and references therein). The overreliance on and oftentimes inappropriate use of cladistic approaches in paleoanthropology has forced an uncomfortable dichotomous perspective on the Central Asian hominins, as they must be identified as either Neandertals or AMH (now we can add Denisovans). Moreover, this approach has supported the notion that a single anatomical area given "special value" is enough to make phylogenetic assessments (Gunz and Bulygina 2012). However, no matter the cause, our field's loyalty to typology with regard to hominin systematics, even when systematics is not the goal of the research, prevents us from successfully describing and explaining hominin spatiotemporal variation. The consequence of this and our dependence on the Out of Africa metanarrative casts human variation in a reductive light, recreating the typological approaches Washburn rebuked as well as hindering the resolution of complex evolutionary processes, such as the mobility patterns resulting in population coalescence, fragmentation, and local adaptations.

Since 2008, my colleagues and I posited in multiple venues that Obi-Rakhmat 1 and Teshik-Tash 1, juvenile hominins from Uzbekistan, departed from the typical European Neandertal morphological pattern, reflecting a mosaic of modern, archaic, and perhaps regional features instead (following Trinkaus 2005). While the conclusion itself is not surprising, it is at odds with the consensus view. The expectation that contemporary humans from Uzbekistan possess the same regional features that define western Europeans is as illogical as this assumption is for late Pleistocene groups unless robust and spatially explicit evidence of long-distance migration exists. Because the metanarrative asserts that only two types of humans existed in the recent past, moderns and archaics, any regional features then get co-opted by this dichotomy and sometimes misidentified as either modern or archaic, when in fact they are neither. The metanarrative also imbues the space separating moderns and archaics with special significance and meaning, a threshold, or a Rubicon to be crossed.

Sample construction is another issue that has shaped the interpretations of Central Asian hominin fossil morphologies, from Gremyatskii's original description of Teshik-Tash in 1949 to that of Obi-Rakhmat 60 years later. Because sample construction presupposes discrete and bounded groups, results tend to support the assumed groupings. The pitfalls of identifying artificially bounded groups by using hominin fossils as proxies for potentially large interbreeding populations can be assuaged analytically by following certain protocols (see Willermet and Hill 1997; Willermet et al. Chapter 8, this volume) – although they are rarely followed. As described earlier, the archaic versus modern dichotomy certainly complicates an appreciation of morphological variation in general and the morphological gradients that track hominin interactions and local adaptation specific to Central Asia.

Historical precedent often dictates that respective specimens be placed in a sample's Neandertal and modern human bins. History also influences the regional human groups to which a newly discovered fossil is compared. Because Teshik-Tash 1 was associated with a Middle Paleolithic toolkit, Gremyatskii (1949) compared the juvenile to other hominins associated with similar toolkits, i.e., the European Neandertals, even though China was a neighboring country with a hominin fossil record of its own (i.e., Zhoukoudian and other localities). The hegemony that privileges western science, born out of the European Enlightenment, encouraged Soviet paleoanthropologists to turn west to validate new discoveries instead of exploring samples from communist Asia. This history is one of the reasons that the Central Asian record is subordinate to the metanarrative in the first place. Appropriate comparative samples ought to include the relevant records from Asia, in addition to the traditional ones (e.g., Buzhilova et al. 2017). Although my colleagues and I have been guilty of this omission as well, we nonetheless acknowledged how our conclusions were limited by sample construction (Glantz 2010).

In 2010, when the Neandertal composite genome was published (Green et al. 2010), the consensus view on late Pleistocene hominin systematics cracked. For those of us working in Central Asia, genomic results gave us one way to interpret the morphological patterns already observed in the record. Although admixture coupled with highly localized drift and selection has long been identified as an underlying driver of morphological gradients (e.g., Wolpoff et al. 1984), it was not until the composite genome was published that the metanarrative became vulnerable. However, recognizing regional variation is dependent on representative samples of a relatively large size, at least larger than the one composite partial genome from Vindjia Cave, Croatia. In this way, the genomic samples from Central Asia (Fu et al. 2014; Kuhlwilm et al. 2016; Meyer et al. 2012; Prüfer et al. 2014; Reich et al. 2010, 2011; Slon et al. 2018) have not improved our ability to describe variation, nor helped us to identify which morphologies are produced by admixture, if any. Although introgression, admixture, and interbreeding were now possible "validated" alternatives to population replacement as explanations for morphological patterns, the genomic sample is hardly representative of the genetic diversity present in a breeding population.

In addition to the conclusion that Neandertals and modern humans must have interbred, ancient DNA sequencing introduced us to new players on the Central Asian landscape, the Denisovans. The Denisovans, represented by a few teeth and a finger bone from Denisova Cave, are ghosts. We have some evidence of their existence in the form of unique strings of base pairs on amplified ancient DNA (aDNA) segments, but have no idea what they looked like, how extensive their population size was, or where it originated. Moreover, given unresolved issues related to site formation processes at Denisova Cave, and the genetic identification of both Neandertals and Denisovans at the site, it is impossible to understand whether differences in the character of the material culture across the stratigraphy is related to its respective makers. This may be a good thing, as it would facilitate another kind of faulty inference that has plagued studies of the Middle Paleolithic to Upper Paleolithic transition in Europe, i.e., the use of stone tools as proxies for specific "types" of humans (Wolpoff et al. 2004).

Because more ancient genomes are from Central Asia than any other place in the Old World, research has shifted to a primary focus on revealing whether hominins were Denisovans, Neandertals, modern humans, or hybrids. In this regard, genomic research has only supported the paleoanthropological research design mainstay of putting hominins into bins as the necessary first step and primary way of reconstructing the history of our species. Although ancient genetics provides a window onto the past that is impossible to open with the bones and stones of traditional paleoanthropological research, this work has only served to entrench one central aspect of the metanarrative, that late Pleistocene hominin variation is still bounded and semi-discrete.

Evidence of intermixture through the genomic analysis of single individuals makes it possible to overturn highly entrenched paleoanthropological theories in one fell swoop. However, competing hypotheses that move beyond the new binary of "admixed or not" have not been forthcoming. It is also important to recognize that the science of paleoanthropology sits much lower in a hierarchical structure that valorizes genetics beyond all other natural sciences. The relative power of geneticists to weigh in on debates embedded in an anthropological literature they are only peripherally aware of is another avenue for the continued subordination of specific datasets and their interpretations. We should be wary of relinquishing narrative control to nucleic acids and base pairs, or decaying isotopes, for that matter. Genomic research is, after all, only one line of evidence used to reconstruct a multidimensional history of our species.

Putting It All Together: Taming the Metanarrative and Future Directions

The metanarrative co-opting the Central Asian Paleolithic record assumes that: (1) the timing and conditions supporting the climate fluctuations during MIS 3 and the arrival of the global Last Glacial Maximum were similar across Eurasia; (2) the character of the Middle Paleolithic record conforms to that of Europe and the Levant; (3) the arrival of the European Upper Paleolithic was either a product of a late migration of AMH into the area or a part of an autochthonous trajectory coupled with the origin of modern humans; and (4) hominin morphologies follow the modern versus archaic binary and are bounded entities, albeit with some introgression. Evidence presented here, however, suggests that these assumptions are faulty and that the metanarrative fails to adequately capture the evolutionary processes that shaped Central Asian hominins during the late Pleistocene.

The metanarrative also provides a structure for describing large-scale hominin migrations into the area that requires a critical review. In this regard, archaic Neandertals were forced to migrate from Western Europe or the Levant because of competition for resources and the pressure put on ecosystems from AMH moving out of Africa. Because modern humans are superior by definition, they displaced Neandertals into the assumed "empty" marginal environments that defined their eastern periphery – Central Asia. Another related narrative has Neandertals fleeing the deteriorating climates of their ancestral homeland as the global Last Glacial Maximum loomed on the horizon. Here, Neandertals are climate migrants, pushed into the secondary ecosystems of Central Asia only to find devious and clever modern humans had expanded into the areas left behind, making a return impossible and population collapse and extinction likely. Adding genetic data to the mix negligibly complicates the metanarrative.

Derevianko and colleagues provide yet another twist on the dominant narrative that relies on actions of non-Neandertal groups in the area. Long proponents of the supremacy of the Altai as an ecosystem, the hominins who lived there, and their material culture, Derevianko and colleagues (2000, 2003, 2008) suggest that the local makers of Eurasia's earliest Initial Upper Paleolithic traditions in southern Siberia forced the relatively new Neandertal émigrés, with their Middle Paleolithic tools, into the region's marginal southern reaches. The forced migration of this archaic human group into subprime real estate by a superior group, even with evidence of some degree of admixture with this group, ultimately led to the same conclusion – Neandertal extinction. Each subtle iteration of the metanarrative conforms to a core set of normalized "beliefs" about late Pleistocene human evolution; namely that bounded human populations inhabited a landscape and, like in the *Hunger Games* (Collins 2008), the landscape presented obstacles that only the superior group could navigate to secure worldwide domination.

To move beyond this dominant narrative, the field needs to stop worrying about hominin identity and related questions about late Pleistocene systematics, highlight variation instead of hiding it in the binary, and look at regional datasets to understand the local dynamics that ultimately produce the hominin morphologies and lithic traditions we describe. Oftentimes research that follows this prescription requires modification by a review process that demands scholars tie their work back into the dominant narrative; this is part of the larger power structure identified here as problematic (see Mott and Cockayne 2017).

How to Move Forward?

The main goal of this review has been to highlight the potential insights gained from assuming a reflexive stance in relation to knowledge production in paleoanthropology. In the best scenario, this stance allows for an appreciation of the power of specific narratives and the myriad ways they manipulate interpretations of evolutionary processes that occur outside the core focus of the dominant perspective: Africa and the Levant. A call for reflexivity does not presuppose that the dominant narrative is wrong or that empirical approaches to the record have failed us. Instead, this critical lens provides the justification to examine actively the impact of bias on the records we analyze and to adjust our conclusions accordingly. This lens also calls for a focus on mid-range regional scales of inquiry, like the ones related to late Pleistocene Central Asia reviewed here. This scale potentially reveals the human–environment interactions unique to a circumscribed set of juxtaposed ecosystems. Single site foci are too easily swept up into the metanarrative and become disembodied entities, used as lines of evidence often to support a continental-scale framework, i.e., the trajectory of AMH migrating out of Africa.

The creation of the metanarrative and the maintenance of its power also determine how we disseminate our research results within paleoanthropology. Over the past 20 years, I have been invited to no fewer than five symposia with similar titles, like *Gaps in Our Knowledge in Paleoanthropology*, *Paleoanthropological Research at the Frontiers*, etc., with almost identical invitee lists. In fact, I co-hosted one myself in 2004. In these sessions, invited scholars, typically from western institutions and other privileged scholarly spaces, who work in areas adjacent to South Africa, East Africa, or the Levant share results through traditional formats (papers/posters) usually to an audience of students or other scholars interested in peripheries. However, these venues often fail to introduce our results and interpretations to scholars whose work is the core focus of the dominant narrative, nor do they provide a stage for local scholars to share their points of view. This problem of audience gets at a larger issue concerning the democratization of science. It seems that paleoanthropology has a long way to go before becoming truly internationalist and decolonized.

Political psychologist and social theorist Ashis Nandy (1998) describes the relationship between the west and Asia, and the impact of colonialism on the individual and collective psychology of Asians. While superficially this topic seems to have little to do with the business of paleoanthropology, I have argued here that contemporary sociopolitical factors influence not only the quality of the data we collect, but also how we analyze those data and the shape of the narratives we construct about the evolution of our species. These factors also have an impact on the character of the professional relationships between western scholars and their Asian counterparts. Central Asia, after all, is geographically a part of Asia with a complicated colonial history of its own.

Nandy (1998:143) suggests:

the modern West finds it particularly difficult to co-exist with other cultures. It may have a well-developed language of co-existence and tolerance and well-honed tools for conversing with other civilizations. It may even have the cognitive riches to study, understand or decode the non-West. But, culturally, it has an exceedingly poor capacity to live with strangers. It has to try to either overwhelm or proselytize them.

This quote alone does not encapsulate the totality of the issues surrounding colonialism, the process of decolonization, and the relationships of power and knowledge production borne out of the tension between the west and the colonized (see Athreya and Ackermann in press). Yet, it can serve as a metaphor for how the dominant metanarrative of human evolution, a product of western-trained scholars, creates subordinate datasets and then assimilates them. It also underscores the potentially fraught nature of collaborative relationships with local scholars when this hegemony goes unacknowledged. The democratization of paleoanthropology will provide, at a minimum, additional conceptual models of human evolution to test and validate; this is likely the only way our science can grow.

References

Asad T (1973) *Anthropology and the Colonial Encounter*. Humanities Press.

Asmerom Y, Polyak V, Wagner J, and Patchett J (2018) Hominin expansion into Central Asia during the last interglacial. *Earth and Planetary Science Letters* 494:148–152.

Athreya S and Ackermann RR (in press) Colonialism and narratives of human origins in Asia and Africa. In Porr M and Matthews J, editors. *Interrogating Human Origins: Decolonisation and the Deep Past*. Routledge. Pp. 23–42.

Babcock B (1980) Reflexivity: definitions and discriminations. *Semiotica* 30(1–2):1–14.

Beeton TA, Glantz MM, Trainer AK, Temirbekov SS, and Reich RM (2014) The fundamental hominin niche in late Pleistocene Central Asia: a preliminary refugium model. *Journal of Biogeography* 41(1):95–110.

Bertens H and Fokkema DW (1997) *International Postmodernism: Theory and Literary Practice.* John Benjamins Publishing.

Buzhilova A, Derevianko A, and Shunkov M (2017) The northern dispersal route: bioarchaeological data from the Late Pleistocene of Altai, Siberia. *Current Anthropology* 58(S17):S491–S503.

Cann R, Stoneking M, and Wilson A (1987) Mitochondrial DNA and human evolution. *Nature* 325 (6099):31–36.

Clifford J and Marcus GE (1986) *Writing Culture: The Poetics and Politics of Ethnography.* University of California Press.

Collins S (2008) *The Hunger Games.* Scholastic Press.

Davis R (1990) Pleistocene climates and migration into Asia: evidence from loess. Unpublished paper, read at the International Symposium on the Chronostratigraphy of Paleolithic in the North, Central, and Eastern Asia and America, Novosibirsk.

Davis RS and Ranov VA (1999) Recent work on the Paleolithic of Central Asia. *Evolutionary Anthropology* 8(5):186–193.

Dennell R (2003) Dispersal and colonisation, long and short chronologies: how continuous is the Early Pleistocene record for hominids outside East Africa? *Journal of Human Evolution* 45 (6):421–440.

Dennell R (2011) The colonization of "Savannahstan": issues of timing(s) and patterns of dispersal across Asia in the Late Pliocene and Early Pleistocene. In Norton C and Braun D, editors. *Asian Paleoanthropology.* Springer. Pp. 7–30.

Derevianko AP and Rybin EP (2003) The earliest representations of symbolic behavior by Paleolithic humans in the Altai Mountains. *Archaeology, Ethnology and Anthropology of Eurasia* 3 (15):27–50.

Derevianko AP, Petrin VT, and Rybin EP (2000) The Kara-Bom site and the characteristics of the Middle–Upper Paleolithic transition in the Altai. *Archaeology, Ethnology and Anthropology of Eurasia* 2:33–52.

Derevianko AP, Shunkov M, and Volkov P (2008) A Paleolithic bracelet from Denisova Cave. *Archaeology, Ethnology and Anthropology of Eurasia* 34(2):13–25.

Dibble H (1987) The interpretation of Middle Paleolithic scraper morphology. *American Antiquity* 52 (1):109–117.

Fahrig L (2003) Effects of habitat fragmentation on biodiversity. *Annual Review of Ecology, Evolution, and Systematics* 34(1):487.

Fitzsimmons K, Iovita R, Sprafke T, et al. (2017) A chronological framework connecting the early Upper Palaeolithic across the Central Asian piedmont. *Journal of Human Evolution* 113:107–126.

Fitzsimmons K, Sprafke T, Zielhofer C, et al. (2018) Loess accumulation in the Tian Shan piedmont: implications for palaeoenvironmental change in arid Central Asia. *Quaternary International* 469(A):30–43.

Flanagan OJ (1981) Psychology, progress, and the problem of reflexivity: a study in the epistemological foundations of psychology. *Journal of the History of the Behavioral Sciences* 17 (3):375–386.

Fu Q, Li H, Moorjani P, Jay F, et al. (2014) Genome sequence of a 45,000-year-old modern human from western Siberia. *Nature* 514(7523):445.

Fuentes A (2010) The new biological anthropology: bringing Washburn's new physical anthropology into 2010 and beyond – The 2008 AAPA Luncheon Lecture. *Yearbook of Physical Anthropology* 53:2–12.

Glantz MM (2010) The history of hominin occupation of Central Asia in review. In Norton C and Braun D, editors. *Asian Paleoanthropology.* Springer. Pp. 101–112.

Glantz MM, Viola B, Wrinn P, et al. (2008) New hominin remains from Uzbekistan. *Journal of Human Evolution* 55(2):223–237.

Glantz MM, Athreya S, and Ritzman T (2009) Is Central Asia the eastern outpost of the Neandertal range? A reassessment of the Teshik-Tash child. *American Journal of Physical Anthropology* 138 (1):45–61.

Glantz MM, Van Arsdale A, Temirbekov S, and Beeton T (2018) How to survive the glacial apocalypse: hominin mobility strategies in late Pleistocene Central Asia. *Quaternary International* 466(A):82–92.

Green RE, Krause J, Briggs AW, et al. (2010) A draft sequence of the Neandertal genome. *Science* 328 (5979):710–722.

Gremyatskii MA (1949) Skull of the Neandertal child from Teshik-Tash Cave, Southern Uzbekistan. In Gremyatskii MA, editor. *Teshik-Tash: Paleolithic Man.* Moscow State University. Pp. 137–182.

Gunz P and Bulygina E (2012) The Mousterian child from Teshik-Tash is a Neanderthal: a geometric morphometric study of the frontal bone. *American Journal of Physical Anthropology* 149 (3):365–379.

Haraway D (1988) Remodelling the human way of life: Sherwood Washburn and the New Physical Anthropology, 1950–1980. In Stocking G, editor. *History of Anthropology Vol. 5. Bones, Bodies, Behavior: Essays on Biological Anthropology.* University of Wisconsin Press. Pp. 206–259.

Hewitt G (1996) Some genetic consequences of Ice Ages, and their role in divergence and speciation. *Biological Journal of the Linnean Society* 58(3):247–276.

Hijmans RJ, Cameron SE, Parra JL, Jones PG, and Jarvis A (2005) Very high resolution interpolated climate surfaces for global land areas. *International Journal of Climatology* 25 (15):1965–1978.

Holderegger R and Thiel-Egenter C (2009) A discussion of different types of glacial refugia used in mountain biogeography and phylogeography. *Journal of Biogeography* 36(3):476–480.

Huttner-Koros A (2015) The hidden bias of science's universal language: the vast majority of scientific papers today are published in English. What gets lost when other languages get left out? *The Atlantic.* www.theatlantic.com/science/archive/2015/08/english-universal-language-science-research/400919.

Kuhlwilm M, Gronau I, Hubisz MJ, et al. (2016) Ancient gene flow from early modern humans into Eastern Neanderthals. *Nature* 530(7591):429–433.

Marks J (2002) *What It Means to be 98% Chimpanzee: Apes, People, and Their Genes.* University of California Press.

Marks J (2009) *Why I am not a Scientist: Anthropology and Modern Knowledge.* University of California Press.

Marks J (2011) *The Alternative Introduction to Biological Anthropology.* Oxford University Press.

Meyer M, Kircher M, Gansauge MT, et al. (2012) A high-coverage genome sequence from an archaic Denisovan individual. *Science* 338(6104):222–226.

Mikels-Carrasco J (2012) Sherwood Washburn's New Physical Anthropology: rejecting the "religion of taxonomy." *History and Philosophy of the Life Sciences* 34(1–2):79–101.

Mitchell T (2002) *Rule of Experts: Egypt, Techno-Politics, Modernity.* University of California Press.

Mott C and Cockayne D (2017) Citation matters: mobilizing the politics of citation toward a practice of "conscientious engagement." *Gender, Place and Culture* 24(7):954–973.

Nandy A (1988) *Science, Hegemony and Violence: A Requiem for Modernity.* Oxford University Press.

Nandy A (1998) A new cosmopolitanism: toward a dialogue of Asian civilizations. In Chen K-H, editor. *Trajectories: Inter-Asia Cultural Studies.* CRC Press. Pp. 142–149.

Otto-Bliesner BL, Brady EC, Clauzet G, et al. (2006a) Last glacial maximum and Holocene climate in CCSM3. *Journal of Climate* 19(11):2526–2544.

Otto-Bliesner BL, Marshall SJ, Overpeck JT, Miller GH, and Hu A (2006b) Simulating Arctic climate warmth and icefield retreat in the last interglaciation. *Science* 311(5768):1751–1753.

Owen LA and Dortch JM (2014) Nature and timing of Quaternary glaciation in the Himalayan–Tibetan orogen. *Quaternary Science Reviews* 88:14–54.

Proctor R (1988) From Anthropologie to Rassenkunde in the German anthropological tradition. In Stocking G, editor. *History of Anthropology Vol. 5. Bones, Bodies, Behavior: Essays on Biological Anthropology.* University of Wisconsin Press. Pp. 138–180.

Prüfer K, Racimo F, Patterson N, et al. (2014) The complete genome sequence of a Neanderthal from the Altai Mountains. *Nature* 505(7481):43.

Pulliam HR and Danielson BJ (1991) Sources, sinks, and habitat selection: a landscape perspective on population dynamics. *The American Naturalist* 137(6):S50–S66.

Ranov V and Davis R (1979) Toward a new understanding of the Soviet Central Asian Paleolithic. *Current Anthropology* 20:249–270.

Ranov VA, Davis RS, Aigner JS, et al. (1979) Toward a new outline of the Soviet Central Asian Paleolithic [and Comments and Reply]. *Current Anthropology* 20(2):249–270.

Reich D, Green R, Kircher M, et al. (2010) Genetic history of an archaic hominin group from Denisova Cave in Siberia. *Nature* 468(7327):1053–1060.

Reich D, Green RE, Kircher M, et al. (2011) Denisova admixture and the first modern human dispersals into Southeast Asia and Oceania. *American Journal of Human Genetics* 89(4):516–528.

Rolland N and Dibble H (1990) A new synthesis of Middle Paleolithic variability. *American Antiquity* 55(3):480–499.

Runge J, Runge M, and Nichols J (2006) The role of local populations within a landscape context: defining and classifying sources and sinks. *American Naturalist* 167(6):925–938.

Schwarcz HP, Grun B, Vandermeersch B, et al. (1988) ESR dates for the hominid burial site of Qafzeh in Israel. *Journal of Human Evolution* 17(8):733–737.

Scott JC (1998) *Seeing Like a State: How Certain Schemes to Improve the Human Condition Have Failed.* Yale University Press.

Slon V, Mafessoni F, Vernot B, et al. (2018) The genome of the offspring of a Neanderthal mother and a Denisovan father. *Nature* 561(7721):113–116.

Smith F, Falsetti A, and Donnelly S (1989) Modern human origins. *Yearbook of Physical Anthropology* 32(S10):35–68.

Stewart JR and Stringer CB (2012) Human evolution out of Africa: the role of refugia and climate change. *Science* 335(6074):1317–1321.

Stringer C (1989) Documenting the origin of modern humans. In Trinkaus E, editor. *The Emergence of Modern Humans: Biocultural Adaptations in the Later Pleistocene.* Cambridge University Press. Pp. 67–96.

Stringer C (1994) Out of Africa: a personal history. In Nitecki M and Nitecki D, editors. *Origins of Anatomically Modern Humans.* Plenum Press. Pp. 149–172.

Stringer C, Grun R, Schwarcz HP, and Goldberg P (1989) ESR dates for the hominid burial site of Es Skhul in Israel. *Nature* 338(6218):756–758.

Trinkaus E (2005) Early modern humans. *Annual Review of Anthropology* 34:207–230.

Trinkaus E and Shipman P (1993) *The Neandertals: Changing the Image of Mankind.* Alfred Knopf.

Villa P and Roebroeks W (2014) Neandertal demise: an archaeological analysis of the modern human superiority complex. *PLoS One* 9(4):e96424.

Vishnyatsky L (1999) The Paleolithic of Central Asia. *Journal of World Prehistory* 13(1):69–122.

Willermet C and Hill B (1997) Fuzzy set theory and its implications for speciation models. In Clark GA and Willermet CM, editors. *Conceptual Issues in Modern Human Research.* Aldine de Gruyter. Pp. 77–89.

Wolpoff M and Caspari R (1997) *Race and Human Evolution: A Fatal Attraction.* Simon and Schuster.

Wolpoff M, Wu XZ, and Thorne AG (1984) Modern *Homo sapiens.* In Spencer F, editor. *The Origins of Modern Humans: A World Survey of the Fossil Evidence.* Alan R. Liss. Pp. 411–483.

Wolpoff M, Mannheim B, Mann A, et al. (2004) Why not the Neandertals? *World Archaeology* 36(4):527–546.

Zilhão J (2011) Aliens from outer time? Why the "Human Revolution" is wrong, and where do we go from here? In Condemi S and Weniger GC, editors. *Continuity and Discontinuity in the Peopling of Europe.* Springer. Pp. 331–366.

3 Anthropology Now

How Popular Science (Mis)Characterizes Human Evolution

Marc Kissel

In this chapter, I examine how scholars, public intellectuals, and popular authors construct and present narratives that explain and explicate human origins. I am interested in how writers from outside of anthropology use anthropological datasets and concepts when discussing who we are, how we behave, and where we came from. While the role of creationism is well-studied (Newport 2012; Number 2006), what has been less studied is what people who accept evolution think about the origins of *Homo sapiens*. Scholars of human origins are often unaware of what the science-literate public thinks about evolution.

However, conversations about who we are and where we come from are relevant to almost everyone. The popularity of *Ancestry.com* and *23andMe* demonstrates this well (both are privately held, but some estimates put the valuation of these at around US$2.5 billion each [Clark 2018]). As Jon Marks reminds us,

Understanding how those human facts differ from, say, cockroach facts, is the first step toward reading the literature on human evolution critically. And the simplest answer is, little is on the line, and few people care about cockroach facts. (Of course urban apartment dwellers and the manufacturers of insecticides may sometimes care strongly about cockroach facts; but those cares are quite specific and localized.) In addition to being facts of nature, human facts are political and ideological; history shows that clearly. It doesn't mean that human scientific facts are unreal and untrue – just that one needs to scrutinize them differently, because there are more variables to consider. (Marks 2015:x)

We see similar reminders of this in public discussions of what it means to be from specific populations. The debate surrounding Senator Elizabeth Warren's DNA testing is just one example of how these facts matter in ways that other facts often do not. In 2018, Warren released results of a genetic ancestry test that purported to indicate she has Native American ancestry, hoping that this would silence critics who have questioned her claim of a family link to Cherokee and Delaware tribes. Her results, however, were used to both support and discredit her claims (Kessler 2018). As Kim TallBear notes, "The broader U.S. public is also invested – as historians, anthropologists, and Ingenious Studies scholars have shown – in making what are ultimately settler-colonial claims to all things indigenous: our bones, blood, land, waters, and ultimately our identities" (TallBear on Twitter, October 15 2018). Privileging settler-colonial definitions over indigenous definitions questions the notions of identity that native peoples have developed.

Similarly, a news report on white supremacists drinking milk to "prove" their whiteness (Harmon 2018) demonstrates how research into what might *appear* to be a purely scientific question of how and when milk-drinking evolved can be used for invidious ends. The racial assumptions here show a misuse and misunderstanding of the science behind lactase persistence (Wiley 2004), but there is a deeper issue here: Do scientists have the responsibility to be aware of how their research is used? In other words, are knowledge production and dissemination our principal aims, or should we be aware of how these data frame debates in the larger social discourse? "Human genetics is inherently an overdetermined science, and therefore, the researcher's responsibility must go beyond the boundaries of the laboratory, and an education in media management is essential" (Perbal 2013:387).

What follows are some examples of what the public learns about our behavior and the past by reading popular accounts of human behavior. When examined critically, it is clear that these popular accounts of our past are often grounded in racist, sexist, and colonialist mentalities and assumptions. These serve as implicit gatekeepers, preventing the inclusion of all voices. It engenders an androcentric view of the past. A more inclusive science that allows for diverse voices is a better science (Page 2008). This is especially true for the study of human origins. In the past, paleoanthropology has often reified marginalized populations as *the other* (Kuljian 2016). As Page (2008) shows, diverse people working together can capitalize on their individuality to yield better outcomes. Yet, this is often unrecognized in popular discourse, especially among many of the leading public intellectuals and non-anthropologists.

When approached this way, I see four themes that either miscategorize what we do or have dangerous/invidious conclusions. They are (1) oversimplifying human behavior and evolutionary theory; (2) reducing models of genotype–phenotype interaction; (3) arguing that science has proven that the *West is Best* with a rational optimism; and (4) imagining males driving much of the evolutionary story. These examples are given to indicate that biological anthropologists must make a concerted effort to be part of that discussion, calling out not just creationism, but racism, sexism, and colonialism (Athreya and Ackermann in press). To show this I discuss three examples of discussions of human behavior that are rooted in ideas about human nature and human origins: the use of personal genomics to understand complex human behaviors; the ideas that men are innately violent and predisposed to war; and the notion that the western Enlightenment has made the world a better place.

Example 1: The Sounds of Our Ancestors

In the fall of 2018, the music-streaming service Spotify partnered with Ancestry.com to provide customers with a custom playlist based on their DNA (Gilmour 2018). Using its customer database, Ancestry.com estimates an individual's genetic background and then provides them with the ability "to explore the soundtrack of their heritage." From a scientific standpoint this is problematic (Terrell 2018). The ability to determine where a person is from ancestrally, based on their genome, is complicated by issues such as sample size and historical migrations. Due to the randomness of meiosis and recombination, the majority of a person's genealogical ancestors

10 generations back are not their genetic ancestors. Yet, for-profit genotype testing services often promise results they cannot deliver on or, even more problematically, provide customers with misleading information. (It might sound impressive to let people know you are a descendant of Charlemagne. Yet, due to the nature of human genetics and pedigree collapse, anyone of European ancestry is going to descend from anyone alive during Charlemagne's time [Ralph and Coop 2013].)

More importantly, services such as these oversimplify human behavior to a reductionist genetic argument. Someone of Swedish descent who was raised in Minnesota in the 1970s might like ABBA, but not because any Swedish genes make them predisposed to liking pop rock. Implying that there are genes *for* behaviors is dangerous as it can lead to misunderstanding more complex studies such as those that examine genetic indicators of intelligence or any other multifactorial behavior (for an anthropologically inclined take on this, see *Behave* by Robert Saplosky [2017]).

The idea that our genetic ancestry can inform our music preferences is not, of itself, problematic. What is concerning is this questionable science leads to improper assumptions, which can be misapplied to other, more significant issues. Too often, we fail to examine the responsibility of the ways in which these conversations are framed. Debates over the genetic influence on behavioral traits are political in nature. It is fairly common to see examples of reductionist models of genotype–phenotype interactions.

However, simplifying models of genotype–phenotype interaction, and overlooking the role the environment has in how these interactions occur, can produce misunderstandings about the nature of genetic data (Tabery 2014). One of the most famous instances of this is the so-called "warrior gene," a genetic variant of the MAOA gene. Researchers have argued that there is a genetic component to aggression and that certain genes can make a person more aggressive (McDermott et al. 2009). The original study on MAOA's effect on aggression is based on a Dutch family in which over a dozen males were known to be aggressive. Scientists suggested a mutation in the gene led to less MAOA production and too much serotonin in the brain. While this particular gene variant was only found in one family (Brunner et al. 1993), other genetic variants, such as variable number tandem repeats, have been correlated with aggression in *some instances* (Caspi et al. 2002, 2003). The label of MAOA as a "warrior gene" comes from a report on a paper given at a professional conference in 2004 (Gibbons 2004) but is based on supposed links between levels of serotonin in the brain and mutations in the MAOA gene.

Others have looked for links between specific MAOA variants and criminal behavior (Beaver et al. 2010, 2014). Yet, many studies do not take into account the individual history of the people involved. Are the differences in the brain the cause of antisocial behavior? Is the environment of violence that is endemic in some populations producing these changes, or is it something else? The interaction of unfair treatment/discrimination and single nucleotide polymorphisms suggests that gene–environment interactions can have significant effects on historically disadvantaged populations (Quinlan et al. 2016). Poverty and inequality may lead to violence for reasons removed from genetics. The environment influences the effect genetic mutations have. A meta-analysis of MAOA, stress, and aggression reports that there is a small effect recorded on the interaction between being mistreated as a child and having low MAOA and subsequent aggression (Weder et al. 2009).

The complex nature is often missed in accounts of this "violence gene." It has been argued that the reason Maōri males have a high crime rate is due to the frequency of the three-repeat version of the MAOA allele. The news media reported on this study and it received a lot of attention. As pointed out by Perbal (2013), the notion that this gene explains why Maōri are violent fits the stereotype associated with this population but does not take into account the context. This, of course, does not stop companies from telling us that they can test for the presence of this gene. Family Tree DNA charges US$99 to test for one of these polymorphisms, while Genovate provides a standalone test for US$129 which "conclusively determines whether you have inherited the warrior gene."

The colonialism evident in the Maōri controversy demonstrates how some scientists generalized from their small number of research participants to an entire population. Europeans have often seen non-western peoples as marginal, both culturally and historically, as compared to people from the west (Saïd 1978). For example, accounts of why political divides are so common suggest that *tribalism* is to blame (e.g., Goldberg 2018). We are told that "from the perspective of our genes, we weren't meant to live like we do today, with wealth, rights, and freedoms . . .. Our natural condition isn't merely poor, it's *tribal* (Goldberg 2018:10). And "as a result of our long evolution of tribal competition, the human mind readily does make dichotomous, us-versus-them thinking" (Lukianoff and Haid 2018:70). While rarely defined, it is seen as the source of much of the world's ills, an example of a primitive institution (Pinker 2018:417) that leads to irrationality. But, as Rosen (2016) notes, when scholars argue that tribal people are inherently violent, it provides justification for their oppression: "We call squabbling groups tribal; we think of them as insular, exclusionary, and archaic. We think of individual tribesmen as submerged in the group and custom as stultifying repetition. The opposite is more often the truth" (Rosen 2016:4).

Moreover, marginalized populations are often used as exemplars of the past. Evolutionary psychologist Steven Pinker refers to the Hadza of Tanzania as people who "live in the ecosystem where modern humans first evolved and probably preserve much of their lifestyle, extract 3,000 daily calories per person from more than 880 species" (Pinker 2018:23). He also writes that "the San hunter-gatherers of the Kalahari Desert (the 'Bushmen'), [are] one of the world's most ancient cultures." Both of these quotes suggest that these populations are closer to nature than state-level societies, which can lead to the assumption that they are less than modern (Barnard 2007).

Example 2: Seeking Better Angles on Our Better Angels

The question of why war exists has been studied by numerous scholars from a multitude of disciplines (Ferguson 2006; Gat 2008; Keeley 1996; Kim and Kissel

2018; Leblanc 2003; Mead 1940; Otterbein 2004). Is it because humans are innately violent or is it epiphenomenal of more recent human inventions such as state-level societies? Yet, the current popular discourse (Gat 2008; Goldberg 2018; Pinker 2011; Shermer 2015) provides a rather simple, two-part narrative, one which views the European West as a civilizing agent that has pacified men's natural aggressive tendencies. In this formulation, men are evolved to compete against each other in order to increase their inclusive fitness.

This fits with a larger theme, critiqued by feminist scholars, that men drive the evolutionary story (for a critique see Watson and Kennedy 1991; Zihlman 1997, 2012). In studies of war, it is often argued that men are the ones who matter. From a group perspective, the more people available to be warriors the better, so why favor a sex-biased war group? Following the controversial work of Chagnon (1988), scholars have argued that men kill in order to increase their genetic fitness. Violence is argued to be a "guy thing." While Chagnon's work has been critiqued (Beckerman et al. 2009; Ferguson 1989), writers such as Steven Pinker, Michael Shermer, Richard Dawkins, and Daniel Dennett often promote his work as objective science while suggesting his critics are unscientific social scientists who ignore the role biology plays in human behavior (Chagnon et al. 2013; Miele 2013; Pinker 2011).

War, especially in the past, seems to be a predominantly male pursuit (e.g., Keeley 1996). Yet *why* this pattern holds is unclear. Gat (2000) has argued that male-biased war is due to body size differences, while others argue differences in fitness costs are the key reason (Van Vugt 2009). Others have suggested more nuanced views (Micheletti et al. 2018), arguing that increased participation in war by one sex disincentivizes involvement by the other. Pre-existing biases toward male aggression, they argue, would lead to war being mostly seen in men (Micheletti et al. 2018).

Science-writer Michael Shermer tells his readers that if you lived 10,000 years ago and were a man "there was about a one in four chance that you would die violently" (Shermer 2015:92), though it is not clear how he came to this estimate. He tells his readers that the "peace and harmony mafia" argue that "war is a recent learned cultural phenomenon and that humans are by nature peaceful, a view they defend with vigor and even ferocity" (Shermer 2015:94). Shermer later explains this mafia consists of "those who adhere to the blank slate theory of human nature and those rather aggressive anthropologists who insist that war is a recent invention and that our ancestors lived in relative peace and harmony with one another and nature" (Shermer 2016). Suggesting that there was a 25 percent chance that men in the Neolithic would be killed violently, even if true, does not really inform on evolutionary origins of violence. Compressing the timeline of evolution in this way makes it difficult to discern just how common interpersonal violence and war was.

In his 2011 bestseller *The Better Angels of Our Nature*, Steven Pinker argues that violence has declined throughout human history. Pinker explains why forms of violence are on the decline. Conflict, the book argues, is becoming less frequent, and when it occurs is less violent, as nation-states spread. Pinker cites statistical trends, datasets, archaeological research, and historical data to support his assertion that a decline in violence is not a fluke but rather the result of the Leviathan of the state. Pinker argues that "we may be living in the most peaceable era in our species' existence" (Pinker 2011:xxi). Pinker bases part of his thesis on the work of Norbert Elias, who argued in his classic text *The Civilizing Process* (Elias 1978) that reforms in medieval and post-medieval Europe led to changes in how people acted and practiced self-restraint. Moreover, power was consolidated from feudal states into a centralized authority. But, as Pinker himself notes, the majority of evidence for this is seen in data from European countries. As anthropologists know, ignoring the non-western world when constructing a model to explain world history is questionable.

Many scholars have pointed out problems with this thesis (Falk and Hildebolt 2017; Ferguson 2013; Kim 2012; Martin and Harrod 2015; Oka et al. 2017). Violence is multifaceted and its definition is complex. Structural violence (Klaus 2012), slow violence (Nixon 2011), and other types of violence (Fuentes 2004) are given short shrift throughout the book. Scholars have shown that poverty, hunger, and humiliation can lead to violence, and these cultural dimensions provide the meaning and the power behind violent practices (Scheper-Hughes and Bourgois 2004). However, these factors cannot be measured in the same way Pinker graphs violence, as he readily admits:

Before the advent of colonialism, large swaths of Africa, the Americas, and Asia were host to predation, feuding, and slave-raiding that slunk beneath the military horizon or fell in the forest without any historian hearing them. Colonialism itself was implemented in many imperial wars that the great powers waged to acquire their colonies, suppress revolts, and fend off rivals. Throughout this era there were plenty of wars. (Pinker 2011:297)

In other words, places where the data do not exist do not exist in the dataset.

Ignoring the fact that archaeological data and non-western sources could provide evidence (Kim et al. 2015), the idea that since structural violence cannot be measured in the same manner as interpersonal violence it simply should not be taken into account is troubling. As noted by Martin and Harrod, "[W]hile there may be some truth to the declining percentage of deaths due to military and wartime combat, this is a very narrow way of viewing violence and is quite misleading" (Martin and Harrod 2015:118).

For a book of this length it is odd to leave out other reasons that crime may be higher, such as insidious state-sponsored practices like redlining, blockbusting, and restrictive covenants that prevented, for example, African Americans in the United States from accruing wealth or living in desirable areas with low mortgage rates (Coates 2014; Rothstein 2017). Economic disparities and life chances are based upon race, class, and where you are born, alongside other factors.

As recently shown by Oka et al. (2017) and Falk and Hildebolt (2017), there is a problem with the dataset Pinker uses to explore long-term trends over time. Pinker relies on data collected by Keeley (1996), who compiled data on population and war group size from foraging populations. He included statistics on the total population and the number of people involved in a war group. Using this data, Pinker argues that the number of people involved in wartime activities dropped from ~40 percent in the past to less than 1 percent today. However, the data on population and war group size from 295 societies, including foraging, farming, and state-level societies, and on war group size and conflict-related casualties from 430 historical conflicts going back to 2500 BC show that population size is a confounding factor (Oka et al. 2017). Trends in proportions of war group size or casualties in relationship to population are described by deeper scaling laws driving group social organization. In other words, in a small group of 100 adults it would be reasonable to have 25 warriors, or one-quarter of the total population. But in a population of 100 million, supporting an army of 25 million soldiers is logistically impossible.

It is not that states prevent violence, but rather that other factors, such as the need to feed, clothe, and arm a war group, drives the proportion of war group size and casualty rates.

While not a science-writer, political analyst Jonah Goldberg also has weighed in on human nature:

This is no longer a debated point among most serious scholars. People who think we once lived in glorious harmony with each other – and the environment – aren't scientists, they're poets and propagandists. The evidence for mankind's blood-soaked past can be found in the archaeological record, DNA analysis, the writings of ancient commentators, and historians, and the firsthand reports of those remaining societies that have so far resisted modernity. (Goldberg 2018:31)

His writing echoes some of Raymond Dart's words about australopithecines. Dart, writing in 1953, argued "Either these Procrustean proto-human folk tore the battered bodies of their quarries apart limb from limb and slaked their thirst with blood, consuming the flesh raw like every other carnivorous beast; or, like early man, some of them understood the advantages of fire as well as the use of missiles and clubs" (Dart 1953:204). Ardrey's (1961) popular account of Dart's work suggests war as the impetus for humans' greatest accomplishments. It also argues that war is deeply rooted in evolutionary history, aspects of which are seen in more recent works such as *Demonic Males* (Peterson and Wrangham 1997), which argues humans, and men especially, have an inborn propensity toward violence.

Suggesting, as Goldberg does, that the only scholars who question our "blood-soaked" past are propagandists is part of the overarching narrative that is grounded in racist, sexist, and colonialist assumptions. Asking if the patterns we see today are the result of the intersection of biology, culture, and history is not only the purview of poets. It is the reason anthropological insight into our past is so important. Our tendency to equate war with men is problematic (Ness 2007; Otto et al. 2006). Evidence of female participation in warfare is ample, if we look in the right place, but this type of competition and aggression is undertheorized (Cross and Campbell 2013). Moreover, models that suggest men are more violent and risky than women simplify a complex issue (Fine 2010). They also frame evolution from an androcentric viewpoint. Giving women active roles, rather than being seen as passive recipients, is critical to evaluating evidence in biological anthropology. Similarly, models that suggest anything is a human universal such as war and aggression must fit all the data, rather than a subset of the data. Colonial models that see peoples from Asia and

Africa as either closer to nature or as stagnant and unchanging have no place in twenty-first-century science.

Example 3: Enlightenment Now or Anthropology Now

Oversimplifying human behavior and evolutionary theory, reducing models of genotype–phenotype interaction, arguing that science has proven that the *West is Best* with a rational optimism, and imagining males driving much of the evolutionary story are problematic themes. For one, they ignore much of the non-western cannon. Scholars from non-western countries may construct knowledge differently, but this does not mean we can ignore it. As argued by Athreya and Ackerman:

> True inclusivity must provide a safe and equal platform for a wide range of voices that have historically been gate-kept from scientific space. This means publishing research by scholars from the Global South, from poor countries, and from non-western countries that have long histories of paleoanthropological research. Many of these communities engage in science and knowledge construction differently than our hypothetico-deductive model, but their facts are no less well-vetted, falsifiable or repeatable. (Athreya and Ackermann in press)

An example of what can happen when sources are biased toward a specific narrative comes from Steven Pinker's follow-up to *Better Angels*, his 2018 book *Enlightenment Now!*. This book argues that the western Enlightenment has made the world a better place. He argues that Americans are influenced by the news media, politicians, and social activists to accept a negative, pessimistic view of the world. People who despair about the environment, poverty, war, and famine are following the headlines, not the trend lines (Pinker 2018).

Echoing the *West is Best* theme, Pinker argues that life is better now due to science and reason. Humans on average live longer, are happier, and have more material goods than ever before. It is the ultimate "glass half-full" book. We are not just living in the most peaceable era but in the best era ever. Pinker's book is in essence a monument to human progress. And a complaint about the "progressophobia" that he says is way too common.

As one critic put it, Pinker's ideals can be summed up as "technocratic neoliberalism" (Bell 2018). Western governments set policy while experts tell us what to do about the problems of the world. We need to divest science from politics, Pinker tells us. If the experts of the world set policy we will make the correct choices since they are unbiased (or at least use science to obtain the unvarnished truth). Yet, Pinker laments, we often do not listen to them. He suggests that if we just talked to experts we would realize we do not know what we are talking about and instead embrace those with superior knowledge. Tellingly, Pinker notes that "Physical scientists, unfortunately, often consider themselves experts in political psychology" (Pinker 2018:310). The Backfire Effect (Nyhan and Reifler 2010) is the hypothesis that people have a cognitive bias which causes them to strengthen their support when confronted with evidence that challenges one of their core beliefs. Convincing others they are incorrect is more than just a matter of citing facts and producing graphs, since emotional facts are harder to change than logical facts. In this case, debates about political, ethical, and even economic issues may not simply be due to the inability of the public to listen to *experts*, but rather may result from more entrenched views. If scholars, policy experts, and authors want to change minds, it would be best to recognize this limitation.

At one level, Pinker is indeed correct that life is better. It is also true that the media tends to focus on the bad rather than the good. As Agustín Fuentes (2012) notes, if 10 people were murdered in New York City on one day, it would be a front-page headline, but a headline that eight million people got along in the Big Apple will never show up, even though it would be equally true. Pinker is upset that we do not concentrate on the good rather than the bad, and this forms an underlying theme of his book. Yes, it is important to keep in mind that peace and cooperation are important aspects of human evolution (Spikins 2015). But in some ways it makes sense to concentrate on the bad. If we do not talk about the refugee crisis, it will disappear from the public discourse but still exist. Cassandras who warn about our impending doom may oversell the idea of a post-apocalyptic future, but we also need to be wary of those who tell us that everything is fine.

It is also not clear for whom the world is getting better. The world may indeed be better for some people. For those who are disenfranchised, subjugated, and discriminated against it probably comes as no solace to know that those in power are doing better. Framed in this way, the argument is a privileged one to take. Any claims of racism, sexism, and colonialism can be dismissed as ignoring the overwhelming benefits that come with the Enlightenment. Rather, readers are told that intellectuals hate any idea of progress. Pinker argues that the effects and popularity of the eugenics movement is an overplayed canard – no one takes eugenics seriously anymore, and those who championed it were "progressives, liberals, and socialists" (2018:400); i.e., the same academics that prevent people today from seeing the light of the Enlightenment. According to Pinker, eugenics was "discredited by its association with Nazism" (Pinker 2018:399) and now simply taints good research. But even a basic reading of the literature shows this is not the case (Black 2003; Etkind 2008; Micklos and Carlson 2000). Eugenic practices survived long past World War II, with states such as North Carolina sterilizing people up to the 1970s.

Yet the lesson Pinker draws is that we have overcorrected. He suggests that review boards such as the IRB are a menace to free speech: "Anthropologists are forbidden to speak with illiterate peasants who cannot sign a consent form, or interview would-be suicide bombers on the off chance that they might blurt out information that puts *them* in jeopardy" (Pinker 2018:402). Not only does that mischaracterize human subjects research, it misses the reason why these boards exist. From the Kallikaks, to Carrie Bell, to the Tuskegee Airmen, to the Havasupai, scientists have often proven unable to police themselves in the search for data (Black 2003; Sterling 2011). But Pinker tells us not to worry, the Tuskegee experiment was a "one-time failure" that only harmed a few dozen people (Pinker 2018:401). In fact, anthropologists have to contend with an issue that many other scientists do not. That is, we are studying and producing facts about human nature and thus our work is emotionally more relevant to people than other fields of knowledge (Marks 2015).

Many scholars have pointed out problems with his thesis. For one, it is not clear what he thinks the Enlightenment actually is. Pinker places this revolution sometime in the late 1700s. But as David Bell (2018) notes, he rarely points to actual thinkers. "Natural selection," Pinker tells us, "consists of competition among genes to be represented in the next generation, and the organisms we see today are descendants of those that edged out their rivals in contests for mates, food and dominance" (Pinker 2018:25). Ignoring recent work in evolutionary biology (Odling-Smee et al. 2003), Pinker adheres to a gene-centric model of evolution, one that assumes simplistic notions of how heredity works.

The theme that the rational optimism of the European west has made the world a better place (Goldberg 2018; Pinker 2018) is, at its face, colonialist in nature, though that does not mean it is wrong. Early in *Enlightenment Now* we are told that "[p]overty, too, needs no explanation. In a world governed by entropy and evolution, it is the default state of humankind" (Pinker 2018:25). Pinker complains that discussions of poverty are about whom to blame rather than celebrating that not *everyone* lives in poverty. It is a very privileged position to take.

Are foraging populations today living in poverty? Perhaps in a globalized economy they are. But what about before farming? Or before the globalization of the world economy?

A few pages later Pinker tells us that life is not that bad for the poor now:

With the usual first-world ingratitude, modern social critics rail against the obesity epidemic with a level of outrage that might be appropriate for famine (that is, when they are not railing against fat-shaming, slender fashion models, or eating-disorders). Though obesity is a public health problem, by the standards of history it's a good problem to have. (Pinker 2018:69)

Of course, the situation is more complex than that. Determining why the poor are overweight is more complex than simply suggesting that they have access to a lot more food than people in the past did. Pinker argues that the stereotype of the "emaciated pauper in rags" (Pinker 2018:117) is no longer true. Yet this may not be the case. Rates of obesity are directly linked to issues of food supply and consumption of energy-dense food. The highest rates of obesity in the USA are seen in groups with high poverty and low education rates (Drewnowski and Specter 2004). As shown by Żukiewicz-Sobczak and colleagues (2014), both the excess of calories and the quality of food affect health and weight. Foods that are cheaper tend to be full of calories and dyes and lack many nutrients, which can lead to obesity. One also needs to have the time to exercise, as sedentary lifestyles lead to more obesity and cardiovascular problems. Yet the working poor have less free time than the middle and upper classes. Researchers suggest more awareness of the importance of daily activity and healthy eating (Drewnowski and Specter 2004). But food deserts and lack of money to buy sports equipment are impediments to this. One wishes Pinker could have addressed this issue in a more nuanced way rather than just using it as a trope that poor people are overweight so that shows lives are better. As Quinlan and colleagues (2016) show, including both sociocultural *and* genetic data allows for better understanding of the etiology of disease. Their work suggests a class of genes "associated with psychosocial distress and mood disorders may be particularly relevant to the manifestation of hypertension in African Americans and underlying racial disparities" (Quinlan et al. 2016:11). Anthropological insights into epigenetic research bolster the notion that we need to study gene–environment interactions in complex ways.

Pinker would not have to look hard to find examples that show he is mistaken. For example, inequality is strongly inherited, while the rates of intergenerational mobility have been mostly flat for decades (Chetty et al. 2018). Approximately 90 percent of Americans born in the 1940s ended up better off than their parents, while by 1984 that percentage had dropped to closer to 50 percent. Even rates of invention (often used by conservative commentators to suggest the West is Best) are driven by income inequality: Inventors are more likely to be raised in high-income families. While the gender gap in invention rate is shrinking, some estimates suggest it will be almost 120 years until gender parity is reached (Bell et al. 2017).

These errors and misrepresentations are not simply wrong. They are part of the narrative arc that is framed by colonialism and racism. It is necessary that scholars address these issues rather than ignore them or suggest that they are problems of the past.

Discussion and Conclusion

There is a broader impact on society when scholars misrepresent or overinterpret the data from a colonialist or sexist perspective, beyond the simple fact that they are wrong. It produces a narrative steeped in anti-scientific notions of human variation that anthropologists have rejected. Rather than suggesting that critics are anti-science or propagandists, everyone who produces or synthesizes scientific data must come to terms with the fact that science is not free of bias.

It is dangerous to assume, as the *West is Best* motif does, that life will continue to get better without the direct action of people who are pushing against these problems. Moreover, this framing suggests that no one should complain because life was worse before. While it is probably true that life is getting better for many people, to argue that because of that we should not worry is false. And to label as a progressophobe anyone who has concerns about where the economy, politics, and the environment are heading misses the point. We never can give up on pointing out the structural inequalities that exist in our society. For the rational optimists who see claims of colonialism and racisms as canards that are no longer valid critiques, the moral arc toward justice occurs because of the Enlightenment and the inherent truths of western science. But it is more complicated than that. Justice increases because people do the hard work of pushing against injustice.

Why do technocrats like Bill Gates love the message of the rational optimists? For one, they suggest that the emphasis on income inequality is misplaced. If, they argue, the overall wealth of the rich is driving growth rather than income disparity then *their* wealth is not a problem. It is novel social Darwinism (with a bunch of eugenics thrown in) in order to appease the elite. It oversimplifies human behavior and evolutionary theory and suggests that the hypothetico-deductive model of western science is the only way to produce knowledge. If you are on the side of the elite you can at the very least be assured of selling some books. Pinker (2018) draws the useful distinction between white lies (told for the listener's benefit) and blue lies (told for the benefit of the in-group). Perhaps the blue lie in these popular accounts is the notion that, since life is getting better and violence is decreasing (for the in-group of consumers of this book), we should not worry about the negative trends we see.

As argued by anthropologist Holly Dunsworth, "human evolution requires a new narrative, both hyper-sensitive to the power of narrative and rooted in science that is light years ahead of Victorian dogma" (Dunsworth 2018:1). If we do not engage with the implicit racist and sexist models/theories that have dominated evolutionary science for the last 150 years, we are not doing our jobs as educators or as scientists (Athreya and Ackermann in press). Creating a more inclusive science is not simply a matter of recruiting students, but of making them feel that they have a place at the table. To do so, we must decolonize our syllabi by adding scholars outside of the western canon to the standard reading lists, listen to indigenous and minority scholars, and prevent harassers (Clancy et al. 2014) from gaining prominence.

This can be accomplished by actively engaging with the current popular literature. Like it or not, Pinker, Shermer, Dawkins, and other public intellectuals are the main source of knowledge on human behavior for the general public. And, as suggested here, much of what they write is problematic.

Engaging in public outreach is often seen by academics as a secondary project, one that is done after our *real work* of teaching students and research is finished (a colleague once told me that my time doing outreach at a high school was an "extracurricular"). Work by Caitlin Schrein (2017) demonstrates that human evolution is inherently interesting to students. As Schrein put it "Withholding the scientific evidence for human origins and evolution from students in K–12 is, in many ways, a social injustice. It deprives students of the opportunity to consider information about their world and their place in it at an age when the development of critical thinking skills is crucial" (Schrein 2017:133).

Having difficult conversations with people who do not share our worldview is not easy and does not come naturally to many of us, which is why it should be taught in graduate school methods courses alongside principal components analysis and how to write a job application covering letter. But it is the only way we can move the conversation forward.

References

Ardrey R (1961) *African Genesis: A Personal Investigation into the Animal Origins and Nature of Man*. Atheneum.

Athreya S and Ackermann RR (in press) Colonialism and narratives of human origins in Asia and Africa. In Porr M and Matthews J, editors. *Interrogating Human Origins: Decolonisation and the Deep Past*. Routledge.

Barnard A (2007) *Anthropology and the Bushman*. Berg Publishers.

Beaver KM, DeLisi M, Vaughn MG, and Barnes JC (2010) Monoamine oxidase A genotype is associated with gang membership and weapon use. *Comprehensive Psychiatry* 1(2):130–134.

Beaver KM, Barnes JC, and Boutwell BB (2014) The 2-repeat allele of the MAOA gene confers an increased risk for shooting and stabbing behaviors. *Psychiatric Quarterly* 85 (3):257–265.

Beckerman S, Erickson PI, Yost J, et al. (2009) Life histories, blood revenge, and reproductive success among the Waorani of Ecuador. *Proceedings of the National Academy of Sciences* 106 (20):8134–8139.

Bell AM, Chetty R, Jaravel X, Petkova N, and Van Reenen J (2017) Who Becomes an Inventor in America? The Importance of Exposure to Innovation. Working Paper 24062. National Bureau of Economic Research.

Bell DA (2018) The PowerPoint Philosophe: Waiting for Steven Pinker's enlightenment. *The Nation*. www.thenation.com/article/waiting-for-steven-pinkers-enlightenment.

Black J (2003) *War Against the Weak: Eugenics and America's Campaign to Create a Master Race*. Dialog Press.

Brunner HG, Nelen M, Breakefield XO, Ropers HH, and van Oost BA (1993) Abnormal behavior associated with a point mutation in the structural gene for monoamine oxidase A. *Science* 262 (5133):578–580.

Caspi A, McClay J, Moffitt T, et al. (2002) Role of genotype in the cycle of violence in maltreated children. *Science* 297(5582):851–854.

Caspi A, Sugden K, Moffitt TE, et al. (2003) Influence of life stress on depression: moderation by a polymorphism in the 5-HTT gene. *Science* 301(5631):386–389.

Chagnon NA (1988) Life histories, blood revenge, and warfare in a tribal population. *Science* 239 (4843):985–992.

Chagnon NA, Pinker S, Wrangham RW, Dennett D, and Haigh J (2013) Blood Is Their Argument: anthropologist Napoleon Chagnon. *Edge*. www.edge.org/conversation/napoleon_chagnon-steven_pinker-richard_wrangham-daniel_c_dennett-david_haig-napoleon.

Chetty R, Hendren N, Kline P, et al. (2018) Is the United States still a land of opportunity? Recent trends in intergenerational mobility. *American Economic Review* 104(5):141–147.

Clancy KB, Nelson RG, Rutherford JN, and Hinde K (2014) Survey of academic field experiences (SAFE): trainees report harassment and assault. *PLoS One* 9(7):e102172.

Clark K (2018) Scoop: 23andMe is raising up to $300M. Pitchbook, July 24. www.pitchbook.com/news/articles/scoop-23andme-is-raising-up-to-300m.

Coates T-N (2014) The case for reparations. *Atlantic* 313(5):54–71.

Cross C and Campbell A (2013) Violence and aggression in women. In Shackelford T and Hansen E, editors. *The Evolution of Violence*. Springer. Pp. 211–232.

Dart R (1953) The predatory transition from ape to man. *International Anthropological and Linguistic Review* 1(4):201–217.

Drewnowski A and Specter S (2004) Poverty and obesity: The role of energy density and energy costs. *American Journal of Clinical Nutrition* 79(1):6–16.

Dunsworth H (2018) It is unethical to teach evolution without confronting racism and sexism. Evolution Institute. https://evolution-institute.org/it-is-unethical-to-teach-evolution-without-confronting-racism-and-sexism.

Elias N (1978) *The Civilizing Process*. Blackwell.

Etkind A (2008) Beyond eugenics: the forgotten scandal of hybridizing humans and apes. *Studies in History and Philosophy of Science Part C: Studies in History and Philosophy of Biological and Biomedical Sciences* 39(2):205–210.

Falk D and Hildebolt C (2017) Annual war deaths in small-scale versus state societies scale with population size rather than violence. *Current Anthropology* 58(6):805–813.

Ferguson B (1989) Do Yanomamo killers have more kids? *American Ethnologist* 16(3):564–565.

Ferguson R (2006) Archaeology, cultural anthropology, and the origins and intensifications of war. In Arkush E and Allen M, editors. *The Archaeology of Warfare: Prehistories of Raiding and conquest.* University of Florida Press. Pp. 469–523.

Ferguson R (2013) Pinker's list. In Fry D, editor. *Peace, and Human Nature: The Convergence of Evolutionary and Cultural Views.* Oxford University Press. Pp. 112–131.

Fine C (2010) *Delusions of Gender: How Our Minds, Society, and Neurosexism Create Difference.* W.W. Norton.

Fuentes A (2004) It's not all sex and violence: integrated anthropology and the role of cooperation and social complexity in human evolution. *American Anthropologist* 106 (4):710–718.

Fuentes A (2012) *Race, Monogamy, and Other Lies They Told You.* University of California Press.

Gat A (2000) Female participation in war: biocultural interactions. *The Journal of Strategic Studies* 23(4):21–31.

Gat A (2008) *War in Human Civilization.* Oxford University Press.

Gibbons A (2004) Tracking the evolutionary history of a "warrior" gene. *Science* 304(5672):818–819.

Gilmour J (2018) Music in your genes? Spotify's turning Ancestry DNA results into custom playlists. *Miami Herald.* www.miamiherald.com/news/nation-world/national/article218939880.html.

Goldberg J (2018) *Suicide of the West: How the Rebirth of Tribalism, Populism, Nationalism, and Identity Politics is Destroying American Democracy.* Crown Forum.

Harmon A (2018) Geneticists see work distorted for racist ends. *New York Times*:A1. www.nytimes.com/2018/10/17/us/white-supremacists-science-dna.html.

Keeley L (1996) *War before Civilization.* Oxford University Press.

Kessler G (2018) Just about everything you've read on the Warren DNA test is wrong. *Washington Post.* www.washingtonpost.com/politics/2018/10/18/just-about-everything-youve-read-warren-dna-test-is-wrong.

Kim N (2012) Angels, illusions, hydras and chimeras: violence and humanity. *Reviews in Anthropology* 41(4):39–272.

Kim N and Kissel M (2018) *Emergent Warfare in Our Evolutionary Past.* Routledge.

Kim N, Kusimba CM, and Keeley LH (2015) Coercion and warfare in the rise of state societies in southern Zambezia. *African Archaeological Review* 32(1):1–34.

Klaus HD (2012) The bioarchaeology of structural violence: a theoretical model and a case study. In Martin DL, Harrod RP, and Perez VR, editors. *The Bioarchaeology of Violence.* University of Florida Press. Pp. 29–62.

Kuljian C (2016) *Darwin's Hunch: Science, Race and the Search for Human Origins.* Jacana.

Leblanc S (2003) *Constant Battles.* St. Martin's Press.

Lukianoff G and Haid J (2018) *The Coddling of the American Mind: How Good Intentions and Bad Ideas Are Setting Up a Generation for Failure.* Penguin Press.

Marks J (2015) *Tales of the Ex-Apes: How We Think about Human Evolution.* University of California Press.

Martin DL and Harrod RP (2015) Bioarchaeological contributions to the study of violence. *American Journal of Physical Anthropology* 156(S59):116–145.

McDermott R, Tingley D, Cowden J, Frazzetto G, and Johnson DDP (2009) Monoamine oxidase A gene (MAOA) predicts behavioral aggression following provocation. *Proceedings of the National Academy of Sciences* 106(7):2118–2123.

Mead M (1940) Warfare is only an invention, not a biological necessity. *Asia* 15:402–405.

Micheletti AJC, Ruxton GD, and Gardner A (2018) Why war is a man's game. *Proceedings of the Royal Society B: Biological Sciences* 285(1884):1–8.

Micklos D and Carlson E (2000) Engineering American society: the lesson of eugenics. *Nature Reviews Genetics* 1(2):153.

Miele F (2013) Savage science: an interview with Napoleon Chagnon. *Skeptic* 18(2):38–48.

Ness C (2007) The rise in female violence. *Daedalus* 136(1):84–93.

Newport F (2012) In U.S., 46% hold Creationist view of human origins. Gall Polit. www.gallup.com/poll/155003/Hold-Creationist-View-Human-Origins.aspx.

Nixon R (2011) *Slow Violence and the Environmentalism of the Poor*. Harvard University Press.

Number R (2006) *The Creationists: From Scientific Creationism to Intelligent Design*. Harvard University Press.

Nyhan B and Reifler J (2010) When corrections fail: The persistence of political misperceptions. *Political Behavior* 32(2):303–330.

Odling-Smee J, Laland KN, and Feldman MW (2003) *Niche Construction: The Neglected Process in Evolution*. Princeton University Press.

Oka RC, Kissel M, Golitko M, et al. (2017) Population is the main driver of war group size and conflict casualties. *Proceedings of the National Academy of Sciences* 114(52):E11101–E11110.

Otterbein KF (2004) *How War Began*. Texas A&M University Press.

Otto T, Thrane H, and Vandkilde H, editors (2006) *Warfare and Society: Archaeological and Social Anthropological Perspectives*. Aarhus University Press.

Page S (2008) *The Difference: How the Power of Diversity Creates Better Groups, Firms, Schools, and Societies*. Princeton University Press.

Perbal L (2013) The "warrior gene" and the Māori people: the responsibility of the geneticists. *Bioethics* 27(7):382–387.

Peterson D and Wrangham RW (1997) *Demonic Males: Apes and the Origins of Human Violence*. Mariner Books.

Pinker S (2011) *The Better Angels of Our Nature: Why Violence Has Declined*. Viking.

Pinker S (2018) *Enlightenment Now: The Case for Reason, Science, Humanism, and Progress*. Viking.

Quinlan J, Pearson LN, Clukay CJ, et al. (2016) Genetic loci and novel discrimination measures associated with blood pressure variation in African Americans living in Tallahassee. *PLoS One* 11:1–22.

Ralph P and Coop G (2013) The geography of recent genetic ancestry across Europe. *PLoS Biology* 11 (5):1001555.

Rosen L (2016) "Tribalism" gets a bum rap. *Anthropology Today* 32(5):3–4.

Rothstein R (2017) *The Color of Law: A Forgotten History of How Our Government Segregated America*. Liveright.

Saïd E (1978) *Orientalism*. Pantheon Books.

Saplosky R (2017) *Behave: The Biology of Humans at Our Best and Worst*. Penguin.

Scheper-Hughes N and Bourgois P (2004) Introduction: making sense of violence. In Scheper-Hughes N, Bourgois P, editors. *Violence in War and Peace: An Anthology*. Blackwell Publishing. Pp. 1–27.

Schrein C (2017) Evolution acceptance among undergraduates in the South. In Lynn C, Glaze A, Evans W, and Reed LK, editors. *Evolution Education in the American South*. Palgrave Macmillan. Pp. 121–133.

Shermer M (2015) *The Moral Arc: How Science Makes Us Better People*. Henry Holt and Co.

Shermer M (2016) On slates and tweets: a reply to David Sloan Wilson on ancient warfare and the blank slate. Evolution Institute. https://evolution-institute.org/blog/on-slates-and-tweets-a-reply-to-david-sloan-wilson-on-ancient-warfare-and-the-blank-slate.

Spikins P (2015) *How Compassion Made Us Human: The Evolutionary Origins of Tenderness, Trust and Morality*. Pen & Sword Books Ltd.

Sterling RL (2011) Genetic research among the Havasupai: a cautionary tale. *Virtual Mentor* 13 (2):113–117.

Tabery J (2014) *Beyond Versus: The Struggle to Understand the Interaction of Nature and Nurture*. MIT Press.

TallBear K @KimTallBear (2018, October 15; 7:04 p.m.) Statement on Elizabeth Warren's DNA test. https://twitter.com/kimtallbear/status/1052017467021651969.

Terrell J (2018) Ancestry tests pose a threat to our social fabric. Sapiens. www.sapiens.org/technology/dna-test-ethnicity.

Van Vugt M (2009) Sex differences in intergroup competition, aggression, and warfare: the male warrior hypothesis. *Annals of the New York Academy of Sciences* 1167(1):124–134.

Watson PJ and Kennedy MC (1991) The development of horticulture in the eastern woodlands of North America: women's role. In Conkey M and Gero JM, editors. *Engendering Archaeology: Women and Prehistory*. Blackwell. Pp. 255–275.

Weder N, Yang BZ, Douglas-Palumberi H, et al. (2009) MAOA genotype, maltreatment, and aggressive behavior: the changing impact of genotype at varying levels of trauma. *Biological Psychiatry* 65(5):417–424.

Wiley AS (2004) "Drink Milk for Fitness": The cultural politics of human biological variation and milk consumption in the United States. *American Anthropologist* 106(3):506–517.

Zihlman A (1997) The Paleolithic glass ceiling. In Hager L, editor. *Women in Human Evolution*. Routledge. Pp. 105–128.

Zihlman A (2012) The real females of human evolution. *Evolutionary Anthropology* 21(6):270–276.

Żukiewicz-Sobczak W, Wróblewska P, Zwoliński J, et al. (2014) Obesity and poverty paradox in developed countries. *Annals of Agricultural and Environmental Medicine* 21(3):590–594.

4 The Strangeness of Not Eating Insects

The Loss of an Important Food Source in the United States

Julie J. Lesnik

About half of the world's countries have cultures that include insects in their diets and there are over 2000 known insect species consumed (Jongema 2017). However, there is a notable lack of insect consumption in the dominant cultures of the USA, Canada, and many members of the European Union that is accompanied by negative attitudes, most notably manifested as disgust (Looy et al. 2014). A common question that follows from this pattern is: Why are insects actively avoided in "western" culture? A satisfactory answer has not been easy to come by.

The disgust that is triggered for many by the thought of eating insects may seem to imply that there is something inherently unsanitary about insects and that consuming them would increase the risk of disease or ailment. However, since there are countless cultures with longstanding practices of including insect foods in their diets, there cannot be something about the taxonomic class Insecta that makes them unfit as food (certainly nothing worse than other commonly consumed animals). Although the disgust trigger may have a deep evolutionary origin for protecting against disease vectors, today the trigger can exist for a variety of reasons, including a persistence of food neophobia into adulthood (Hartmann et al. 2015). Many people react negatively to what they do not know, and most westerners do not know insects to be food.

In looking to address why insects were never food to westerners, some researchers have suggested that beginning with the origins of agriculture, insects have been viewed as pests to food crops, changing general opinion of insects from one of nuisance to one of vitriol (Harris 1998; Van Huis et al. 2013). Since the vast majority of world cultures are agricultural, this viewpoint seems less rooted in correlates of agriculture and more on a history of considering foragers "uncivilized" (Earle 2010). I tested (Lesnik 2017) whether there was any relationship between agricultural productivity and insect consumption by assessing the percentage of arable land and the recorded number of consumed insect species for each country; I found no correlation. I also found no correlation with insects consumed and population density, which suggests that they are not being used as a fallback food when population sizes are so great they risk outstripping other resources.

The variables in the 2017 study that correlated with insect consumption were latitude and per capita gross domestic product (GDP; an estimate of a country's wealth). Although these results suggest that insects are consumed in poorer countries, the greatest predictor of insect consumption is latitude. Further investigation found that latitude could correctly predict presence/absence of insect consumption in

80 percent of the cases. Additionally, it was found that consumption of insects reduces along a gradient as distance from the equator increases, confirming that insects are most commonly food in tropical regions. I argue that ecological factors, notably the relative abundance of insect species at varying degrees latitude (Gaston 2007), played a major role in shaping the insect consumption patterns we see around the world today; however, there is a great difference between not eating insects and scorning them.

In western countries, GDP tends to be high while insect consumption tends to be actively avoided, so this relationship may be driving the negative correlation between per capita GDP and insect consumption. And since latitude also correlates with GDP, which is evident from the concept of the Global North/Global South socioeconomic divide, the statistically significant geographic pattern of reduced insect consumption further from the equator could be driven by the fact that most western countries reside past 40 degrees latitude. The negative attitude toward insect foods commonly held in western society must be more carefully considered in determining global patterns.

Rediscovery of Evidence in Anthropology

In anthropology, just as with any academic discipline, we build on the knowledge generated by our predecessors. However, if we do not rediscover this knowledge and proceed by just accepting it as true, then we risk perpetuating information that may not only be inaccurate, but also can be harmful. One notable way we can rediscover the meaning of the data we often cite is to acknowledge the colonial history of our nation and of our discipline.

Anthropologists began conducting regular, organized ethnographic research of other cultures in the late nineteenth and early twentieth centuries. The subjects of this research were most commonly the indigenous peoples who had been conquered and colonized by the anthropologist's nation of origin. Lewis Henry Morgan, who was described by Bohannan and Glazer (1973:29) as "one of the most influential thinkers of the nineteenth century," famously detailed what he called the periods of "savagery" and "barbarism" that he argued preceded "civilization" (Morgan 1877). These categories reflect the "animal-like" impressions early explorers conveyed in their journals and letters. Diego Álvarez Chanca (1493 [1906]:312), companion of Columbus on his second voyage, wrote:

They eat all the snakes, and lizards, and spiders, and worms, that they find upon the ground; so that, to my fancy, their bestiality is greater than that of any beast upon the face of the earth.

Although we train students today to recognize the absurdity of Morgan's categories and to avoid ethnocentrisms in their own work, we may not emphasize enough how the views of that time still color our impressions today. Edible insects are particularly illustrative of this problem because the disdain of westerners for them is most certainly tied to these concepts of primitive and savage. Even in contemporary anthropological thought, insects are commonly conveyed as a fallback food, consumed only when other preferred items are not available. Nutritionally, they do not belong in this category because fallback foods are generally items like starchy tubers that are not nutritionally dense (Marshall et al. 2009), while insects offer complete protein, fat, and an assortment of essential micronutrients. The high nutritional values of insects are evident in Dufour's (1987) research of the Tukanoan of the southwest Amazon Basin. For one season of the year, the Tukanoan acquire up to one-quarter of their total protein from insect foods. Dufour notes (1987:394): "The high level of insect consumption recorded in May–June coincided with a seasonal peak in the abundance of alate ants and a relative low point in fish and game availability." When cited (for example, Moran 1991:371), the fact that insects provide up to one-quarter of dietary protein during this season is almost always qualified with the fact that hunting and fishing yields are lowest at this time but rarely with the fact that it is the high season for preferred insect prey. When looking beyond the Tukanoan to other foraging peoples around the world, regular routines are often disrupted to focus on harvesting large numbers of insects when they come into season (Kneebone 1991; Nonaka 1996). By some metrics, this would indicate this resource is highly valued when it becomes available (Lesnik 2018).

The truth is that we know very little about how insects were traditionally utilized or valued as a food source in traditional diets, including those of Native Americans. We need to remember that by the time anthropologists were establishing study sites, Native Americans had already been displaced from their native lands onto constrained reservations in new environments that were not conducive for foraging for their traditional foods (Lesnik 2018). For example, the environment best suited for edible insects is the subtropical southeastern United States, but the Indian Removal Act of 1830 forcibly relocated the major tribes of this region – Chickasaw, Choctaw, Creek, Seminole, and Cherokee – west of the Mississippi River to much more temperate zones (Foreman 1953). The best accounts of insects as food for Native Americans come from the Great Basin region, where colonial settlement came relatively late in US history with the arrival of the Mormons in 1847. Although tribes such as the Northern Paiute were ultimately forced onto reservations that required them to shift subsistence to domesticated foods, they were notably resistant to assimilation and became known for their displays of cultural identity, such as the Ghost Dance (Kehoe 2006). Therefore, the persistence of insects in the traditional diets of the region today, and its visibility to outsiders, is also reflective of this dedication to self despite colonial oppression.

Investigating Global Patterns of Insect Consumption

This chapter aims to improve upon the limitations of the 2017 study and re-evaluate the impacts of western society on global patterns of insect eating. Analyses here will be run twice: once with all of the available global data, and a second time after the removal of data for western countries to determine their influence on the initial analysis. Additionally, another limitation of the original dataset will be addressed, the probable inconsistencies of working with species-level taxonomies.

The scholarly record of insects consumed around the world is enormously piecemeal. The literature extends across many disciplines – anthropology, geography, and entomology to name a few – and each utilizes its own research framework which leads to a lack of standardization and thus great inconsistencies in how data is reported (Bodenheimer 1951). Yet, in 2013, entomologist Yde Jongema at the Wageningen University and Research Center in the Netherlands took on the enormous task of compiling the *World List of Edible Insects* from across these disparate resources. Jongema has made this work available online and has since published two updated versions, the most recent published in April 2017. The database compiles published taxonomic information for insects consumed in each country as well as the taxonomic classifications for edible insects Jongema was able to deduce based on contextual information. My previous study used data from the 2015 version, so this chapter will utilize the most up-to-date version of the database. However, relying on these species-level designations for assessing global patterns may be problematic for a number of reasons. First, there is likely a skew in available data based on research interest in each country. For instance, Mexico has the largest number of known edible insect species in the world, but it also has one of the most detailed records thanks to the work of entomologist Julieta Ramos-Elorduy (see Pino Moreno 2016). Second, Jongema does not report the exact number of insects consumed in each country, only ordinal groups (0, 1–5, 5–10, 10–25, etc.), which limits the types of statistical analyses for which they can be used without transforming the data. Lastly, species-level identification of insects is difficult. The only sure way to know the species-level designation of insects consumed in a country is to have an entomologist assess each one. However, even entomologists are limited in their expertise, often specializing in taxonomic orders. Therefore, the species-level designations in Jongema's database are estimates and will be variable in accuracy depending on the quality of research presented in each individual study cited in his work. Therefore, taxonomic order may be a more useful metric since this category can be accurately identified by anyone with some education on the topic. Most people are able to distinguish insects such as beetles, caterpillars, ants, etc. from each other. Comparing orders of insects consumed in countries of varying latitudes may more accurately reflect how insects are consumed differently in different environments by controlling for some of the human error associated with generating data to the genus/species level.

This chapter reviews the global data for insect consumption and tests whether countries that are considered western, thus with longstanding European colonial histories, are driving the patterns, such as the negative correlations of insect consumption with latitude and per capita GDP.

Methods

Databases and Variables

The following variables come from Jongema's World List of Edible Insects (2017):

Insect species rank. Ranked estimates of insect species consumed per country were categorized into nine ordinal groups representing the following categories created by Jongema: 0, 1–5, 5–10, 10–25, 25–50, 50–100, 100–200, 200–300, and 300+. The values were obtained for this study by referencing Jongema's published map (Figure 4.1). The "0" category reflects no known edible insects, which can be from either their avoidance or underreporting.

Insect species binary. This is coded as presence (1) or absence (0) of edible insects in each country.

Insect orders. This classifies the number of known insect orders consumed in each country, with the category names reflecting some modifications from Jongema's publications. The categories for Homoptera and Heteroptera were combined into Hemiptera (true bugs), which reflects the current understanding of the phylogenetic order. The few instances of Psopetera and Phthiraptera in the database were combined into the superorder Psocodea (lice). Conversely, Jongema's categories of Isoptera and Dictyoptera were maintained although they do not represent monophyletic groups. Isoptera is the defunct taxonomic order for termites; they now belong in Blattodea along with cockroaches. Dictyoptera is a superorder that includes the orders Blattodea (termites and cockroaches) and Mantodea (mantises). For this chapter, termites remain in their own category because the social nature of these insects makes them a very different food resource than the rest of Dictyoptera. Jongema includes Araneae (spiders) in his database, and although they are technically not insects, the order is included here as well. Other orders represented in this chapter are: Coleoptera (beetles), Dermaptera (earwigs), Diptera (true flies), Ephemeroptera (mayflies), Hymenoptera (ants/bees/wasps), Ixodida (ticks), Lepidoptera (butterflies/moths), Megaloptera (alderflies/dobsonflies/fishflies), Odonata (dragonflies/damselflies), Orthoptera (grasshoppers/locusts/crickets), Phasmida (stick insects), Plecoptera (stoneflies), and Trichoptera (caddisflies).

The *World Factbook* (Central Intelligence Agency 2018) is a coordinated effort of the US intelligence community reporting information on people, economy, geography, etc. These databases are available free online through www.cia.gov. For 165 countries identified in the *World List of Edible Insects*, the following variables from the *World Factbook* (2018) were used in this study:

Latitude. This is the rounded latitude coordinate for the centroid or center point of a country. This value is based on reports from the Geographic Names Server maintained by the National Geospatial-Intelligence Agency on behalf of the US Board on Geographic Names. The values are reported in degrees and minutes north and south but converted to absolute value decimal degrees for this study.

Latitude lot. Ordinal categories for each country's latitude were created by rounding down the latitude value to the tens position, resulting in categories reflecting degrees latitude as 0s, 10s, 20s, 30s, 40s, 50+.

Population density. This variable was estimated by dividing population by the total area of the country, resulting in a figure measured as the number of people per square kilometer.

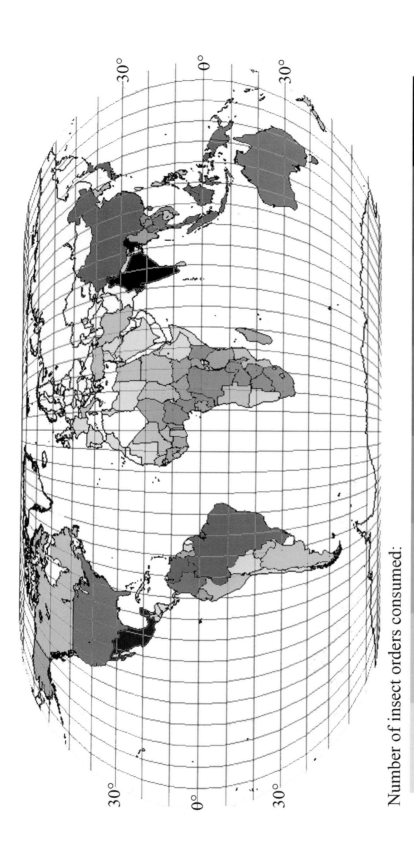

Number of insect orders consumed:

| | | | | | | | |
|1|2-3|4-5|6-7|8-9|10-11|12-13|14+|

Figure 4.1 Number of insect orders consumed per country. Categorical data from Jongema (2017).

Gross domestic product per capita (per capita GDP). GDP is the estimated value of all final goods and services produced within a nation in a given year. Per capita GDP is calculated by dividing GDP by population, recorded in US dollars.

Definition of "Western"

"Western" is difficult to define. Etymologically, the word refers to nations across Europe, but the term's meaning has been broadened to include countries with a history of European colonization and continued European migrations. However, some countries with a European colonial history, such as those in Latin America, are not typically described as western. Here, the countries removed from the analysis in order to understand the western influence on the data include all European countries, including those in the Caucasus region, plus the United States, Canada, Australia, and New Zealand, totaling 47 countries: Albania, Armenia, Australia, Austria, Azerbaijan, Belarus, Belgium, Bosnia and Herzegovina, Bulgaria, Canada, Croatia, Czech Republic, Denmark, Estonia, Finland, France, Georgia, Germany, Greece, Hungary, Iceland, Ireland, Italy, Latvia, Liechtenstein, Lithuania, Luxembourg, Macedonia, Malta, Moldova, Montenegro, Netherlands, New Zealand, Norway, Poland, Portugal, Romania, Serbia, Slovakia, Slovenia, Spain, Sweden, Switzerland, Turkey, Ukraine, United Kingdom, and the United States.

Analyses

All statistics were run in IBM SPSS Statistics v. 21 (IBM Corp. 2012). Multicollinearity tests were conducted to check that the independent variables in this study were independent of each other. Logistic regression was performed to ascertain the effects of the independent variables (latitude, density, and per capita GDP) on the presence of edible insects (insect species binary). One-tailed Spearman rank-order correlations were generated for each pair of continuous variables. Since multiple analyses on the same dependent variable increases the likelihood of Type I errors, a Bonferroni correction was used when assessing the significance of the Spearman correlations. Lastly, the effect of latitude on insect consumption (insect species binary) was explored in more detail by using paired Mann–Whitney U tests and related Bonferroni corrections to assess whether insect consumption is different at different latitude lots.

Insect order data were included in the above analyses along with species-level statistics. Additional investigations of the insect order data include a Kruskal–Wallis H test to assess whether different orders are consumed differently across latitude and an assessment of whether the orders consumed outside the tropics represent a subset of the orders consumed in the tropics.

Results

Tolerance and VIF (variance inflation factor), both measures of multicollinearity in SPSS, suggest that there is little to no influence of the independent variables on each

Table 4.1 Results of the one-tailed Spearman rank-order correlations of insect species or orders with latitude, population density, or per capita GDP

	Species All countries	Orders All countries	Species WoW countries[a]	Orders WoW countries
Latitude	**$p < 0.001$**[b]	**$p < 0.001$**	**$p < 0.001$**	**$p < 0.001$**
Density	$p = 0.139$	$p = -0.250$	$p = 0.344$	$p = 0.126$
Per capita GDP	**$p < 0.0001$**	**$p < 0.001$**	$p = 0.027$	$p = 0.590$

[a] "WoW countries" indicates the analyses without the inclusion of western countries.
[b] Significant correlation indicated by bold font.

other. As described by Chen et al. (2003), tolerance values less than 0.10 may indicate problematic multicollinearity since only a small amount of variance in the predictor cannot be accounted for by other predictors. A common threshold for VIF, which is calculated as 1/tolerance, suggests that values greater than 10 may be cause for concern. The range of values obtained in this study for tolerance is 0.797–1.00, which is well over 0.10, and the range of values obtained for VIF is 1.00–1.254, which is well under 10.

The binary logistic regression model using data for all 165 countries was statistically significant (chi-square value 79.3, df = 3, $p < 0.001$). The model explained 52 percent of the variance in the presence of edible insects (Nagelkerke pseudo R^2 of 0.515) and correctly classified 80 percent of cases. Latitude was the only variable showing significant individual chi-squared value (Wald 38.45, $p < 0.001$), thus is the driving force behind the predictive power of the model. When this analysis was run again after removing the 47 western countries, the results were essentially the same. Although the model explained only 35 percent of the variance, it correctly classified 81 percent of the cases, with latitude again being the only significant variable.

Spearman correlations for insect species rank and orders from the entire database revealed a negative correlation with per capita GDP ($p < 0.001$ for both) but not any correlation with population density. When the analysis was run again without the data from western countries, insect species still appear to negatively correlate with per capita GDP ($p = 0.027$), but this does not hold up to a Bonferroni correction whereby the *alpha* of 0.05 is divided by the number of comparisons (in this case four comparisons after removing density from the analysis) which results in a new p-value of 0.0125. When the analysis incorporates number of orders instead of species, all appearances of a significant relationship with per capita GDP dissolve ($p = 0.059$). Spearman comparisons are available in Table 4.1.

Mann–Whitney U test results for latitude lots and insect species binary are given in Table 4.2. When using the data for all of the countries, the general pattern that adjacent lots tend not to be significantly different from each other seems to hold, with one exception comparing 30 degrees and 40 degrees. However, when the analysis is run again without the western countries (that reside mostly at 40 degrees and above), there is no significant difference between the 30 and 40 lots, although significant differences in general are fewer because of the lower sample sizes at higher latitudes.

Lastly, a Kruskal–Wallis H test found no difference in how latitude affects which orders of insects are consumed (chi-square value 12.8, df = 17, $p = 0.75$). Most of the

Table 4.2 Results of Mann–Whitney U tests comparing mean rank of insect species pairwise by latitude lot

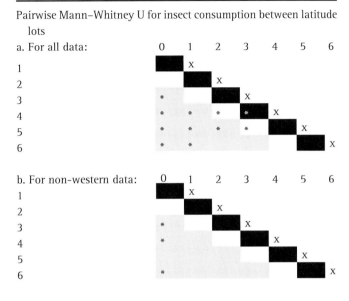

Pairwise Mann–Whitney U for insect consumption between latitude lots

a. For all data:

b. For non-western data:

Note: The analyses were done twice, once with all the data (a), and again with the removal of data for western countries (b). Rows and columns create a matrix pairing latitude lots for comparison. The numbers 0, 1, 2, etc. represent 10-degree latitude lots: respectively 0–9.99°, 10–19.99°, 20–29.99°, etc. The Bonferroni corrected *alpha* level is 0.002 and significance at this level for a pair indicated by the matrix row and column is marked with an asterisk (*). The cells marked with black shading indicate pairs that are geographically adjacent to each other and thus predicted to not be significantly different in a gradient pattern. The cells marked with lighter gray shading indicate pairs that are more than two lots away from each other and thus predicted to show the most significant differences in a gradient pattern.

orders consumed outside of the tropics are also consumed within the tropics, with two exceptions: Plecoptera and Dermaptera (Figure 4.2).

Discussion

Interpretation of Data

The data suggests that latitude is the strongest predictor of insect consumption even when the effects of western countries are accounted for. Conversely, the negative correlation of insect consumption with per capita GDP appears to be steered by the high per capita GDP of western countries. However, the population density still does not correlate with insect consumption even when the western countries are removed from the analyses.

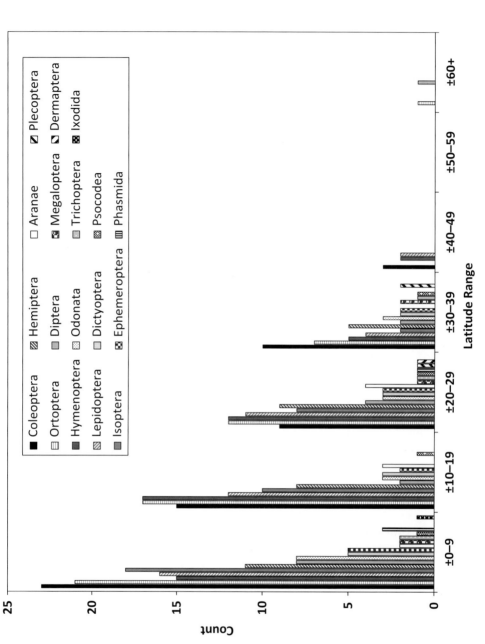

Figure 4.2 Insect orders consumed by latitude. 'Count' represents the number of countries from that latitude range that consume insects from each order. Data from Jongema (2017).

These results are compatible with the findings of the Lesnik (2017) study, but now include a more nuanced view of how western culture influences global patterns. Without the tandem analyses run here it was uncertain whether the relationship between latitude and insect consumption was reflective of ecological patterns across latitudes or whether the concentration of insect-avoidant countries in Europe was influencing the findings. But with nearly the same results in the binary logistic regression for both the complete dataset and the dataset without western countries, it can be stated with certainty that transitioning outside of the tropics increasingly lowers the likelihood of insect consumption. This pattern mimics that of the latitudinal gradient of biodiversity, which is the phenomenon that terrestrial species richness is greatest at the equator, and reduces with increasing latitude (Gaston 2007). Therefore, the same ecological factors (sunlight, seasonality, etc.) contributing to species diversity are likely affecting the availability and accessibility of edible insect species.

The tandem Mann–Whitney U analyses were unable to elucidate the fitness of the data to a gradient pattern. Although the data from the original study supported the hypothesis that insect consumption gradually reduces with increased latitude, there was an indication that insect consumption across the 40th parallel was significantly different, suggesting a possible disruption to the gradient at this latitude. Since most of the western countries are located past 40 degrees, I hypothesized their tight grouping was responsible for this result. In this study, the analysis utilizing the full dataset reproduced this finding, with a significant difference between insect consumption identified between the 30s and 40s latitude lots (Table 4.2a). Although this significant difference disappears when the analysis is run without the western countries, so do most of the significant differences, including many of the pairs that are more than two lots away (Table 4.2b). These results suggest that removing 47 of the 165 countries from the analysis weakens the reliability of the data. It is likely that this rough transition at 40 degrees is influenced by western culture, but it is not necessarily the only cause. The lack of human-inhabited landmass past the 45S parallel and the constraint of using centroid latitudes to represent entire countries may also be affecting this result.

The influence of western countries on the data is most evident with the analyses of per capita GDP. Like the 2017 study, the Spearman test (Table 4.1) found that per capita GDP correlated with insect consumption and latitude, but that it was not a significant variable in the binary logistic regression ($p = 0.343$). However, in this study I hypothesized that this finding would disappear when the western countries were removed from the Spearman analysis, and the results of the tandem Spearman test support this. There is some indication of a relationship between insect species consumed and per capita GDP, but the correlation is not significant at the Bonferroni correct *alpha* value. When the analysis was run using insect orders instead of insect species, there was no correlation, even at the level of the uncorrected *alpha*.

The categorization of the data by insect order as opposed to insect species did not affect the results in any statistically significant way. However, this variable is useful for visual representations of the data since diversity of insect consumption can be

Table 4.3 Summary of data compiled by latitude lot

Absolute degrees latitude	0–9.9°	10–19.9°	20–29.9°	30–39.9°	40–49.9°	50–59.9°	60°+
Number of countries	32	33	27	22	31	11	8
Number of countries with insect foods	31 (97%)	27 (82%)	19 (70%)	14 (64%)	6 (19%)	0 (0%)	1 (12%)
Number of "western" countries	0 (0%)	1 (3%)	5 (18%)	5 (23%)	25 (81%)	10 (100%)	5 (62%)
Number of orders consumed	16	12	17	14	3	0	2

assessed in a way the data have not previously allowed. The general trends seen in Figure 4.2 and Table 4.3 confirm the reduction of insect consumption with increasing latitude, both in number of orders consumed (number of bars) and in number of each order consumed (height of bars). The Kruskal–Wallis H test confirmed that there is no significant difference in how the different insect orders are consumed across latitudes. However, a few interesting things can be gleaned from the data. First, the largest number of consumed orders is not at the equator, but at 20–29 degrees. It was at this latitude that insects from the orders Plecoptera (stoneflies) and Dermaptera (earwigs) were first reported as consumed, in the USA and India, respectively. Second, even though the Mann–Whitney U tests could not confirm that it was western countries responsible for the disruption of the gradient pattern at 40 degrees latitude, the presence of only three consumed orders at the 40s lot appears to be a drop-off from the trend started at the equator, and since 81 percent of the countries at 40–49 degrees are western, there is a strong likelihood that culture is responsible. Lastly, it is worth noting that there are two orders consumed past 60 degrees latitude. Both of these records are from Canada. One is Orthoptera and represents the now extinct Rocky Mountain grasshopper, which would have been consumed closer to 50 degrees, near the border with the USA; the other is Diptera for parasitic warble fly larvae that infect caribou, and hunters such as the Tlicho of the Northern Territories valued consuming them while butchering the meat (Felt 1918). The global pattern reflects a reduction in frequency of insect consumption at northern latitudes, but not its total absence in these regions.

Environment and Colonial History

Insects are well known as a tropical food resource, but their avoidance in non-tropical areas is rarely described in these terms. Instead the lack of insect consumption in areas far from the tropics, such as Europe, has historically been described as a feature of modern civilization. Even today, these notions persist, indicating how badly perceptions of this valuable food source have been marred by colonial history. However, by identifying the strong correlation of insect foods with latitude and acknowledging that European countries are situated in environments that are not the most suitable for insect abundance and diversity, these perceptions can be historically contextualized.

In classical antiquity, Aristotle (third century BC) and Pliny the Elder (first century AD) wrote positively about a few insect foods, including cicadas, locusts, and grasshoppers (DeFoliart 2002). Over time these foods disappeared, likely lost during the chaos that followed the fall of the Western Roman Empire, but they certainly did not survive the cooling period known as the Little Ice Age that began in the thirteenth century, which brought unpredictable weather including cold summers and harsh winter storms across Europe (Mann 2002). By the time explorers such as Columbus began to traverse the seas in the fifteenth century, insects were anything but food. However, when these explorers reached the Americas they encountered different peoples with practically unrecognizable diets that often included insects. Earle (2010:703) explains that Spanish settlers feared that eating the unfamiliar foods in the Americas would make them ill and that "the consumption of insects attracted particular scorn." Food became a critical component of how European settlers differentiated themselves from the peoples they encountered. Although early colonial conceptions of the human body were fluid, such that settlers feared deteriorating their European forms if they ate non-European foods, this discrimination against indigenous peoples was the seed from which the eighteenth-century fixed, immutable-form racism grew (Chaplin 1997).

In the USA today, the dominant culture is derived from these European settlers and the scorn against insect consumption has persisted. However, environmentally, the region is well suited for these foods. With centroid latitude of 38 degrees, the mainland encompasses the transition from subtropical to temperate zones. Of the other countries with similar positioning around the world, 64 percent have some use of insect food. And according to the *World List of Edible Insects*, so does the USA.

Although the USA is included in the list of western countries removed here for some analyses, there is a deep history of insect foods for many of the indigenous cultures that were thriving before European colonization. These insects represent nine taxonomic orders, which encompass some of the greatest taxonomic diversity in the database, falling into the top 8 percent of countries. This result, like the rest of the study, likely reflects a combination of environmental and cultural factors: the USA crosses a wide range of ecozones that yield different preferred prey, and also there is more data for the region since it has been continually studied by anthropologists since the establishment of the field.

Indigenous peoples of North America, like thousands of other different cultures around the world, have benefited from utilizing insects as a food source. Insects are abundant, nourishing, and with their position at the bottom of the terrestrial fauna food chain, they are an efficient way to extract energy from the environment. Through the circumstance of Europe occupying some of the highest latitudes habitable by humans, this resource was not utilized by the culture that has grown to have such global influence. However, western culture's negative opinion toward insect foods needs to be decolonized, not only in order to eliminate the perpetuation of negative opinions toward indigenous peoples, but also to make the food source desirable to everyone around the world as we look for ways to feed the ever-growing global population. We need to recognize that *not* eating insects may be the "strange" behavior in places like the USA because environmental, nutritional, and ethnographic data all suggest that insects are a smart food choice.

Conclusion

This study confirms that latitude is the best predictor of insect consumption, with the greatest prevalence of insect foods in the lower latitudes of tropical regions. As distance from the equator increases, use of edible insects reduces. Included in this pattern is the widespread aversion that people in western culture feel toward insects as food. The absence of this food in their diets can be traced back to their European origins in high-latitude areas where insect foods are the least reliable. As European conquests took over more variable regions of the world, the settlers maintained their preferences for foods from home and stigmatized as primitive the foods from the cultures they contacted. This irrational, discriminatory opinion still persists today, and moving past the negative conception of edible insects will contribute to decolonizing western culture and creating a more inclusive space for indigenous identities.

References

Bodenheimer FS (1951) *Insects as Human Food: A Chapter of the Ecology of Man.* Junk.

Bohannan P and Glazer M, editors (1973) *Highpoints in Anthropology.* Alfred A. Knopf.

Central Intelligence Agency (2018) *The World Factbook.* www.cia.gov/library/publications/resources/the-world-factbook.

Chanca DÁ (1906) Letter of Dr. Chanca on the second voyage of Columbus (1493). In Olson JE and Bourne EG, editors. *The Voyages of the Northmen; The Voyages of Columbus and of John Cabot.* Charles Scribner's Sons. Online facsimile edition. www.americanjourneys.org.

Chaplin JE (1997) Natural philosophy and an early racial idiom in North America: comparing English and Indian bodies. *The William and Mary Quarterly* 54(1):229–252.

Chen X, Ender P, Mitchell M, and Wells C (2003) *Regression with SPSS.* SPSS Web Books.

DeFoliart GR (2002) The human use of insects as food and as animal feed. *Bulletin of the Entomological Society of America* 35(1):22–36.

Dufour DL (1987) Insects as food: a case study from the northwest Amazon. *American Anthropologist* 89(2):383–397.

Earle R (2010) "If you eat their food…": diets and bodies in early colonial Spanish America. *The American Historical Review* 115(3):688–713.

Felt EP (1918) Caribou warble grubs edible. *Journal of Economic Entomology* 11:482.

Foreman G (1953) *Indian Removal: The Emigration of Five Civilized Tribes of Indians.* University of Oklahoma Press.

Gaston KJ (2007) Latitudinal gradient in species richness. *Current Biology* 17(15):R574.

Harris M (1998) *Good to Eat: Riddles of Food and Culture.* Waveland Press.

Hartmann C, Shi J, Giusto A, and Siegrist M (2015) The psychology of eating insects: a cross-cultural comparison between Germany and China. *Food Quality and Preference* 44:148–156.

IBM Corp. (2012) *IBM SPSS Statistics for Windows, Version 21.0.* IBM Corp.

Jongema Y (2017) *World List of Edible Insects.* Wageningen University.

Kehoe AB (2006) *The Ghost Dance: Ethnohistory and Revitalization.* Waveland Press.

Kneebone E (1991) Interpreting traditional culture as land management: Aboriginal involvement in parks and protected areas. In Birkhead J, DeLacy T, and Smith LJ, editors. *Papers Presented to a Conference Organized by the Johnstone Centre for Parks, Recreation, and Heritage at Charles Sturt University, Albury, New South Wales, 22–24 July 1991.* Canberra Aboriginal Studies Press. Pp. 227–238.

Lesnik JJ (2017) Not just a fallback food: global patterns of insect consumption related to geography, not agriculture. *American Journal of Human Biology* 29(4):e22976.

Lesnik JJ (2018) *Edible Insects and Human Evolution.* University Press of Florida.

Looy H, Dunkel FV, and Wood JR (2014) How then shall we eat? Insect-eating attitudes and sustainable foodways. *Agriculture and Human Values* 31(1):131–141.

Mann ME (2002) Little Ice Age. *Encyclopedia of Global Environmental Change* 1:504–509.

Marshall AJ, Boyko CM, Feilen KL, Boyko RH, and Leighton M (2009) Defining fallback foods and assessing their importance in primate ecology and evolution. *American Journal of Physical Anthropology* 140(4):603–614.

Moran EF (1991) Human adaptive strategies in Amazonian blackwater ecosystems. *American Anthropologist* 93(2):361–382.

Morgan LH (1877) *Ancient Society.* Holt.

Nonaka K (1996) Ethnoentomology of the central Kalahari San. *African Study Monographs* 22:29–46.

Pino Moreno J (2016) The career of Dr. J. Ramos-Elorduy Blásquez. *Journal of Insects as Food and Feed* 2(1):3–14.

Van Huis A, Van Itterbeeck J, Klunder H, et al. (2013) *Edible Insects: Future Prospects for Food and Feed Security.* Food and Agriculture Organization of the United Nations (FAO).

5 Methods without Meaning

Moving Beyond Body Counts in Research on Behavior and Health

Robin G. Nelson

Biological anthropology is an intentionally integrative discipline incorporating methods from various fields. As such, data collection techniques ranging from morphometric analyses of hominin fossils to assessments of human cardiac output via fitness trackers are being added to the methodological catalog. This reflects a trend toward an increased reliance on quantifiable data. These data enable researchers to identify ever more finite differences in individual physiologies, and to discover the threads that connect this variability to our evolutionary past. Thus, it is attractive in its appeal to seemingly more objective scientific approaches to our most enduring areas of inquiry. However, it also signals movement in the field away from a reliance on and confidence in qualitative and descriptive methods, and our unwillingness to ask experiential questions differently in evolutionary anthropological research than our peers in other biological sciences. Thus, these methodological innovations both enhance our findings and limit the plurality of the data that is valued in the field.

In this chapter, I examine how the emerging methodological tensions in biological anthropology are anchored in a disciplinary history that made sense of human difference via faulty science, and the ways that scholars have responded to pressure to reframe their research while still investigating the core questions in human evolution. The lure of quantifiable metrics comes at the cost of labor-intensive qualitative methods, including ethnography and participant observation, that allow for more nuanced assessments of behavior, cultural practice, and life's daily challenges as articulated by study participants. I use this space to reflect on work that achieves this balance, while discussing what is lost when long-term qualitative work is marginalized, and thus slowly excluded from the canon within biological anthropology. While this trend is present in research throughout our subdiscipline, I will pay particular attention to this shift within studies of survivorship, reproduction, and health in contemporary human populations. Finally, I will address the cost of this fixation on long-term field-based studies, and how some scholars have centered both participant narratives and measurements in their analyses of social behavior and health.

Making Meaning of Difference

Before anthropology divided itself firmly into subdisciplines, scholars who were focused on the physical body sought to make sense of phenotypic differences by creating and codifying the race concept. Folk conceptualizations of racial hierarchies were made real through quantitative measurements of human populations living in different geographical spaces. According to one of the discipline's principal founders, a central aim of physical anthropology was the establishment of a system of measurements of the human body (Ellison 2018; Hrdlička 1918). Hrdlička (1918:8) decreed that anthropology is largely an investigation of "man's anatomical and physiological variation." In a list of changes necessary to advance the science of our field, standardizing anthropometric measurements was viewed as important, and as necessary as unifying scholars across the world. Thus, quantitative assessments of the human body became the central way to systematize our understanding of human difference. These earliest studies of the human body contained spurious biologically deterministic claims about the link between behavior, ability, and phenotypic appearance (Blakey 1987; Caspari 2003). As physical anthropology has become less singularly focused on measurements of the human form for purposes of recordkeeping and categorization, it has moved toward the goal of better understanding the interdependent relationship between behavior and individual biology.

With its origins in the nineteenth century, biological anthropology has been steeped in scientific racism for longer than it has not. Race was made real by scientific studies that used craniometry and anthropometry to create hierarchically weighted and legitimate meaning out of adaptive (and sometimes neutral) phenotypic differences (Brace 2005). These biological race narratives in science persisted and were put to use by policy makers well into the twentieth century (Silver 2003; Stern 2005). Citing Haeckel's belief in a polygenic origin of races, Madison Grant, eugenicist and zoologist, actively advocated for restrictions on the numbers of immigrants arriving into the USA, and supported anti-miscegenation laws in the US South (Sussman 2014). However, there have always been scholars – most famously Boas – who understood the troubling implications and misuses of racial typologies and made attempts to counter this popular narrative (Boas 1940). Before Washburn called for a focus on adaptation and evolution, Boas and others theorized that the most pragmatic and effective argument against the well-established racial typologies of the day would be an equally quantitative and statistically rigorous argument for phenotypic variability via adaptation (Caspari 2009; Kasten 2010; Oppenheim 2010). Thus, from the outset of this newly fledged and differentiating subdiscipline, quantitative analyses became the standard of rigor. What was once simply one way of creating categorical truth out of human difference became physical anthropology's defining feature. This was perhaps most apparent during the discipline's identity crisis of the latter twentieth century.

Rather than serving as complementary investigations of human variability, physical anthropology and cultural anthropology moved further apart in their assessments of what counted as meaningful conceptualizations of the human condition. At this moment, cultural anthropology moved decisively toward a more self-reflexive and postmodern turn (Marcus et al. 1999). Physical anthropology understood its mission as an investigation of the core conditions underlying human evolution and contemporary human diversity. In this vein, the subdiscipline more explicitly expanded beyond estimations of variability in physical form. What had always been housed within physical anthropology, but also under the umbrella of broader discipline (primatology, human ecology, paleoanthropology, human biology, and anthropological genetics) began to differentiate itself further from the cultural wing of the field (Fuentes and Wiessner 2016). This was particularly true for studies of the relationship between human behavior and biology as sociobiology came to prominence (Lieberman 1989). This broadening rift between the subdisciplines resulted in fractured departments, thus shaping the education of at least two generations of scholars. There was an undercurrent of belief that this divide was a reasonable conclusion as anthropology was never as holistic as proclaimed (Borofsky 2002).

Implicit within this disciplinary argument was a conversation about whether the field was big enough for theoretical contributions that, in some cases, directly challenged the validity of the others. Physical anthropology began explicitly reimagining itself as biological anthropology, as the former term has its origins in a historical moment that is focused on the link between race concepts and morphological measurements. However, the core aim of understanding human evolution and the human condition via our biology and that of our closest living relatives, nonhuman primates, remained a central goal. In this same postmodern turn, cultural anthropologists problematized the pursuit of a unifying understanding of the human condition, and even questioned the utility of ethnography as a method by which we can speak about other communities (Trouillot 2003). This critique was also made by anthropologists who interrogated the relationship between feminist and anthropological theory (Carsten 2000; Yanagisako and Collier 1987). As cultural anthropology wrestled with these questions, human ecologists and biologists within biological anthropology moved beyond sociobiology's prescribed focus on the evolution of human behavior to a more expansive emphasis on human reproduction and survivorship that accounted for ecological and environmental variability, proximate cultural practice, and species-specific behavioral practice (Ellison 2018).

Bodies in Flux

In what has been deemed a resurgence of Darwinian approaches to studies of human evolution (Ellison 2018), research in the field remained centered on measuring bodies. While the earliest iterations of what could be recognized as human biology were pseudo-scientific studies focused on making real faulty race hierarchies, a definitive shift toward research anchored in assessments of human variability in individual bodily adaptations to selective pressures in the environment was evident by the mid-twentieth century. A suite of papers on high-altitude adaptation pursued the idea that we could use the human body as a guide to direct our understanding of experiences of migration and species-specific adaptive capacity to extreme environments (Baker 1969; Beall 2000; Frisancho 1977; Moore 1989, 2001). High altitude serves as one early example of these new studies of human variability. It also demonstrates the ways that methods within biological anthropology and adjacent fields came to lead research questions in a race to uncover ever more finite differences in human variability.

Mirroring methodological advances in biology writ large, the earliest studies of human high-altitude adaptation were anchored in analyses of mechanistic variability at the level of the organ, and eventually shifted to explorations of the human genome. Classic studies of high-altitude dwelling populations living in Peru used anthropometry and analyses of work physiology to explore chest size, oxygen consumption, and growth (Baker 1978; Beall 2002; Beall et al. 1977). There was a wave of studies examining how the growth and development of populations experiencing this specific environmental stressor differed from that of their sea-level counterparts (Frisancho and Baker 1970; Pawson 1976). Until Leonard's influential piece highlighting the role of low socioeconomic status in further amplifying this environmental stressor, it was presumed that high-altitude stress alone caused a delayed adolescent growth spurt (Leonard 1989). As studies within broader biological anthropology shifted focus toward birth and reproduction, high-altitude investigations followed suit. What were primarily analyses of adolescent growth shifted to investigations of fetal growth and maternal compensation (Moore 1990; Moore et al. 2004). Compensation for higher risk of intrauterine growth retardation via genetic adaptations ranging from enlarged lung volumes to increased blood flow to the uterus reflect variability in ancestral duration at high altitude (Moore et al. 1998). It is worth noting that this research on high altitude served as only one lens through which researchers studied human adaptation to various environments. Parallel to this work, there was a growing body of literature exploring body mass adaptation to both cold and tropical environments (Bailey and DeVore 1989; Hanna and Brown 1983; Mazess and Mather 1974, 1975; Thompson and Gunness-Hey 1981). Through this early research, we observe the ways that these investigations of human adaptation reflect a neo-Darwinian shift in biological anthropology.

Reimagining the body and adaptive function as more than simply a sum of organs and parts required a shift in our conceptions of what counted as a useful metric by which to study human evolution. Once the field had definitely moved beyond the race concept (and onto what some would argue was a muddier and yet still categorical idea about populations) (Billinger 2007), ideas about human survivorship shifted toward examinations of what I conceptualize as *body counts*. These studies are exemplified by examinations of completed fertility rate, child survivorship, and sex-specific reproductive strategies. They reflected not only a broadening of ideas about how to best understand evolutionary resilience of a population, but also a diversity of perspectives as more women joined the ranks of principal investigators within the discipline (Lancaster 1991). Evolution in contemporary human populations, and specifically reproductive fitness, is often articulated as a three-part process: (1) reproduction, (2) survival to maturity, and (3) reproduction of individuals in the next generation. This centering of reproduction in analyses of human evolution necessitated a move toward understanding how many children were conceived, born, and survived in various communities around the world, and what the proximate mechanisms were that contributed to their survival.

As studies of human evolution came to center on reproductive processes, and thus the lives of mothers and their children, there was also an accompanying interest in natural fertility populations. Natural fertility populations are communities in which the women use no hormonal contraception. It is, perhaps, not entirely surprising that one of the earliest references to this concept appears in a publication that was also devoted to exploring reproduction, a journal entitled *Eugenics Quarterly* (Henry 1961). Although subsequently there has been considerable interrogation of this central premise, the particular focus on natural fertility populations hinged on their presumed resemblance and proximity to our ancestral condition (Wallace 1870). Much of this early writing about these communities is done in the ethnographic present, reflecting the idea that these populations were symbolically frozen in time and thus representative of human prehistory (Hastrup 1990; Sanjek 1991). From this vantage point, some theorized that we would be able to gain an understanding of our species' baseline risk of maternal morbidity and mortality, child survivorship, resource acquisition, and parental strategies.

Due to legacies of imperialism and colonialism, these natural fertility populations are limited in number and restricted to geographical areas that were either difficult to access or set aside by the government. At the outset of this increased interest in reproduction and survival, several influential studies were conducted with the San in southern Africa (Konner 1976; Lee 1972; Lee and DeVore 1976). Centered in the intellectual moment following the Man the Hunter conference, this research codified the relationship between subsistence and reproduction (Washburn et al. 1968). A primary area of interest was the mechanism underlying birth spacing in these natural fertility populations (Bentley 1985; Blurton Jones 1986; Cashdan 1985). Women were described primarily as gatherers and reproducers (Lee 1979, 1980). Thus, specific attention was paid to the energetics of gestation and lactation in light of a foraging and hunting diet and hormonal variability across the duration of reproductive status (Bentley 1985; Konner and Worthman 1980; Pennington and Harpending 1988; Spielmann 1989). The San served as the primary model of natural fertility populations, and thus as a proxy for the baseline state of bodily energetics and reproductive decision-making.

The framing of this early research on natural fertility populations established codified parameters and scope of these studies. They validated ways of quantifying each member's evolutionary value in the form of calories and babies. This focus on energetics and reproduction was anchored in life history theory, which conceptualizes the balance between current and future reproduction as a central trade-off in humans (Stearns 1989). Underlying these investigations was the idea that we could make numerical sense of each individual's contribution to the society and thus their evolutionary contribution to their own or their child's survival, and to their community. In short order, the field became saturated with information on a relatively limited number of natural fertility populations.

In this moment of theory production, research with natural fertility populations expanded to include other foraging populations. In addition to studies with Australian Aboriginal communities, the Mbuti, Aka, and Efe in Central Africa and the Hadza in Southern Africa received considerable attention after the first wave of research on the San. While these kinds of exploratory studies all but disappeared in other aspects of anthropology, they remained central in studies of resource acquisition and reproduction in foraging communities. Early influential research on the Mbuti was centered on social behavior, cooperation, and community-specific diversity in hunting strategies (Hart and Hart 1986; Ichikawa 1981; Milton 1985; Noss and Hewlett 2001; Wilkie and Curran 1991). While much research on the Mbuti examined subsistence patterns and interactions with neighboring communities, research on the Aka and Efe often included a focus on reproductive strategies rather than the energetics of lactation or gestation (Hewlett 1987; Hewlett and Lamb 2000; Meehan 2005). In this way, research on the Aka and Efe are a representative example of research in evolutionary anthropology exploring parental behavior, in addition to energetic allotment and subsistence.

Like research on their continental neighbors, early studies on the Hadza were dominated primarily by quantitative inquiries into demography, caloric balance, dietary practice, and the relationship between energetic availability and reproduction (Blurton Jones et al. 1992). There was also that familiar call to use the Hadza as an analogy for our ancestral condition (O'Connell et al. 1988). However, there was also a suite of studies investigating both paternal and maternal parental behavior (Crittenden and Marlowe 2008; Hawkes et al. 1995; Marlowe 1999; Wood and Marlowe 2011). One of the most influential theoretical contributions of this era, Hawkes' Grandmother hypothesis, was developed from data gathered among the Hadza (Hawkes et al. 1989, 1998). It serves as an illustrative model of the merging of energetics and reproductive analyses of daily life in foraging communities. Many studies building upon this frame have reintegrated ethnographic data into our quantitative models of energetics and resource allocation in small-scale communities.

The above-mentioned studies serve only as examples of the breadth of studies on foraging populations that emerged following the shift away from race studies within the discipline. Like biological anthropologists, archaeologists have long been engaged with questions surrounding the place of foraging communities in our understanding of the diversity of the human condition (Sheehan 2004; Winterhalder 1981). These reproductive data from foraging populations living in variable environmental contexts enable researchers to explore our understanding of the social dynamics and ecological challenges that shape the experiences of these people. Comparative studies challenge the idea that we can understand the human primeval condition through close study of a relatively small group of people (Kelly 2013; Kent 1992). They problematize the idea of a universal experience of early human evolution, instead recognizing that humans across space and time have been navigating environmentally specific selective pressures. Others have challenged the idea that life in foraging communities was somehow less symbolically and culturally rich than those of their counterparts living in industrialized settings (Bird-David 1996; Mosko 1987), and responded to the seeming inevitability of women's roles as reproducers and gatherers (Brightman 1996). There is also evidence that foraging communities are not all egalitarian and experience considerably more within- and between-group violence than was once imagined (Ember 1978; Fitzhugh 2003; Kelly 2013). That this simplified view of the lives of foragers gained any traction is curious, considering the wealth of data supporting symbolically and culturally complex lives from the outset of our species (McBrearty and Brooks 2000).

Beyond Foraging

Data from ecological contexts other than what was thought to be our ancestral condition provide additional ways to understand humanity, and highlight the limitations of reductionist body counting. Human behavior, specifically reproductive behavior, has always been culturally complex and ecologically specific. Research in varied anthropological field contexts problematizes the use of typologies, and introduces much-needed diversity to our analyses. In one example, influential research with the Aché in South America helped to both contextualize issues of demography and cultural practice, and to grapple with the relationship between foraging communities and the colonial government that was restricting their movements in areas in which they had historically traveled (Hill and Hurtado 1989, 1996; Kaplan et al. 1984). In these studies, we also observe an explicit integration of theorizing regarding individual survivorship, resource acquisition, and the evolution of human behavior, specifically kin and parental investment (Allen-Arave et al. 2008).

While research among the Aché provides a much-needed exception, this framing of resource availability, risk, and parenting was and remains largely dependent on a conceptualization of foraging communities, specifically natural fertility populations, as existing outside of the forces that shape reproductive choice and survivorship in "modernizing" and industrialized communities. It is useful to clearly identify what information from natural fertility populations can help us to better understand these phenomena, and what information is obscured by our dependence on relatively few communities as the standard bearer of access to and information about our pre-industrialized evolutionary past.

Demographic questions regarding population size and completed family size provide one kind of snapshot of the risk experienced by individuals in their daily lives. Qualitative data provide a different set of information on the ways that individuals mediate this risk in their daily decisions regarding food acquisition, maintenance of good health, reproduction and mate choice, and the navigation of social relationships. Recent research within evolutionary anthropology has retained, and in some cases reintroduced, qualitative and quantitative mixed-methods approaches to long-term studies of both foraging and industrialized populations. By necessity, this work often foregrounds the perspectives of study participants in defining terms and ideas like cost, benefit, trauma, love, and joy. By centering the participants' understandings of their own lives, we are able to provide additional rigor to analyses of the interdependence between individual health outcomes, and experiences of social relationships and the local environment. This integration of life history narratives and proximate cultural contexts counteracts a growing trend of measuring the body in ever more finite biometric analyses that come to serve as a proxy for individual lived experience.

The Value in the Proximate

A suite of studies investigating classic theoretical questions within evolutionary anthropology regarding mate choice, reproduction, and survivorship were better situated within the broader sociopolitical context of their study participants' daily lives. Shenk's research in India identifies ways to explore parental investment and mate choice beyond utilizing classic variables that permeated this same research in foraging communities (Shenk 2005, 2007). In one study, a close examination of the role of education, marriage, and income allowed for nuanced analyses of the influence of socioeconomic class on proximate-level decisions regarding parental investment (Shenk 2004). In this way, child survivorship gets defined more broadly, and more in line with the plurality of challenges facing these communities. In research with the Shodagor, Starkweather and Keith (2018) demonstrate that nutritional outcomes for women and children are mixed, and vary based on the level of market integration in this mixed-cash economy. These studies underscore the need to diversify what variables matter, and how they are defined in order to best understand classic anthropological questions in a broader range of contemporary human populations.

Beyond accounting for the diversity in the experiences of communities that are in the midst of demographic, political, and social change, increasingly researchers are allowing the experiences of their study participants to help structure the research questions as much as the evolutionary theory upon which their testable hypotheses are based. Pike's long-term research among the Turkana provides an instructive example of mixed-methods research on a population in flux. As a community becomes involved in small-scale warfare, individual experiences of stress, health, nutrition, and resilience are variable and mediated by culturally specific practices (Pike 2004, 2018; Pike and Straight 2011; Pike et al. 2010). In enabling the study community to lead in the creation of research questions and the very definition of the applicable variables, researchers like Pike are able to get to a different sort of truth regarding survivorship and reproduction that incorporates everyday decision-making, and the relevance of cultural practice and symbolic meaning.

Many scholars who are committed to understanding these quintessential species-level questions of reproduction and survival in diverse contemporary human populations ranging from small-scale to industrialized are confronted with communities that are in transition, and thus do not fit neatly within classic anthropological terminology. In an inadvertent reference to the same stifling practice that resulted in African foraging communities being used as a prototypical analogy of early humans and despite methods that are increasingly diverse, a short-hand label of "traditional" and "modernizing" has come to describe the persistence or erosion of social behaviors that are considered less adulterated by contact or market integration. In using the terms "traditional" and "modernizing," we risk revisiting etic anthropological practices in which the scholars determined the authenticity of particular cultural practices and individual behaviors. Our operationalization of the idea of modernization needs to be checked against the emic constructs of change, rather than modernization per se. The entire venture of studying modernization has fallen under critique as being neocolonialist due to its inherent directionality and suggestions of progress (Gladwin 1971). Cross-verification within the community enables us to evaluate the relevance of these ideas, and whether or not they conflict with emic representations of meaningful change.

If researchers are primarily concerned with reproduction, survivorship, and health, they can assess their disciplinary understanding of modernization and related health outcomes against emic conceptions of what has caused these changes, and whether or not the shifts in health outcomes have been beneficial. To address questions of modernization and human health, some have anchored their investigations in populations experiencing transition from locally mediated foraging or pastoral subsistence practices to increasing integration in local markets that are connected to global trade (Blackwell et al. 2009; Byron 2003; Godoy 2012; McAllister et al. 2012). There is evidence that the changes in health associated with modernization can be generally positive as they can reduce the risk of disease (Dockery 2010; Reyes-García et al. 2005; Veile et al. 2014). However, they also can increase risk of chronic diseases, and shift social dynamics and local knowledge within the community in ways that result in unexpected poor health outcomes (Frenk et al. 1991; Simonelli 1987; Urlacher et al. 2016). One potential intersection of participant-directed research on health and modernization are studies of changing practices regarding parental investment and childrearing. There is a dearth of research on modernization and parental investment (Mattison et al. 2016). There are, however, a few studies that address the ways that this social change can influence perception of risk regarding child survivorship and success, and thus influence the distribution of capital (Gibson and Lawson 2011; Hedges et al. 2016). In a mixed-methods study that utilized open-ended interviews to understand domains of health knowledge and breastfeeding practices in a recently settled pastoralist community, Miller (2011) found that western and indigenous models of health overlapped and that this maternal knowledge was protective against illness in infants. These studies reveal that modernization in and of itself is a non-linear process often complicated by individual integration and participation in the global market dynamics.

Perhaps the most innovative work being done in anthropology are those studies that upend the foundational structure of scientific research by engaging directly with participant communities in the construction of the research questions (Willyard et al. 2018). This framework interrogates the colonial foundation that relegated study participants to study subjects, and designated the researcher as the single knowledge holder. With knowledge of and active communication with their participants, Gravlee and Dressler developed research programs exploring the interaction between anti-Black racism and health outcomes experienced by Black communities in Puerto Rico and the American South (Gravlee et al. 2005, 2009). Pike's research among East African pastoralists best illustrates this kind of community-led research. These studies on warfare, nurturing, and women's experiences of vulnerability were developed from ethnographically grounded initial rounds of data collection. Ethnographic data provided information that was then used to structure the questions and methods employed in later research (Pike 2018; Pike et al. 2010, 2018). Such research requires a multi-year commitment to a tiered methodological model that may shift from year to year, and thus may require diverse funding streams. Due to its fluidity, this kind of study presents different challenges but may be more intellectually robust due to its ability to better reflect the dynamics experienced by community members. The shift has been more firmly established in other subdisciplines, most notably archaeology, where legislation has changed power dynamics and ownership of materials (Clifford et al. 2004; Den Ouden and O'Brien 2013; Douglass et al. 2018). Rather than jettisoning long-held theoretical models, these studies often can serve both the needs of the researcher and the communities.

Biological anthropology has historically centered the physical body as the locus through which we can understand all aspects of the human experience, ranging from adaptation to reproduction. Having largely embraced a move away from race science and toward investigations of adaptation, scholars created new rigor by atomizing the human experience in a reification of body counts – literal quantifications of who does and does not survive. Early studies met the call for a better understanding of human evolution by focusing primarily on natural fertility populations. While we were able to gain insight into social practice, reproduction, and resource acquisition, our ability to understand the plurality of the human experience was limited by a focus on a relatively small set of communities. Our disciplinary emphasis on quantitative assessments of bodies has foregrounded and privileged these numerical data, while relegating the substantive and informative information regarding proximate decision-making, change, and quality of life to the footnotes.

In this chapter, I have explored how the history of our discipline shaped investigations into cultural diversity and individual knowledge of reproduction, social relationships, and health, resulting in a dependence on quantitative methods and measurements of bodies but not experiences. Recent tests of hypotheses derived from evolutionary theories of human behavior, like optimal foraging theory, mate choice, and parental investment theory, are born of data that were anchored in nuanced understandings of daily life. Although the focus has shifted away from sex-specific examinations of biological reproduction, many studies still remain anchored in a quantification of bodies. These bodies often serve as a proxy for success. A nimbler interrogation of quality of life for those individuals who were doing this very particular work of gathering food and keeping children alive must be reintegrated into the dominant narrative. An overreliance on quantitative methods removes the participant from analyses of their own lives, and thus consigns them to a body that can be measured and thus explained, much like the work of our earliest disciplinary forefathers. By allowing study participants to guide both research questions and methodological inquiry, we gain better anthropological insight into the interrelatedness of conceptions of self and community, and the embodiment of life experience. Who is born and who survives remain vitally important questions. To fully address these themes, we must engage with data that are not easily operationalized, but that can inform our understanding of the proximate-level mechanisms that shape long-term dynamics of population- and species-level survival.

Acknowledgments

Thank you to Cathy Willermet and Sang-Hee Lee for organizing and inviting me to participate in the sessions that led to this volume, and thank you to the anonymous reviewers for your helpful comments. All errors or mistakes are my own.

References

Allen-Arave W, Gurven M, and Hill K (2008) Reciprocal altruism, rather than kin selection, maintains nepotistic food transfers on an Ache Reservation. *Evolution and Human Behavior* 29(5):305–318.

Bailey RC and DeVore I (1989) Research on the Efe and Lese populations of the Ituri Forest, Zaire. *American Journal of Physical Anthropology* 78(4):459–471.

Baker PT (1969) Human adaptation to high altitude. *Science* 163(3872):1149–1156.

Baker PT (1978) *The Biology of High-Altitude Peoples.* Cambridge University Press.

Beall CM (2000) Tibetan and Andean patterns of adaptation to high altitude hypoxia. *Human Biology* 72(1): 201–228.

Beall CM (2002) Tibetan and Andean contrasts in adaptation to high-altitude hypoxia. In Lahiri S, Prabhakar NR, and Forster RE, editors. *Oxygen Sensing: Advances in Experimental Medicine and Biology.* Springer. Pp. 63–74.

Beall CM, Baker PT, Baker TS, and Haas JD (1977) The effects of high altitude on adolescent growth in Southern Peruvian Amerindians. *Human Biology* 49(2):109–124.

Bentley GR (1985) Hunter-gatherer energetics and fertility: a reassessment of the !Kung San. *Human Ecology* 13(1):79–109.

Billinger MS (2007) Another look at ethnicity as a biological concept: moving anthropology beyond the race concept. *Critique of Anthropology* 27(1):5–35.

Bird-David N (1996) Hunter-gatherer research and cultural diversity. In Kent S, editor. *Cultural Diversity Among Twentieth-Century Foragers: An African Perspective.* Cambridge University Press. Pp. 297–304.

Blackwell AD, Pryor III G, Pozo J, Tiwia W, and Sugiyama LS (2009) Growth and market integration in Amazonia: a comparison of growth indicators between Shuar, Shiwiar, and nonindigenous school children. *American Journal of Human Biology* 21(2):161–171.

Blakey ML (1987) Intrinsic social and political bias in the history of American physical anthropology: with special reference to the work of Aleš Hrdlička. *Critique of Anthropology* 7(2):7–35.

Blurton Jones N (1986) Bushman birth spacing: a test for optimal interbirth intervals. *Ethology and Sociobiology* 7(2):91–105.

Blurton Jones NG, Smith LC, O'Connell JF, Hawkes K, and Kamuzora CL (1992) Demography of the Hadza, an increasing and high density population of savanna foragers. *American Journal of Physical Anthropology* 89(2):159–181.

Boas F (1940) Changes in bodily form of descendants of immigrants. *American Anthropologist* 42 (2):183–189.

Borofsky R (2002) The four subfields: anthropologists as mythmakers. *American Anthropologist* 104 (2):463–480.

Brace CL (2005) *"Race" Is a Four-Letter Word: The Genesis of the Concept.* Oxford University Press.

Brightman R (1996) The sexual division of foraging labor: biology, taboo, and gender politics. *Comparative Studies in Society and History* 38(4):687–729.

Byron E (2003) *Market Integration and Health: The Impact of Markets and Acculturation on the Self-Perceived Morbidity, Diet, and Nutritional Status of the Tsimane' Amerindians of Lowland Bolivia* (Doctoral Dissertation). University of Florida.

Carsten J (2000) *Cultures of Relatedness: New Approaches to the Study of Kinship.* Cambridge University Press.

Cashdan EA (1985) Natural fertility, birth spacing, and the "first demographic transition." *American Anthropologist* 87(3):650–653.

Caspari R (2003) From types to populations: a century of race, physical anthropology, and the American Anthropological Association. *American Anthropologist* 105(1):63–74.

Caspari R (2009) 1918: three perspectives on race and human variation. *American Journal of Physical Anthropology* 139(1):5–15.

Clifford J, Dombrowski K, Graburn N, et al. (2004) Looking several ways: anthropology and native heritage in Alaska [and Comments and Reply]. *Current Anthropology* 45(1):5–30.

Crittenden AN and Marlowe FW (2008) Allomaternal care among the Hadza of Tanzania. *Human Nature: An Interdisciplinary Biosocial Perspective* 19(3):249–262.

Den Ouden AE and O'Brien JM (2013) *Recognition, Sovereignty Struggles, and Indigenous Rights in the United States: A Sourcebook*. UNC Press Books.

Dockery AM (2010) Culture and wellbeing: the case of indigenous Australians. *Social Indicators Research* 99(2):315–332.

Douglass K, Antonites AR, Morales EMQ, et al. (2018) Multi-analytical approach to zooarchaeological assemblages elucidates Late Holocene coastal lifeways in Southwest Madagascar. *Quaternary International* 471(A):111–131.

Ellison PT (2018) The evolution of physical anthropology. *American Journal of Physical Anthropology* 165(4):615–625.

Ember CR (1978) Myths about hunter-gatherers. *Ethnology* 17(4):439–448.

Fitzhugh B (2003) *The Evolution of Complex Hunter-Gatherers*. Springer.

Frenk J, Bobadilla JL, Stern C, Frejka T, and Lozano R (1991) Elements for a theory of the health transition. *Health Transition Review* 1(1):21–38.

Frisancho AR (1977) Developmental adaptation to high-altitude hypoxia. *International Journal of Biometeorology* 21(2):135–146.

Frisancho AR and Baker PT (1970) Altitude and growth: a study of the patterns of physical growth of a high altitude Peruvian Quechua population. *American Journal of Physical Anthropology* 32 (2):279–292.

Fuentes A and Wiessner P (2016) Reintegrating anthropology: from inside out. An introduction to Supplement 13. *Current Anthropology* 57(S13):S3–S12.

Gibson MA and Lawson DW (2011) "Modernization" increases parental investment and sibling resource competition: evidence from a rural development initiative in Ethiopia. *Evolution and Human Behavior* 32(2):97–105.

Gladwin T (1971) Modernization and anthropology. *Anthropology News* 12(8):9–10.

Godoy R (2012) *Indians, Markets, and Rainforests: Theoretical, Comparative, and Quantitative Explorations in the Neotropics*. Columbia University Press.

Gravlee CC, Dressler WW, and Bernard HR (2005) Skin color, social classification, and blood pressure in southeastern Puerto Rico. *American Journal of Public Health* 95(12):2191–2197.

Gravlee CC, Non AL, and Mulligan CJ (2009) Genetic ancestry, social classification, and racial inequalities in blood pressure in southeastern Puerto Rico. *PLoS One* 4(9):e6821.

Hanna JM and Brown DE (1983) Human heat tolerance: an anthropological perspective. *Annual Review of Anthropology* 12(1):259–284.

Hart TB and Hart JA (1986) The ecological basis of hunter-gatherer subsistence in African rain forests: the Mbuti of eastern Zaire. *Human Ecology* 14(1):29–55.

Hastrup K (1990) The ethnographic present: a reinvention. *Cultural Anthropology* 5(1):45–61.

Hawkes K, O'Connell JF, and Blurton Jones NG (1989) Hardworking Hadza grandmothers. In Standen V and Foley RA, editors. *Comparative Socioecology: The Behavioral Ecology of Humans and Other Mammals*. Blackwell. Pp. 341–366.

Hawkes K, O'Connell JF, and Blurton Jones NG (1995) Hadza children's foraging: juvenile dependency, social arrangements, and mobility among hunter-gatherers. *Current Anthropology* 36 (4):688–700.

Hawkes K, O'Connell JF, Blurton Jones N, Alvarez H, and Charnov EL (1998) Grandmothering, menopause, and the evolution of human life histories. *Proceedings of the National Academy of Sciences* 95(3):1336–1339.

Hedges S, Mulder MB, James S, and Lawson DW (2016) Sending children to school: rural livelihoods and parental investment in education in northern Tanzania. *Evolution and Human Behavior* 37 (2):142–151.

Henry L (1961) Some data on natural fertility. *Eugenics Quarterly* 8(2):81–91.

Hewlett BS (1987) Intimate fathers: patterns of paternal holding among Aka Pygmies. In Lamb ME, editor. *The Father's Role: Cross-Cultural Perspectives.* Lawrence Erlbaum. Pp. 295–330.

Hewlett BS and Lamb ME (2000) Parental investment strategies among Aka foragers, Ngandu farmers, and Euro-American urban industrialists: an anthropological perspective. In Cronk K, Chagnon N, and Irons W, editors. *Adaptation and Human Behavior: An Anthropological Perspective.* Aldine de Gruyter. Pp. 155–178.

Hill K and Hurtado AM (1989) Hunter-gatherers of the New World. *American Scientist* 77(5):437–443.

Hill K and Hurtado AM (1996) *Ache Life History.* Aldine de Gruyter.

Hrdlička A (1918) Physical anthropology: its scope and aims; its history and present status in America. *American Journal of Physical Anthropology* 1(2):133–182.

Ichikawa M (1981) Ecological and sociological importance of honey to the Mbuti net hunters, eastern Zaire. *African Study Monograph* 1:55–68.

Kaplan H, Hill K, Hawkes K, and Hurtado A (1984) Food sharing among Ache hunter-gatherers of eastern Paraguay. *Current Anthropology* 25(1):113–115.

Kasten E (2010) Franz Boas: culture, language, race. Through an anti-racist anthropology. *Anthropos* 105(2):668–670.

Kelly RL (2013) *The Lifeways of Hunter-Gatherers: The Foraging Spectrum.* Cambridge University Press.

Kent S (1992) The current forager controversy: real versus ideal views of hunter-gatherers. *Man* 27 (1):45–70.

Konner MJ (1976) Maternal care infant behavior and development among the !Kung. In Lee RB and Devore I, editors. *Kalahari Hunter-Gatherers: Studies of the !Kung San and Their Neighbors.* Harvard University Press. Pp. 218–45.

Konner MJ and Worthman C (1980) Nursing frequency, gonadal function, and birth spacing among !Kung hunter-gatherers. *Science* 207(4432):788–791.

Lancaster JB (1991) A feminist and evolutionary biologist looks at women. *American Journal of Physical Anthropology* 34(S13):1–11.

Lee RB (1972) *Population Growth and the Beginnings of Sedentary Life among the !Kung Bushmen.* MIT Press.

Lee RB (1979) Production and reproduction. In Lee RB, editor. *The !Kung San.* Cambridge University Press. Pp. 309–332.

Lee RB (1980) *Lactation, Ovulation, Infanticide and Women's Work.* Yale University Press.

Lee RB and DeVore I, editors (1976) *Kalahari Hunter-Gatherers: Studies of the !Kung San and Their Neighbors.* Harvard University Press.

Leonard WR (1989) Nutritional determinants of high-altitude growth in Nuñoa, Peru. *American Journal of Physical Anthropology* 80(3):341–352.

Lieberman L (1989) A discipline divided: acceptance of human sociobiological concepts in anthropology. *Current Anthropology* 30(5):676–682.

Marcus GE, Fischer MM, and Fischer M (1999) *Anthropology as Cultural Critique: An Experimental Moment in the Human Sciences.* University of Chicago Press.

Marlowe FW (1999) Showoffs or providers? The parenting effort of Hadza men. *Evolution and Human Behavior* 20(6):391–404.

Mattison SM, Smith EA, Shenk MK, and Cochrane EE (2016) The evolution of inequality. *Evolutionary Anthropology: Issues, News, and Reviews* 25(4):184–199.

Mazess RB and Mather WE (1974) Bone mineral content of north Alaskan Eskimos. *The American Journal of Clinical Nutrition* 27(9):916–925.

Mazess RB and Mather WE (1975) Bone mineral content in Canadian Eskimos. *Human Biology* 47 (1):45–63.

McAllister L, Gurven M, Kaplan H, and Stieglitz J (2012) Why do women have more children than they want? Understanding differences in women's ideal and actual family size in a natural fertility population. *American Journal of Human Biology* 24(6):786–799.

McBrearty S and Brooks AS (2000) The revolution that wasn't: a new interpretation of the origin of modern human behavior. *Journal of Human Evolution* 39(5):453–563.

Meehan CL (2005) The effects of residential locality on parental and alloparental investment among the Aka foragers of the Central African Republic. *Human Nature* 16(1):58–80.

Miller EM (2011) Maternal health and knowledge and infant health outcomes in the Ariaal people of northern Kenya. *Social Science & Medicine* 73(8):1266–1274.

Milton K (1985) Ecological foundations for subsistence strategies among the Mbuti Pygmies. *Human Ecology* 13(1):71–78.

Moore LG (1989) Comparative high-altitude adaptation. *American Journal of Physical Anthropology* 78(2):178.

Moore LG (1990) Maternal O_2 transport and fetal growth in Colorado, Peru, and Tibet high-altitude residents. *American Journal of Human Biology* 2(6):627–637.

Moore LG (2001) Human genetic adaptation to high altitude. *High Altitude Medicine and Biology* 2 (2):39–47.

Moore LG, Niermeyer S, and Zamudio S (1998) Human adaptation to high altitude: regional and life-cycle perspectives. *Yearbook of Physical Anthropology* 41:25–64.

Moore LG, Shriver M, Bemis L, et al. (2004) Maternal adaptation to high-altitude pregnancy: an experiment of nature – a review. *Placenta* 25(S):S60–S71.

Mosko MS (1987) The symbols of "forest": a structural analysis of Mbuti culture and social organization. *American Anthropologist* 89(4):896–913.

Noss AJ and Hewlett BS (2001) The contexts of female hunting in central Africa. *American Anthropologist* 103(4):1024–1040.

O'Connell JF, Hawkes K, and Blurton Jones N (1988) Hadza scavenging: implications for Plio/Pleistocene hominid subsistence. *Current Anthropology* 29(2):356–363.

Oppenheim R (2010) Revisiting Hrdlicka and Boas: asymmetries of race and anti-imperialism in interwar anthropology. *American Anthropologist* 112(1):92–103.

Pawson IG (1976) Growth and development in high altitude populations: a review of Ethiopian, Peruvian, and Nepalese studies. *Proceedings of the Royal Society London B* 194(1114):83–98.

Pennington R and Harpending H (1988) Fitness and fertility among Kalahari !Kung. *American Journal of Physical Anthropology* 77(3):303–319.

Pike IL (2004) The biosocial consequences of life on the run: a case study from Turkana District, Kenya. *Human Organization* 63(2):221–235.

Pike IL (2018) Intersections of insecurity, nurturing, and resilience: a case study of Turkana women of Kenya. *American Anthropologist* 121(1):126–137.

Pike IL and Straight BS (2011) Unpacking resilience in extreme circumstances: a mixed-method, longitudinal case study from Turkana pastoralists of northern Kenya. *American Journal of Human Biology* 23(2):272.

Pike IL, Straight B, Oesterle M, Hilton C, and Lanyasunya A (2010) Documenting the health consequences of endemic warfare in three pastoralist communities of northern Kenya: a conceptual framework. *Social Science & Medicine* 70(1):45–52.

Pike IL, Hilton C, Österle M, and Olungah O (2018) Low-intensity violence and the social determinants of adolescent health among three east African pastoralist communities. *Social Science & Medicine* 202:117–127.

Reyes-García V, Vadez V, Byron E, et al. (2005) Market economy and the loss of folk knowledge of plant uses: estimates from the Tsimane' of the Bolivian Amazon. *Current Anthropology* 46 (4):651–656.

Sanjek R (1991) The ethnographic present. *Man* 26(4):609–628.

Sheehan MS (2004) Ethnographic models, archaeological data, and the applicability of modern foraging theory. In Barnard A, editor. *Hunter-Gatherers in History, Archaeology and Anthropology*. Berg. Pp. 163–173.

Shenk MK (2004) Embodied capital and heritable wealth in complex cultures: a class-based analysis of parental investment in urban south India. *Socioeconomic Aspects of Human Behavioral Ecology*. Emerald Group Publishing Limited. Pp. 307–333.

Shenk MK (2005) Kin investment in wage-labor economies. *Human Nature* 16(1):81–113.

Shenk MK (2007) Dowry and public policy in contemporary India. *Human Nature* 18(3):242–263.

Silver MG (2003) Eugenics and compulsory sterilization laws: providing redress for the victims of a shameful era in United States history. *George Washington Law Review* 72(4):862–891.

Simonelli J (1987) Defective modernization and health in Mexico. *Social Science & Medicine* 24 (1):23–36.

Spielmann KA (1989) A review: dietary restrictions on hunter-gatherer women and the implications for fertility and infant mortality. *Human Ecology* 17(3):321–345.

Starkweather KE and Keith MH (2018) Estimating impacts of the nuclear family and heritability of nutritional outcomes in a boat-dwelling community. *American Journal of Human Biology* 30(3): e23105.

Stearns SC (1989) Trade-offs in life-history evolution. *Functional Ecology* 3(3):259–268.

Stern AM (2005) Sterilized in the name of public health: race, immigration, and reproductive control in modern California. *American Journal of Public Health* 95(7):1128–1138.

Sussman RW (2014) Physical anthropology in the early twentieth century. In Sussman RW, editor. *The Myth of Race*. Harvard University Press. Pp. 165–199.

Thompson D and Gunness-Hey M (1981) Bone mineral-osteon analysis of Yupik-Inupiaq skeletons. *American Journal of Physical Anthropology* 55(1):1–7.

Trouillot M-R (2003) Anthropology and the savage slot: the poetics and politics of otherness. In *Global Transformations*. Springer. Pp. 7–28.

Urlacher SS, Liebert MA, Snodgrass J, et al. (2016) Heterogeneous effects of market integration on sub-adult body size and nutritional status among the Shuar of Amazonian Ecuador. *Annals of Human Biology* 43(4):316–329.

Veile A, Martin M, McAllister L, and Gurven M (2014) Modernization is associated with intensive breastfeeding patterns in the Bolivian Amazon. *Social Science & Medicine* 100:148–158.

Wallace AR (1870) Researches into the early history of mankind and the development of civilisation. *Nature* 2(44):350.

Washburn SL, Lancaster C, Lee RB, and DeVore I (1968) *Man the Hunter*. Routledge.

Wilkie DS and Curran B (1991) Why do Mbuti hunters use nets? Ungulate hunting efficiency of archers and net-hunters in the Ituri Rain Forest. *American Anthropologist* 93(3):680–689.

Willyard C, Scudellari M, and Nordling L (2018) How three research groups are tearing down the Ivory Tower. *Nature* 562(7725):24–28.

Winterhalder B (1981) Optimal foraging strategies and hunter-gatherer research in anthropology: theory and models. In Winterhalder B and Smith EA, editors. *Hunter-Gatherer Foraging Strategies: Ethnographic and Archaeological Analyses*. University of Chicago Press. Pp. 13–35.

Wood BM and Marlowe FW (2011) Dynamics of postmarital residence among the Hadza: a kin investment model. *Human Nature: An Interdisciplinary Biosocial Perspective* 22(1–2):128–138.

Yanagisako SJ and Collier JF (1987) Toward a unified analysis of gender and kinship. In Collier JF and Yanagisako SJ, editors. *Gender and Kinship: Essays Toward a Unified Analysis*. Stanford University Press. Pp. 14–50.

Part II

(Re)Discovery of Evidence

New Thinking About Data, Methods, and Fields

6 (Re)Discovering Paleopathology

Integrating Individuals and Populations in Bioarchaeology

Ann L. W. Stodder and Jennifer F. Byrnes

The past decade has been a time of significant growth in paleopathology, and also a time of transition in the relationship between paleopathology – "the investigation of diseases and related conditions in skeletal and soft tissue remains" (Paleopathology Association 2018) – and the broader field of bioarchaeology – the "integrative, contextualized study of human skeletal remains derived from archaeological settings" (Larsen 2018:865). These trends are driving a real florescence in paleopathology as this work, which starts from the study of individual bones, finds an integral role in larger-scale contextualized explorations of life in the past (Buzon 2012; Grauer 2018a, 2018b). In this chapter, we review the underpinnings of the enhanced articulation of paleopathology and bioarchaeology, especially in regard to studies of disability and care. We address the difficulties attendant to discussions of disability that stem from the epistemologies and semantics of disability studies and the cross-cultural (and temporal) differences in the experience of illness, the perceived sources of illness, and attitudes toward the ill or disabled. These are significant issues in contemporary society and global epidemiology, as well as in the interpretation of pathologies identified in skeletal and soft tissue remains. Returning to the role of paleopathology, we review current approaches to quantifying impairment and interpreting disability in the bioarchaeological record, highlighting the role of interpreting evidence for the provision (and withholding) of care – care of the very young and the very old, of the ill and disabled, and care of the dead – as a bridge between paleopathology and the broader studies that represent significant developments in bioarchaeology.

Paleopathology and Bioarchaeology, Individuals and Populations

Paleopathology was traditionally a domain of dentists, pathologists, and medical historians whose case reports were not typically of interest to bioarchaeologists (Buikstra and Roberts 2012; Cook and Powell 2006). However, since the 1970s several encyclopedic texts on paleopathology (Aufderheide and Rodriguez-Martin 1998; Ortner 2003; Ortner and Putschar 1981; Roberts and Manchester 2005; Steinbock 1976) have supported the efforts of bioarchaeologists to diagnose pathologies in skeletal remains. Additional volumes on the paleopathology of specific diseases and disease groups are joined by electronic resources like *Digitized Diseases* (2018), *Osteoware* (Smithsonian National Museum of Natural History 2018), the *Index of Care* (Tilley and Cameron 2014), and the Paleopathology Association's *The*

International Journal of Paleopathology. The growth and professionalization of paleopathology is evident in the number of students trained and in the move to systematic data collection and methodological rigor in the identification and recording of pathologies. Buikstra and colleagues (2017) enumerate the range of skills required for best practice in paleopathology, including the anatomical and biological knowledge to go beyond paleopathology textbooks and use primary sources (e.g., forensic studies, clinical texts, and other biomedical literature), understanding the archaeological contexts and the representativeness of bioarchaeological assemblages, critical skills in data interpretation, and the breadth of interest to consult anthropological and historical resources for contextual information. Paleopathology has become "the quintessential interdisciplinary subject" (Grauer 2018a:447).

The field of bioarchaeology, initiated by Buikstra and others in the 1970s (Blakely 1977; Buikstra 1977) and synthesized by Buikstra and Beck (2006), Martin et al. (2013), and Larsen (2015, 2018) is defined by the importance of context and by an analytical emphasis on sample-based studies of archaeological skeletal assemblages to address broad questions about human biocultural evolution and adaptation. The interpretive basis of bioarchaeology rests largely on the statistical detection of trends and patterns in otherwise nondiagnostic reactive changes, collectively referred to as nonspecific stress indicators (Armelagos and Goodman 1991; Goodman et al. 1984, 1988; Grauer 2018a, 2018b; also see DeWitte, Chapter 7 this volume). These include dental enamel defects, periosteal inflammation, and cranial lesions related to inadequate dietary intake or absorption of iron and vitamin B. Observable on all sufficiently preserved skeletons, these yield large datasets on the presence and extent of physiological stress and growth disruption. Along with the prevalence of skeletal fractures, dental pathology, and degenerative joint wear, these continue as core data in bioarchaeological analyses of health in skeletal assemblages.

Armelagos succinctly identified the divide between paleopathology and bioarchaeology: "Although the individual is the unit of *diagnosis*, the population is the unit of *analysis*" (2003:29). As a result of the focus on nonspecific stress indicators and population data, skeletal pathologies diagnosed in one or two individuals have been left out of many bioarchaeological studies because they did not fit into the statistical portraits of population health, nor were they considered important for paleodemography because skeletal lesions reflect the response to relatively long-term, chronic conditions rather than acute conditions that cause death (Stodder 2016, 2017).

New approaches in bioarchaeology integrate paleopathology, maximizing this information rather than discarding carefully researched and documented case studies as merely descriptive and qualitative. Paleopathologists are working on ways to treat these works as data that can be used to track the significance of skeletal pathologies, and the conditions and comorbidities they represent, on multiple scales. There is broad agreement that morbidity – the departure from optimal health – is a critical aspect of every individual's life and also of the collective well-being, functionality, and resilience of every family, community, and population today and in the past.

This multiscalar humanist perspective is apparent in the archaeological and bioarch-aeological literature (e.g., Glowacki 2015; Hegmon 2016; Hegmon et al. 2008; Juengst and Becker 2017; Milner and Boldsen 2017). The individual and collective morbidity reflected in skeletal assemblages reveals genetic, epigenetic, and environmental factors affecting health, and the social and political forces that drive differential access to health and longevity.

The conceptual transition that accommodates more than nonspecific stresses and situates paleopathology in social and political contexts is captured by the evolving stress model that has been used since the 1980s to explicate the linkage between skeletal data and biocultural adaptation (Armelagos and Goodman 1991; Goodman et al. 1984, 1988; Martin et al. 2013). Figure 6.1 shows the top-level labels; for more detail see the various published versions (especially in Martin et al. 2013:16–17). In the 1984 version (Goodman et al. 1984:14), the environment is buffered by culture. A recent version of the model from an essay on structural violence (Klaus 2012:34) has a subtle, but significant, modification. In Klaus's model, culture is presented first as a stress factor on the same level as environmental constraints. Culture creates social inequality and other impediments to optimal health that must be buffered by other cultural systems. Bioarchaeological research explicitly acknowledges that cultural variables may have a greater impact on morbidity than the physical environment, as reflected in patterns and prevalence of trauma (interpersonal and intergroup), social status based on sex, sociopolitical role, and social class.

Another significant development in the integration of paleopathology is the adoption of the life course approach in which social and biological processes are seen as impacting individual life histories as well as crossing generations, thereby tying individual frailty to larger biocultural trends (Agarwal 2016; Agarwal and Beauchesne 2011; Gowland 2015). Sofaer's (2006) characterization of the skeleton as a socially created entity links the themes of life course, embodiment, and agency and has reinvigorated interest in osteobiography (Saul and Saul 1989) as a way to understand life in the past through the study of a single individual's remains, integrating archaeological, ethnographic, epigraphical, and historical evidence (e.g., Boutin 2016; Hawkey 1998; Robb 2002; Stodder and Palkovich 2012). The newly formalized field of forensic biohistory (Stojanowski and Duncan 2017) carries osteobiography into public awareness through the study of known individuals. The structured integration of osteological, paleopathological, archaeological, historical, and clinical data forms the basis for the structured osteobiographies formulated in the bioarchaeology of care approach (Tilley 2015), which we discuss further below.

These new approaches provide the broad framework for a more humanistic bioarchaeology that includes individuals and populations, and goes beyond the largely economic and ecological adaptationist themes of processualist archaeology (Grauer 2012; Zuckerman et al. 2012). Current bioarchaeological research considers the creation of identity and personhood (Boutin 2016; Knudson and Stojanowski 2009), the roles and experiences of children (Beauchesne and Agarwal 2018; Kamp 2002, 2009; Lewis 2016, 2018; Mays et al. 2017; Thompson et al. 2014) and the elderly in past societies (Gowland 2016a), gender and identity construction (Agarwal

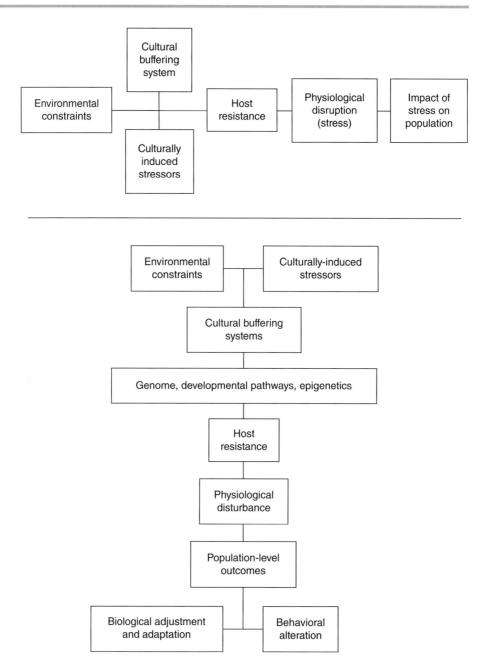

Figure 6.1 Models for interpreting stress in bioarchaeology. Top: based on data from Goodman et al. (1984: fig. 2.1). Bottom: based on data from Klaus (2012: fig. 2.2).

and Wesp 2017; Geller 2017), the lives of displaced and colonized peoples (Baker and Tsuda 2015; Murphy and Klaus 2017), the scope of bioarchaeological evidence for overt and structural violence (Martin 1997, 2008; Martin and Tegtmeyer 2017; Martin et al. 2012), and the immediate and long-term effects of social inequality on health and frailty (Agarwal 2016; Agarwal and Beauchesne 2011; Gowland 2015).

Larsen captures the sense of current bioarchaeology, and the trend toward understanding life in the past through more than statistical profiles, in the title of his essay in the centennial issue of the *American Journal of Physical Anthropology*: "Bioarchaeology in perspective: from classifications of the dead to conditions of the living" (Larsen 2018). A similar theme is reflected in Milner and Boldsen's (2017) paper, "Life not death: epidemiology from skeletons," in which they build on their earlier consideration of the importance of community health and morbidity (Boldsen and Milner 2012), and make some progress in linking population-based paleoepidemiology to paleopathology. The importance of well-being and quality of life experience is integral to current humanistic approaches in archaeology, as exemplified in *The Archaeology of the Human Experience* (Hegmon 2016), which includes sociopolitical issues such as the consequences of inequality, violence, the collapse of social systems, migration and diaspora, and pain and suffering resulting from any and all of these, providing strong links between archaeology and bioarchaeology (Hegmon 2016:13). In that volume, Martin and Harrod echo the individual/population dichotomy regarding the implementation of "a (bio)archaeology of pain and suffering: . . . analyses must move between individual-level data on pain and disability and population-level data that can indicate patterns of suffering that crosscut subgroups such as age, sex, and class" (Martin and Harrod 2016:165). This work requires deeply contextualized paleopathology data and theoretically framed interpretation of the *meaning* of that data at larger social scales. This is the essential bridge between diagnosis and analysis, individual and population, that is also implemented in studies of disability and care in bioarchaeology.

Interpreting Paleopathology: Theory and Terminology in the Bioarchaeology of Disability and Care

The link between clinical data and the evidence for the functional and epidemiological consequences of the conditions we see in human remains provides the empirical grounding for both scientific and humanistic interpretations of well-being in the past. In all of these areas of inquiry, we face the sometimes contentious issues of how to define and identify disability, and how to interpret skeletal data to make broader inferences about the treatment of, and attitudes toward, health, impairment, and disability, in the past. In the US Americans with Disabilities Act, impairment is defined as a disorder or condition affecting one or more body systems, in contrast to disability, which is defined as an impairment that substantially limits participation in one or more major life activities. As shown in Table 6.1, there are different, more nuanced, versions of these understandings of impairment and disability.

Disability is a relatively recent western, sociopolitical concept, albeit one mapped onto biological characteristics. The binary categories of normal and disabled were developed during the Industrial era to differentiate people who were able to work from those who could not (Davis 1995). Historical and bioarchaeological evidence indicate that people in the past were also treated differently based on various physical, mental, or emotional capabilities (cf. Finlay 1999; Hubert 2000).

Table 6.1 Definitions of impairment and disability

Americans With Disabilities Act (2008)	Medical model (World Health Organization 1980)	Social model (Disabled Peoples' International 1982)	Biopsychosocial model (International Classification of Functioning, Disability and Health, World Health Organization 2001)
Impairment			
"A physical impairment is a physiological disorder or condition, cosmetic disfigurement or anatomical loss impacting one or more body systems. A mental impairment is a mental or psychological disorder."	"[A]ny loss or abnormality of psychological, physiological, or anatomical structure or function."	"[I]s the functional limitation within the individual caused by physical, mental, or sensory impairment."	"[P]roblems in body function or structure such as a significant deviation or loss."
Disability			
"A physical or mental impairment that substantially limits one or more major life activities."	"[A]ny restriction or lack (resulting from an impairment) of ability to perform an activity in the manner or within the range considered normal for a human being."	"[I]s the loss or limitation of opportunities to take part in the normal life of the community on an equal level with others due to physical and social barriers."	"[A]n umbrella term for impairments, activity limitations and participation restriction. It denotes the negative aspects of the interaction between an individual (with a health condition) and that individual's contextual factors (environmental and personal factors)."

Source: modified from Bethard et al. (2017).

The challenge, and indeed the usefulness, of investigating disability through paleopathology and bioarchaeology is the fact that the experience and perception of disability and disease varies substantially; "what may be classed as a disease in the western sense could be viewed as an illness that, in the eyes of the person experiencing the illness and their community more generally, does not need treatment" (Roberts 2017:105). The varied experiences exist cross-culturally and across the life course of the affected individual, since disability identities are created and embodied in dynamic physical and sociopolitical contexts. Impairments may be progressive or congenital; even in one cultural setting, age of onset and duration can significantly alter the potentially disabling experience and social perception of the person (Gowland et al. 2016:218; Lewis 2016:34).

There are two main schools of thought within the academic discipline of disability studies – the medical model and social model (see Table 6.1). The medical model frames physical, mental, or emotional impairments as functional deficits that lead to disability, for which the individual should be medically treated (Siebers 2008). The development of the medical model of disability can be traced to the professionalization of medicine in the nineteenth century (Davis 1995, 2013a). This model does not consider sociocultural factors like the built physical environment, transportation options that could impact the extent to which impairment is disabling, or the question of whether a given impairment is considered a disability or something quite different, like a special gift, in different cultures.

In the social model, disability is understood as a sociopolitical construct (Oliver 1983). Hence, this model describes disability as the marginalization of people based on perceived differences in their ability as restricted by the physical and social barriers that exist in the environment. The social model does not suggest a direct connection between impairment and disability (Goodley 2011; Shakespeare 2013), and instead links disabling effects experienced by a person to "physical and social barriers." This can be read to mean that within any given culture, individuals who have palpable differences (including chronic illnesses) that are perceived to affect the common good or otherwise do not fit into preset societal norms, will result in that person experiencing disability within the community. When applied in bioarchaeology, the social model understanding of disability can help to draw attention to the potential range of experiences and agency of disabled people in the past.

Since its emergence in the 1980s, Disability Studies scholars who adhere to a variety of theoretical persuasions (e.g., dismodernism, post-structuralism) have continued to critique and refine the social model (Davis 2013b; Goodley et al. 2012; Shakespeare 2013; Swain et al. 2014; Watson et al. 2012). A potentially useful revision for bioarchaeologists proposed by Kasnitz and Shuttleworth (2001) is referred to as the "sociocultural model." This model focuses more on cultural particulars and symbolism. In this model, they refer to "impairment-disability" as "anomalous embodiment," which can lead to four possible outcomes (see Roberts 1999:82 for a similar discussion): (1) elevation of social status when positively perceived; (2) societal integration when not perceived; (3) societal integration when neutrally perceived; or (4) adverse responses when negatively perceived. These various cultural outcomes present a useful framework for bioarchaeologists thinking about the potentially negative (disabling), neutral (integration), or positive (elevation) experiences of persons with differences (e.g., impairments) in the past. For example, leprosy was stigmatized in medieval Europe (e.g., Knüsel 1999), but a study of pre-Colombian Andean individuals with skeletal indicators of leishmaniasis, another disfiguring disease, revealed no evidence of stigmatization in mortuary practice (Marsteller et al. 2011).

The field of Critical Disability Studies articulates with other critical studies, such as queer, race, and feminist, to enhance the focus on intersectional identities that contribute to societal marginalization (Shildrick 2012). Critical disability scholars consider disability and impairment to be "sociocultural responses to anomalous embodiment and impairments," which can result in dis-ablization and marginalization, depending on context and intersectionality (Shuttleworth and Meekosha 2017:25). They do not deny that past peoples with impairments could have experienced negative reactions, but they argue that bioarchaeologists should appreciate the range of reactions that people could have experienced (Shuttleworth and Meekosha 2017). For example, using the historical case of Kojo, an eighteenth-century Jamaican Maroon leader, Ingleman (2017) demonstrates how bodily differences, such as kyphosis, could have been variously interpreted by differently situated historical actors as well as retrospectively reimagined by historians, anthropologists, descendant communities, and the public.

The current World Health Organization (WHO) biopsychosocial model (also referred to as the interactional model) of disability appears to strike a compromise between the biologically bound medical model and the socially constructed social model. According to the WHO *International Classification of Functioning, Disability and Health* (ICF), "[i]mpairments are problems in body function or structure such as a significant deviation or loss" (WHO 2001:10; Table 6.1). Also, the ICF states "Disability is an umbrella term for impairments, activity limitations and participation restriction. It connotes the negative aspects of the interaction between an individual (with a health condition) and that individual's contextual factors (environmental and personal factors)" (WHO 2001:213). Impairments and disability are assessed in reference to four constructs: body functions and structures, activities and participation, environmental factors, and personal factors (WHO 2001). The ICF also attempts to quantify impairment and disability using "Qualifiers," which "specify information about functioning status: the magnitude, the location and the nature of any problem" (WHO 2013:26).

Critics of the ICF note that the measures of impairment may be less useful when applied to non-western and historical contexts (Shuttleworth and Meekosha 2017), and that the focus on the individual may be inappropriate when applied to societies with fundamentally different concepts of individuality. Quantifying the impact of a given impairment cross-culturally is also at the heart of criticism of the multi-decade Global Burden of Disease Project methods for deriving the disability weights associated with specific conditions that are used when calculating regional and global morbidity burdens (Jelsma et al. 2000; Reidpath et al. 2003; Salomon 2010). As the underlying construct to all of these models and arguments attests, conditions considered impairments and disabilities in modern contexts might not have been perceived as such from another cultural worldview (Goodley 2014). For example, in Lovell's (2016) osteobiography of a man who lived in Roman Italy in the first to second century AD, she presents skeletal evidence that his gait would have been quite distinctive due to a malaligned healed hip fracture. His burial, however, was similar to others in his community; thus, while his visibly different gait, or physical impairment, would likely have been recognized, socially he was likely not excluded and therefore not considered disabled by others.

Historically, theoretically, and in global health policy, the understanding of what constitutes an impairment and who is considered disabled are varied and subject to critique. However, these distinctions are worthy of our attention, and the terms should not be conflated in bioarchaeology (Shakespeare 1999; Southwell-Wright 2013) since the very act of distinguishing between impairment and disability is part of our research process (e.g., Byrnes and Muller 2017a). Bioarchaeological contributions where the distinction is maintained include papers in *Disability and Archaeology* (Finlay 1999), Byrnes and Muller's edited volume (2017b), and studies by Lovell (2016), Marsteller and colleagues (2011), and van Duijvenbode and colleagues (2015).

Care as Controversy, Care as Unifying Concept

In the 1980s, paleoanthropologists and bioarchaeologists began to interpret paleopathological evidence as evidence of care and compassion in the past. Studies of the Neandertals from Shanidar Cave, Iraq (Trinkaus and Zimmerman 1982), an Upper Paleolithic juvenile with dwarfism recovered from Italy (Frayer et al. 1987), and an Early Archaic juvenile with severe neural tube defect recovered from Florida (Dickel and Doran 1989) are commonly cited as evidence of compassionate care. Dettwyler (1991) criticized these interpretations as an anachronistic projection of modern ideals into the past. She acknowledged that care would have been necessary for some individuals described in paleopathology case studies, but maintained that it is impossible to discern the motivations of caregivers from skeletal remains. In the decades following her critique, bioarchaeological interest and engagement with disability and care in the past waxed and waned. In current bioarchaeology, the provision of care in the past is explored through the linkage between skeletal pathology and social and physical context. However, the question of "our ability to meaningfully recognize and discuss the existence and nature of compassionate attitudes in the past remains contentious" (Southwell-Wright et al. 2016:4).

Roberts uses the *Oxford English Dictionary* definition of care: "[t]he provision of what is necessary for the health, welfare, maintenance, and protection of someone or something" (2016:xv). Care is provided by choice, "culturally constituted, and with its limits defined by the historical, economic, and social circumstances in which individuals operate" (Gowland et al. 2016:215). Research in the history and anthropology of medical care examines social attitudes toward disability and "disease culture" (e.g., Fay 2006; Meltzer 1999), a critical component of context for studies of care in the past. Medical archaeology (Arnott 2013; Baker and Carr 2002) addresses healing practices in a diversity of times and places, from shamans to surgeons. Many of the individual works mentioned below (and many not represented here) incorporate archaeological, historical, and ethnographic information on material culture related to healing, attitudes toward disease (Marsteller et al. 2011), and traditional healing practices (Jolly and Kurin 2017; Willet and Harrod 2017).

The care of people whose remains were excavated from archaeological sites is addressed in the method set out by the Index of Care (Tilley and Cameron 2014). At the community scale, care is examined through studies of "normative care" for children and the elderly (Gowland et al. 2016; Southwell-Wright et al. 2016), and care for the chronically ill and disabled. Archaeological evidence for the treatment in death of those who were ill or disabled can also reveal attitudes toward the affected and culturally specific beliefs about disease.

The Index of Care

Tilley deploys the ICF, also referred to as the interactional or biopsychosocial model of disability, in an approach known as the *Bioarchaeology of Care* (Tilley 2015). In this innovative framework, ethnographic and clinical analogs are used along with attention to details of archaeological context (i.e., the built environment, topography, material culture, household and community organization, division of labor) to ask meaningful questions about the care requirements of individuals with skeletal evidence of impairment and potentially disabling conditions. Studies of care combine "the perspective of 'disability experienced' and 'care provided'" (Tilley 2015:145). The methodology is presented in detail on the website *Index of Care* (http://indexofcare.org). Numerous applications utilizing the method appear in a growing array of edited volumes and articles (e.g., Nystrom and Tilley 2018; Tilley 2015; Tilley and Cameron 2014; Tilley and Oxenham 2011; Tilley and Schrenk 2017; Worne 2017a).

This approach has been used to explore the care-related implications of skeletal pathologies in a quadriplegic in Neolithic Vietnam (Tilley and Oxenham 2011), Neandertals, and British Neolithic farmers (Tilley 2015). An extraordinary application of this method addresses the social and political significance of the provision of cranial surgery (trepanation) and the long-term consequences of cranial trauma in the Chanka of Peru (Jolly and Kurin 2017). Other studies explore the experience of severe kyphoscoliosis in eighteenth-century London (Conlogue et al. 2017), and the social implications of individuals surviving severe trauma in twelfth- and thirteenth-century New Mexico (Willett and Harrod 2017) and in Mississippian Tennessee (Worne 2017b). Several new studies apply the Index of Care at the community scale (e.g., Tremblay and Schrenk 2018). Casserly and Moore (2018) explore the implications of injured persons, and those with otherwise impaired mobility, in a Late Archaic non-sedentary community in Kentucky. Gardner and colleagues (2018) consider the impact of various injuries on social identity, economic roles, and care provisioning among the prehistoric Ohlone, sedentary hunter-fisher-foragers in Central California.

The number and variety of studies employing the Index of Care speaks to its inherent flexibility, and the importance of the approach for both paleopathology and bioarchaeology. Buikstra (2017) situates the bioarchaeology of care as an approach whose time has come, in concert with renewed interest in osteobiography, the legitimacy of case studies in paleopathology, and the theoretical emphasis on bioarchaeology of the body as created through lived experience. Tilley notes that "For many scholars, the appeal resides in the approach's clearly structured framework for analysis. The methodological, incremental approach to assessing the level and impact of disability and the ability to use these as the basis for identifying likely components of a care response, allows extraction of additional meaning from descriptive skeletal data" (Tilley 2015:31). The interpretive, humanistic stage of the Index invokes "careful critical thought, coupled with creativity" (Buikstra et al. 2017:82). Tilley (2015) emphasizes that the bioarchaeology of care is, and should continue to be, a work in progress, with adjustments as needed for particular studies, but also that this approach is broadly applicable to bioarchaeology studies including those that are not focused on the provision of care. The larger message is that thinking about care and the implications of care for recipients, caregivers, and other community members should be a regular part of bioarchaeology and paleopathology.

Normative Care

The provision of care across the life course touches on a remarkably broad range of human behavior and beliefs. Care as "a normalized aspect of infancy and early childhood, and to some extent ... an expected sequelae of increased frailty in older age" (Southwell-Wright et al. 2016:8) is the foundation for recognizing difference in care, as emphasized in the volume *Care in the Past* (Powell 2016). The "sociobioarch-acology of children" (Mays et al. 2017) is a dynamic and growing subfield that brings paleopathology into the consideration of parenting and childhood in the past. Isotopic data and the prevalence and age patterns of conditions like scurvy and rickets provide insights into weaning strategies and other aspects of infant and child care (Kendall 2016; Lewis 2016, 2018), and particular injuries in neonates can reveal birthing practices (Merbs 2012). Clinical documentation supports a skeletal signature of child abuse (Gaither 2012; Lewis 2018; Love et al. 2011), and children's remains also hold evidence of ritual violence and child sacrifice (e.g., Klaus et al. 2010; Wilson et al. 2013).

Evidence of care for children is marshaled from nuanced and critical reading of historical sources and funerary evidence (e.g., toys in children's graves). To demonstrate the provision of care through skeletal pathology, "the child would need to have survived beyond infancy with a visible deformity for a sustained period of time ... the severity or physical disability of any impairments and the child's eventual age at death may help to elucidate the level of care provided" (Lewis 2016:24). Lewis noted that congenital conditions would have had a different impact on a child's life, and those of parents or other caregivers, compared to conditions that develop gradually or resulted from injury. These could also have invoked different stigma for mother and child (e.g., Sargent 1988). Reaction to physically different and disabled children, and the nature of healing treatments provided, should be assumed to be as situationally specific as analogous reactions to adults. Lewis (2016) reviews cases of normative, honorific, and derogatory interments of disabled children.

Evidence for care and abuse of the elderly is a new focus in paleopathology that aims to understand social practice and attitudes toward this important stage of the life course. Gowland (2016b) identifies skeletal and dental injuries that, in combination, are most indicative of elder abuse. She describes possible cases of elder abuse from Roman period sites in Britain, identified on the basis of non-normative burial location and skeletal evidence of impairment or trauma, and interprets these in the context of the nuclear household, and the likelihood that care for the elderly would have been provided by adult children (Gowland 2016a, 2017). As with the study of child abuse, there are many cultural and situational contingencies that could alter the interpretation of these injuries, including our own experiences with aging and the elderly.

The experience and impact of disability of individuals is dynamic with regard to age as well as context: "old age has the power to subsume the stigma of 'disablement', replacing it instead with the construct of 'frailty'" or infantilization (Gowland 2017:248). To date, there has been more investigation of physical abuse than care of the young and elderly in bioarchaeology. This reflects the data that we collect: many skeletal traumas are evidence of something other than care. The relative *infrequency* of these in a community presumably reflects the fact that most individuals experienced the normative provision of care, and there are carefully drawn studies of care of the elderly and of children. But, as Thorpe (2016) observes, cruelty in the past seems to be far less controversial than compassion.

Institutional Care: Historical Bioarchaeology and Paleopathology

The excavation of historic cemeteries associated with institutions such as poorhouses, tuberculosis and leprosy sanitaria, and asylums provide bioarchaeologists with an opportunity to examine care in the past through institutions that were explicitly designed to provide care. Historical bioarchaeology provides a means for those who did not write history to contribute their story through their remains as well as the archival documents and artifactual evidence that inform us of past social, political, and economic context. Acknowledging that these documents tell the dominant social group's point of view is important in order to properly contextualize them within bioarchaeological data; the dominating social or political group's narrative is substantially different from that of people who were marginalized, colonized, or displaced (Murphy and Klaus 2017). Perry (2007) provides an important summary of these points and more, drawing attention to the ways that bioarchaeologists investigating historical periods should try to approach interpreting multiple lines of evidence, and Mitchell (2012) addresses some of the issues attendant to the use of historical sources in paleopathology.

The bioarchaeological research on the Dunning Poorhouse in Chicago presented some of the first contextualized data on people who entered, and ultimately died within, the confines of a historical institute (Grauer and McNamara 1995; Grauer et al. 1998). Because many of the institutions cared for those who were disenfranchised and marginalized, paleopathology within these cemetery samples can create an inherent bias in rates and prevalence of disease in the past (Grauer 2018a). Institutional documents are the creation of those who supervised and implemented institutional policies, while those who lived within the confines of these institutes had their experiences written into their bodies. Thus, bioarchaeologists are able to use historical and biological data of institutes to more vividly portray how sociopolitical power was wielded through concepts such as structural violence, biopower, and other forms of institutionalized oppression (e.g., Muller 2017; Nystrom et al. 2017).

The paleopathology of people who resided in institutes also provides an understanding of care administered by the state. For example, Phillips (2017) provides a few osteobiographical examples from the Oneida County Asylum, providing historical archival documents that may coincide with the skeletal remains of people who have skeletal differences and received institutional care. Roberts's (2017) essay on leprosy care in late medieval London is one of several wherein the bioarchaeology of care is applied to the provision of care to individuals and classes of individuals in special hospitals and sanitaria, insane asylums, and other institutions. Milligan and Bright (2018) examine evidence for differential access to care, especially to the immigrants among the urban poor, in a Santa Clara Valley indigent cemetery used from 1875 to 1935. In a study that exemplifies the usefulness of care as a focal point for broader exploration of the history of beliefs about illness, the body, and the motivations for healthcare delivery in a colonial context, Wesp (2017) integrates archival, historical, and skeletal data from a hospital founded by missionaries in early colonial Mexico City, where the interaction and separation of indigenous and European belief systems impacted the nature of care sought and provided, and the agency of caregivers and patients.

Care of the Dead

Treatment in death provides a lens into the role and persona of the deceased, and the attitudes of survivors, from family to community (or the state) (Carr 1995; Parker Pearson 2000), and the articulation of mortuary archaeology and paleopathology provides another dimension of insight into cultural perceptions of the sick, disabled, or disfigured. The recognition of distinctive treatment in death is predicated on understanding the normative treatment for a cemetery or population "in order to observe any identity-related shifts as a consequence of impairment" (Gowland et al. 2016:216).

A number of studies address the mortuary treatment of people with leprosy (Fay 2006; Roberts 2011, 2017; Schug 2016), and these do not find evidence for segregation or special funerary treatment in death. In burials of leprous individuals in late medieval Norwich, Fay concluded "no single leprous identity or monolithic response to the disease existed in the period" (2006:202). In contrast, Klaus and Ortner (2014) report the distinctly aberrant burial of an individual with advanced, disfiguring tertiary treponemal infection in Early Colonial Peru. These two diseases result in significant facial disfigurement; together these studies certainly reinforce the importance of context in our attempts to understand the impact of disease on social identity and funerary treatment. The burials of many individuals with skeletal pathologies have been examined for evidence of stigmatization, segregation, disrespectful, or honorific and special treatment (e.g., papers in Murphy 2008).

Quantifying and Measuring Morbidity in Bioarchaeology

Other new studies by bioarchaeologists employ methodological approaches explicitly based on clinical and epidemiological metrics for the analysis of impairment (e.g., Byrnes 2017; Plomp 2017; Stodder 2017; Young and Lemaire 2017). Plomp (2017) and Young and Lemaire (2014, 2017) apply current clinical findings on the association of pain and impairment to the interpretation of degenerative joint changes typically observed in skeletal assemblages. Plomp provides detailed information from clinical research on back pain associated with lesions that are regularly observed and recorded in bioarchaeological assemblages. Young and Lemaire draw from clinical literature measuring arthritis patients' knee pain and functionality limitations to develop the Clinical Archaeological Osteoarthritis Scale (CAOS) for bioarchaeological assemblages. Given appropriate attention to physical environment and social context, the clinical data on the pain associated with specific paleopathologies can be used to more completely understand how and if lesions resulted in pain, impairment, and possibly disability if their activity was limited in a socially unacceptable way.

Traumatic injuries, especially fractures, provide information about the nature of violence in the past, and about the kinds of injuries associated with regular activity. The functional limitations resulting from fractures are typically mentioned as an afterthought, particularly in population-based studies, after the study's main "big" question(s) have been addressed. Thus, quantification of traumatic injuries to assess functionality and impairment in the past has been limited. Byrnes (2017) applied a modified clinical methodology to assess impairment from traumatic injuries. This data was subsequently contextualized within the broader cultural framework from the nineteenth- and twentieth-century Erie County Poorhouse in Buffalo, NY. The impairment assessments were used to discuss how the intersectionality of these injuries with the social identities of an individual could either mitigate or amplify how/if a person in the past was understood as being viewed as disabled. Ethnicity and gender were strong social identity factors that, based on historical documentation, contributed to differential risk of injury, socioeconomic/occupation statuses, and seeking relief from the poorhouse institute. Specifically, Byrnes found that the intersecting identities of Irish male immigrants were most at risk of acquiring traumatic injuries in their low-wage, high-risk jobs, and subsequently were overrepresented within the poorhouse compared to other groups living in Buffalo at the same time.

A method developed to incorporate a wide range of individual skeletal pathologies recorded in bioarchaeological assemblages employs disability weights from the Global Burden of Disease Project (Institute for Health Metrics and Evaluation 2009; Murray et al. 2012) to quantify the functional impacts of fractures, anemia, tuberculosis, edentulism, periodontal disease, and other conditions recorded in skeletal remains. This method can be used to generate morbidity scores for individuals, and is particularly useful for understanding the multidimensional impacts of conditions like acromegaly (Stodder 2016). At the community level, prevalence-based disability weights for specific conditions can be compared for men and women, or to examine morbidity load over time within or between regions (Stodder 2016, 2017). The use of disability weights also facilitates incorporation of comorbidities not expressed in the skeleton, like the cognitive deficit and growth stunting attendant to severe childhood anemia associated with parasitic infections, diarrheal disease, dietary insufficiency, and malaria. Disability weights can be translated into a prevalence-based measure of years lived with disability, an intuitively meaningful portrayal of morbidity burden that is based on metrics generated by the largest epidemiology project in the world. However, as mentioned above, use of disability weights also puts the paleopathologist into the significant debate about the relative significance (i.e., weight) of different conditions in different contexts. As a project of global scope, the strength of the data is predicated on comparability and consistency in metrics, but this is difficult to reconcile with the reality that many conditions have different impacts on life in contemporaneous rural and urban communities, and of course, in different settings in the past. As with the bioarchaeology of care, skeletal pathologies and their impacts must be interpreted in context.

Conclusion

In this chapter, we have reviewed research strategies and interpretive frameworks that integrate paleopathology and bioarchaeology by bridging the gap between individual and population data and interpretation. In these studies, population-level data take on a different role, as the background against which we recognize the significance of different lives (Stodder 2012), and the agency, heterogeneity, and variation in the experience of disease, impairment, and disability and in the provision of care that would be invisible in population data (Blom 2017; Kendall 2016). The integration of paleopathology, clinical findings, bioarchaeology, and disability studies has stimulated new approaches to the quantification of morbidity and functional impairment in individuals and groups, as well as new ways of thinking critically about how the departure from health affected people differently. These studies consider the physical and social significance of impairment and disability in what may be familiar historical settings and well-documented archaeological cultures, but we are compelled to acknowledge and investigate the unfamiliar realms of cross-cultural health and the situationally complex perceptions and reactions to the differently abled and the "other."

In the volume *New Developments in the Bioarchaeology of Care* (Tilley and Schrenk 2017), the philosopher David Doat opines that while the range of scientific, intellectual, and moral issues attendant to the interpretation of care in the past should not be minimized, interpretation and even speculation have an essential role in the archaeological reconstruction of the past: "it is not only impossible to avoid speculation, but necessary to attempt interpretation at some stage as a condition for theoretical progress and further discoveries in the field" (Doat 2017:331). Thorpe also stresses that "[i]f paleopathology is to be properly integrated into an archaeological discussion of past societies then interpretation cannot be an optional extra" (Thorpe 2016:101). The challenge to further interpretation is not an insignificant one for paleopathologists. Even as we understand the skeleton to be a socially created entity (Sofaer 2006), we consider our data to be empirical and biological, and because bony responses are limited and general, paleopathology maintains a conscientious conservatism that is reflected in the Index of Care methodology.

The bioarchaeological record is large, cross-cultural, and trans-historical. Our work has the potential to illuminate the wide range of responses to human variation, many of which may be historically unattested. Because our research looks at human variation and biocultural stress across time and space, we have much to offer the larger field of Disability Studies with the breadth of comparative human experiences across human history. Anchoring bioarchaeological interpretations with Critical Disability Studies and constraining interpretations based on cultural context encourages hypothesis testing. Bioarchaeologists who work within the context of Critical Disability Studies are well positioned to challenge the "highly questionable orthodoxies," which, as Gleeson observed, naturalize "disabled people's contemporary social marginality and poverty by depicting them as fixed, historical conditions that have been present in most, even all, past human societies" (1999:23).

Bioarchaeological research on impairment, disability, and care provides unique insights into the range of the human experience of departure from health. There is no question that approaches to interpreting disability in the past will be subject to debate and ongoing re-evaluation, and as anthropologists we should keep our minds open to the seemingly infinite ways human culture influences and changes our social and biological bodies. The problems we face in endeavoring to understand the roles of disability and impairment in the past are not unique to social bioarchaeology (e.g., gender, ethnicity); questions about the cross-cultural understandings of health and morbidity pose fundamental questions about the universality of human experience.

Acknowledgments

We are grateful to the editors for including this topic in their 2016 American Anthropological Association session, (Re)Discovery of Evidence in Biological Anthropology: A Critical View, and for their thoughtful critiques and patience during the review process. We would also like to thank the anonymous reviewers for their insightful comments on an earlier draft of this work.

References

Agarwal S (2016) Bone morphologies and histories: Life course approaches to bioarchaeology. *Yearbook of Physical Anthropology* 159:S130–S149.

Agarwal S and Beauchesne P (2011) It is not carved in bone: development and plasticity of the aged skeleton. In Agarwal S and Glencross BA, editors. *Social Bioarchaeology*. Wiley-Blackwell. Pp. 213–332.

Agarwal S and Wesp JK, editors (2017) *Exploring Sex and Gender in Bioarchaeology*. University of New Mexico Press.

Americans with Disabilities Act (ADA) Amendments Act of 2008 (2008) Pub. L. No. 110-325 § 3406.

Armelagos GJ (2003) Bioarchaeology as anthropology. *Archeological Papers of the American Anthropological Association* 13:27–41.

Armelagos GJ and Goodman AH (1991) Concept of stress and its relevance to studies of adaptation in prehistoric populations. *Collegium Antropologicum* 15(1):45–58.

Arnott R, editor (2013) *The Archaeology of Medicine*. Archaeopress.

Aufderheide A and Rodriguez-Martin (1998) *The Cambridge Encyclopedia of Human Paleopathology*. Cambridge University Press.

Baker BJ and Tsuda T, editors (2015) *Migration and Disruptions: Toward a Unifying Theory of Ancient and Contemporary Migrations*. University Press of Florida.

Baker PA and Carr G, editors (2002) *Practitioners, Practices and Patients: New Approaches to Medical Archaeology and Anthropology*. Oxbow Books.

Beauchesne P and Agarwal S, editors (2018) *Children and Childhood in Bioarchaeology*. University Press of Florida.

Bethard JD, DiGangi EA, and Sullivan LP (2017) Attempting to distinguish impairment from disability in the bioarchaeological record: an example from Dearmond Mound (40re12) in east Tennessee. In Byrnes JF and Muller JL, editors. *Bioarchaeology of Impairment and Disability: Theoretical, Ethnohistorical, and Methodological Perspectives*. Springer. Pp. 249–267.

Blakely RL, editor (1977) *Biocultural Adaptation in Prehistoric America*. University of Georgia Press.

Blom D (2017) A bioarchaeological perspective on community and the tension between individual and population. *Archeological Papers of the American Anthropological Association* 28:104–111.

Boldsen JL and Milner GR (2012) An epidemiological approach to paleopathology. In Grauer AL, editor. *A Companion to Paleopathology*. Blackwell. Pp. 114–132.

Boutin AT (2016) Exploring the social construction of disability: an application of the bioarchaeology of personhood model to a pathological skeleton from ancient Bahrain. *International Journal of Paleopathology* 12:17–28.

Buikstra JE (1977) Biocultural dimensions of archeological study: a regional perspective. In Blakely RL, editor. *Biocultural Adaptation in Prehistoric America*. University of Georgia Press. Pp. 67–84.

Buikstra JE (2017) Conclusion: new developments in the bioarchaeology of care. In Tilley L and Schrenk A, editors. *New Developments in the Bioarchaeology of Care*. Springer. Pp. 365–375.

Buikstra JE and Beck LA, editors (2006) *Bioarchaeology: The Contextual Analysis of Human Remains*. Academic Press.

Buikstra JE and Roberts CA, editors (2012) *The Global History of Paleopathology*. Oxford University Press.

Buikstra JE, Cook DC, and Bolhofner KL (2017) Introduction: scientific rigor in paleopathology. *International Journal of Paleopathology* 19:80–87.

Buzon M (2012) The bioarchaeological approach to paleopathology. In Grauer AL, editor. *A Companion to Paleopathology*. Wiley-Blackwell. Pp. 58–75.

Byrnes JF (2017) Injuries, impairment, and intersecting identities: the poor in Buffalo, NY 1851-1913. In Byrnes J and Muller J, editors. *Bioarchaeology of Impairment and Disability: Theoretical, Ethnohistorical, and Methodological Perspectives*. Springer. Pp. 201–222.

Byrnes JF and Muller JL (2017a) Mind the gap: bridging disability studies and bioarchaeology – an introduction. In Byrnes JF and Muller JL, editors. *Bioarchaeology of Impairment and Disability: Theoretical, Ethnohistorical, and Methodological Perspectives*. Springer. Pp. 1–15.

Byrnes JF and Muller JL, editors (2017b) *Bioarchaeology of Impairment and Disability: Theoretical, Ethnohistorical, and Methodological Perspectives*. Springer.

Carr C (1995) Mortuary practices: their social, philosophical-religious, circumstantial, and physical determinants. *Journal of Archaeological Method and Theory* 2(2):105–200.

Casserly A and Moore BR (2018) The bioarchaeology of care for individuals with reduced mobility in non-sedentary societies. *American Journal of Physical Anthropology* 165(66S):43.

Conlogue G, Viner M, Beckett R, et al. (2017) A post-mortem evaluation of the degree of mobility in an individual with severe kyphoscoliosis using direct digital radiography (Dr) and multi-detector computed tomography (Mdct). In Tilley L and Schrenk A, editors. *New Developments in the Bioarchaeology of Care*. Springer. Pp. 153–174.

Cook DC and Powell ML (2006) The evolution of American paleopathology. In Buikstra JE and Beck LA, editors. *Bioarchaeology: The Contextual Analysis of Human Remains*. Elsevier. Pp. 281–322.

Davis LJ (1995) *Enforcing Normalcy: Disability, Deafness, and the Body*. Verso.

Davis LJ (2013a) Introduction: disability, normality, and power. In Davis L, editor. *The Disability Studies Reader*. 4th ed. Routledge. Pp. 1–16.

Davis LJ, editor (2013b) *The Disability Studies Reader*. 4th ed. Routledge.

Dettwyler KA (1991) Can paleopathology provide evidence for "compassion"? *American Journal of Physical Anthropology* 84(4):375–384.

Dickel DN and Doran GH (1989) Severe neural tube defect syndrome from the early Archaic of Florida. *American Journal of Physical Anthropology* 80(3):325–334.

Digitised Diseases (2018). Digitised diseases. www.digitiseddiseases.org.

Disabled Peoples' International (1982) "Agreed statement", at Human Rights plenary meeting in support of European Day of Disabled Persons. Disabled Peoples' International.

Doat D (2017) What ethical considerations should inform bioarchaeology of care analysis? In Tilley L and Schrenk A, editors. *New Directions in the Bioarchaeology of Care*. Springer. Pp. 319–342.

Fay I (2006) Text, space, and the evidence of human remains in English late Medieval and Tudor disease culture: some problems and possibilities. In Gowland R and Knüsel C, editors. *Social Archaeology of Funerary Remains*. Oxbow Books. Pp. 190–208.

Finlay N (1999) Disability and archaeology. *Archaeological Review from Cambridge* 15(2):55–67.

Frayer DW, Horton WA, Macchiareli R, and Mussi M (1987) Dwarfism in an adolescent from the Italian Late Upper Paleolithic. *Nature* 330(6143):60–62.

Gaither C (2012) Cultural conflict and the impact on non-adults at Puruchuco-Huaquerones in Peru: the case for refinement of the methods used to analyze violence against children in the archaeological record. *International Journal of Paleopathology* 2(2–3):69–77.

Gardner KS, Bartelink EJ, Martinez A, Leventhal A, and Cambra R (2018) Social identity and disability in prehistoric central California: evidence for community support, accommodation, and care at the Yukisma Mound (Ca-Scl-38). *American Journal of Physical Anthropology* 165(66S):94.

Geller PL (2017) *The Bioarchaeology of Socio-Sexual Lives: Queering Common Sense About Sex, Gender, and Sexuality*. Springer.

Gleeson B (1999) *Geographies of Disability*. Routledge.

Glowacki D (2015) *Living and Leaving: A Social History of Regional Depopulation in Thirteenth Century Mesa Verde*. University of Arizona Press.

Goodley D (2011) *Disability Studies: An Interdisciplinary Introduction*. Sage.

Goodley D (2014) *Disability Studies: Theorising Disablism and Ableism*. Routledge.

Goodley D, Hughes B, and Davis L, editors (2012) *Disability and Social Theory: New Developments and Directions*. Palgrave Macmillan.

Goodman AH, Martin DL, Armelagos GJ, and Clark G (1984) Indications of stress from bone and teeth. In Cohen MN and Armelagos GJ, editors. *Paleopathology at the Origins of Agriculture.* Academic Press. Pp. 13–49.

Goodman AH, Thomas RB, Swedlund AC, and Armelagos GJ (1988) Biocultural perspectives on stress in prehistorical, historical, and contemporary population research. *Yearbook of Physical Anthropology* 31:169–202.

Gowland R (2015) Entangled lives: implications of the developmental origins of health and disease hypothesis for bioarchaeology and the life course. *American Journal of Physical Anthropology* 158(4):530–540.

Gowland R (2016a) That "tattered coat upon a stick the ageing body": evidence for elder marginalisation and abuse in Roman Britain. In Powell L, editor. *Care in the Past: Archaeological and Interdisciplinary Perspectives.* Oxbow Books. Pp. 71–91.

Gowland R (2016b) Elder abuse: evaluating the potentials and problems of diagnosis in the archaeological record. *International Journal of Osteoarchaeology* 26(3):514–523.

Gowland R (2017) Growing old: biographies of disability and care in later life. In Tilley L and Schrenk A, editors. *New Developments in the Bioarchaeology of Care.* Springer. Pp. 237–252.

Gowland R, Powell L, and Southwell-Wright W (2016) Concluding thoughts and future directions. In Powell L, editor. *Care in the Past: Archaeological and Interdisciplinary Perspectives.* Oxbow Books. Pp. 215–220.

Grauer AL (2012) The scope of paleopathology. In Grauer AL, editor. *A Companion to Paleopathology.* Wiley-Blackwell. Pp. 1–14.

Grauer AL (2018a) Paleopathology: from bones to social behavior. In Katzenberg MA and Grauer AL, editors. *The Biological Anthropology of the Human Skeleton.* 3rd ed. Wiley. Pp. 447–465.

Grauer AL (2018b) A century of paleopathology. *American Journal of Physical Anthropology* 165 (4):904–914.

Grauer AL and McNamara E (1995) A piece of Chicago's past: exploring subadult mortality in the Dunning Poorhouse Cemetery. In Grauer AL, editor. *Bodies of Evidence: Reconstructing History through Skeletal Analysis.* Wiley-Liss. Pp. 91–103.

Grauer AL, McNamara EM, and Houdek DV (1998) A history of their own: patterns of death in a nineteenth-century poorhouse. In Grauer AL and Stuart-Macadam P, editors. *Sex and Gender in Paleopathological Perspective.* Cambridge University Press. Pp. 149–164.

Hawkey DE (1998) Disability, compassion and the skeletal record: using musculoskeletal stress markers (MSM) to construct an osteobiography from early New Mexico. *International Journal of Osteoarchaeology* 8(5):326–340.

Hegmon M (2016) Archaeology of the human experience: an introduction. *Archeological Papers of the American Anthropological Association* 27(1):7–21.

Hegmon M, Peeples MA, Kinzig AP, et al. (2008) Social transformation and its human costs in the prehispanic U.S. Southwest. *American Anthropologist* 110(3):313–324.

Hubert J, editor (2000) *Madness, Disability and Social Exclusion: The Archaeology and Anthropology of "Difference."* Routledge.

Ingleman DA (2017) Kojo's dis/ability: the interpretation of spinal pathology in the context of an eighteenth-century Jamaican maroon community. In Byrnes J and Muller J, editors. *Bioarchaeology of Impairment and Disability: Theoretical, Ethnohistorical, and Methodological Perspectives.* Springer. Pp. 95–117.

Institute for Health Metrics and Evaluation (2009) *Global Burden of Disease Study Operations Manual January 2009.* University of Washington. www.healthdata.org/GBD.

Jelsma J, Chivaura V, Mhundwa K, De Weerdt W, and de Cock P (2000) The global burden of disease disability weights. *The Lancet* 355(9220):2079–2080.

Jolly S and Kurin D (2017) Surviving trepanation: approaching the relationship of violence and the care of "war wounds" through a case study from prehistoric Peru. In Tilley L and Schrenk A, editors. *New Developments in the Bioarchaeology of Care.* Springer. Pp. 175–197.

Juengst SL and Becker SK (2017) The bioarchaeology of community. *Archeological Papers of the American Anthropological Association* 28:6–12.

Kamp KA, editor (2002) *Children in the Prehistoric Puebloan Southwest.* University of Utah Press.

Kamp KA (2009) Children in an increasingly violent landscape: a case study from the American Southwest. *Childhood in the Past* 2(1):71–85.

Kasnitz D and Shuttleworth RP (2001) Engaging anthropology in disability studies. In Rogers LJ and Swadener BB, editors. *Semiotics and Dis/Ability: Interrogating Categories of Difference.* State University of New York Press. Pp. 19–42.

Kendall E (2016) The "Terrible Tyranny of the Majority": recognising population variability and individual agency in past infant feeding practices. In Powell L, editor. *Care in the Past: Archaeological and Interdisciplinary Perspectives.* Oxbow Books. Pp. 39–51.

Klaus HD (2012) The bioarchaeology of structural violence: a theoretical model and case study. In Martin DL, Harrod RP, and Perez VR, editors. *The Bioarchaeology of Violence.* University Press of Florida. Pp. 29–62.

Klaus HD and Ortner DJ (2014) Treponemal infection in Peru's Early Colonial period: a case of complex lesion patterning and unusual funerary treatment. *International Journal of Paleopathology* 4:25–36.

Klaus HD, Centurion J, and Curo M (2010) Bioarchaeology of human sacrifice: violence, identity, and the evolution of ritual killing at Cerro Cerrillos, Peru. *Antiquity* 84(326):1102–1122.

Knudson KJ and Stojanowski C, editors (2009) *Bioarchaeology and Identity in the Americas.* University Press of Florida.

Knüsel C (1999) Orthopaedic disability: some hard evidence. *Archaeological Review from Cambridge* 15(2):31–53.

Larsen CS (2015) *Bioarchaeology: Interpreting Behavior from the Human Skeleton.* Cambridge University Press.

Larsen CS (2018) Bioarchaeology in perspective: from classifications of the dead to conditions of the living. *American Journal of Physical Anthropology* 165(4):865–878.

Lewis M (2016) Childcare in the past: the contribution of palaeopathology. In Powell L, editor. *Care in the Past: Archaeological and Interdisciplinary Perspectives.* Oxbow Books. Pp. 23–37.

Lewis M (2018) *Paleopathology of Children: Identification of Pathological Conditions in the Human Skeletal Remains of Non-Adults.* Academic Press.

Love JC, Derrick JA, and Wiersema JM (2011) *Skeletal Atlas of Child Abuse.* Humana Press.

Lovell NC (2016) Tiptoeing through the rest of his life: a functional adaptation to a leg shortened by femoral neck fracture. *International Journal of Paleopathology* 13:91–95.

Marsteller SJ, Torres-Rouff C, and Knudson KJ (2011) Pre-Columbian Andean sickness ideology and the social experience of leishmaniasis: a contextualized analysis of bioarchaeological and paleopathological data from San Pedro De Atacama, Chile. *International Journal of Paleopathology* 1(1):24–34.

Martin DL (1997) Violence against women in a Southwestern series (AD 1000–1300). In Martin DL and Frayer DW, editors. *Troubled Times: Violence and Warfare in the Past.* Gordon and Breach. Pp. 45–75.

Martin DL (2008) Reanalysis of trauma in the La Plata Valley (AD 900–1300): strategic social violence and the bioarchaeology of captivity. In Stodder ALW, editor. *Reanalysis and Reinterpretation in Southwestern Bioarchaeology.* Anthropological Papers No. 59. Arizona State University. Pp. 167–184.

Martin DL and Harrod RP (2016) The bioarchaeology of pain and suffering: human adaptation and survival during troubled times. *Archeological Papers of the American Anthropological Association* 27(1):161–174.

Martin DL and Tegtmeyer C, editors (2017) *Bioarchaeology of Women and Children in Times of War: Case Studies from the Americas.* Springer.

Martin DL, Harrod RP, and Perez VR, editors (2012) *The Bioarchaeology of Violence.* University Press of Florida.

Martin DL, Harrod RP, and Perez VR (2013) *Bioarchaeology: An Integrated Approach to Human Remains.* Springer.

Mays S, Gowland R, Halcrow S, and Murphy E (2017) Child bioarchaeology: perspectives on the past 10 years. *Childhood in the Past* 10(1):38–56.

Meltzer I (1999) The palaeopathology of disability in the Middle Ages. *Archaeological Review from Cambridge* 15(2):55–67.

Merbs CF (2012) Thumbprints of a midwife: birth and infant death in an ancient Pueblo community. In Stodder ALW and Palkovich AM, editors. *The Bioarchaeology of Individuals.* University Press of Florida. Pp. 229–241.

Milligan CF and Bright LN (2018) Population level approaches to differential caregiving at a historic hospital. *American Journal of Physical Anthropology* 165(66S):178.

Milner GR and Boldsen JL (2017) Life not death: epidemiology from skeletons. *International Journal of Paleopathology* 17:26–39.

Mitchell P (2012) Integrating historical sources with paleopathology. In Grauer AL, editor. *A Companion to Paleopathology.* Blackwell. Pp. 310–323.

Muller JL (2017) Rendered unfit: "defective" children in the Erie County Poorhouse. In Byrnes JF and Muller JL, editors. *Bioarchaeology of Impairment and Disability: Theoretical, Ethnohistorical, and Methodological Perspectives.* Springer. Pp. 119–138.

Murphy E, editor (2008) *Deviant Burial in the Archaeological Record.* Oxbow Books.

Murphy MS and Klaus HD, editors (2017) *Colonized Bodies, Worlds Transformed: Toward a Global Bioarchaeology of Contact and Colonialism.* University Press of Florida.

Murray CJL, Ezzati M, Flaxman AD, et al. (2012) GBD 2010: design, definitions, and metrics. *Lancet* 380(9859):2063–2066.

Nystrom KC and Tilley L (2018) Mummy studies and the bioarchaeology of care. *International Journal of Paleopathology.* https://doi.org/10.1016/j.ijpp.2018.06.004

Nystrom KC, Sirianni J, Higgins R, Perrelli D, and Liber Raines JL (2017) Structural inequality and postmortem examination at the Erie County Poorhouse. In Nystrom KC, editor. *The Bioarchaeology of Dissection and Autopsy in the United States.* Springer. Pp. 279–300.

Oliver M (1983) *Social Work with Disabled People.* MacMillan.

Ortner DJ (2003) *Identification of Pathological Conditions in Human Skeletal Remains*, 2nd edition. Academic Press.

Ortner DJ and Putschar WG (1981) *Identification of Pathological Conditions in Human Skeletal Remains.* Smithsonian Institution Press.

Paleopathology Association (2018) https://paleopathology-association.wildapricot.org.

Parker Pearson M (2000) *The Archaeology of Death and Burial.* Texas A&M University Press.

Perry MA (2007) Is bioarchaeology a handmaiden to history? Developing a historical bioarchaeology. *Journal of Anthropological Archaeology* 26(3):486–515.

Phillips SM (2017) "A long waiting for death": dependency and the care of the disabled in a 19th century asylum. In Powell L, Southwell-Wright W, and Gowland R, editors. *Care in the Past: Archaeological and Interdisciplinary Perspectives.* Oxbow Books. Pp. 125–140.

Plomp K (2017) The bioarchaeology of back pain. In Byrnes JF and Muller JL, editors. *Bioarchaeology of Impairment and Disability: Theoretical, Ethnohistorical, and Methodological Perspectives.* Springer. Pp. 141–157.

Powell L, editor (2016) *Care in the Past: Archaeological and Interdisciplinary Perspectives.* Oxbow Books.

Reidpath DD, Allotey PA, Kouame A, and Cummins RA (2003) Measuring health in a vacuum: examining the disability weight of the DALY. *Health Policy and Planning* 18(4):351–356.

Robb J (2002) Time and biography: osteobiography of the Italian Neolithic. In Hamilakis M, Pluciennick M, and Tarlow S, editors. *Thinking through the Body: Archaeologies of Corporeality.* Kluwer Academic/Plenum. Pp. 153–171.

Roberts CA (1999) Disability in the skeletal record: assumptions, problems and some examples. *Archaeological Review from Cambridge* 15(2):79–97.

Roberts CA (2011) The bioarchaeology of leprosy and tuberculosis: a comparative study of perceptions, stigma, diagnosis, and treatment. In Agarwal S and Glencross B, editors. *Social Bioarchaeology*. Wiley-Blackwell. Pp. 252–281.

Roberts CA (2016) Navigating approaches to impairment, "disability" and care in the past: the need for reflection. In Powell L, editor. *Care in the Past: Archaeological and Interdisciplinary Perspectives*. Oxbow Books. Pp. xi–xvii.

Roberts CA (2017) Applying the index of care to a person who experienced leprosy in Late Medieval Chichester, England. In Tilley L and Schrenk A, editors. *New Directions in the Bioarchaeology of Care*. Springer. Pp. 101–124.

Roberts CA and Manchester K (2005) *The Archaeology of Disease*, 3rd edition. Sutton Publishing.

Salomon J (2010) New disability weights for the global burden of disease. *Bulletin of the World Health Organization* 88:879.

Sargent CF (1988) Born to die: witchcraft and infanticide in Bariba culture. *Ethnology* 27(1):79–95.

Saul F and Saul MB (1989) Osteobiography: a Maya example. In Iscan MY and Kennedy KAR, editors. *Reconstructing Life from the Skeleton*. Alan R. Liss. Pp. 287–302.

Schug GR (2016) Begotten of corruption? Bioarchaeology and "othering" of leprosy in south Asia. *International Journal of Paleopathology* 15:1–9.

Shakespeare T (1999) Commentary: observations on disability and archaeology. *Archaeological Review from Cambridge* 15(2):99–101.

Shakespeare T (2013) *Disability Rights and Wrongs Revisited*, 2nd edition. Taylor and Francis.

Shildrick M (2012) Critical disability studies: rethinking the conventions for the age of postmodernity. In Watson N, Roulstone A, and Thomas C, editors. *Routledge Handbook of Disability Studies*. Routledge. Pp. 30–41.

Shuttleworth RP and Meekosha H (2017) Accommodating critical disability studies in bioarchaeology. In Byrnes JF and Muller JL, editors. *Bioarchaeology of Impairment and Disability: Theoretical, Ethnohistorical, and Methodological Perspectives*. Springer. Pp. 19–38.

Siebers T (2008) *Disability Theory*. University of Michigan Press.

Smithsonian National Museum of Natural History (2018) Osteoware: Standardized Skeletal Documentation Software. https://osteoware.si.edu.

Sofaer J (2006) *The Body as Material Culture: A Theoretical Osteoarchaeology*. Cambridge University Press.

Southwell-Wright W (2013) Past perspectives: what can archaeology offer disability studies? In Wappett M and Arndt K, editors. *Emerging Perspectives on Disability Studies*. Palgrave Macmillan. Pp. 67–95.

Southwell-Wright W, Gowland R, and Powell L (2016) Foundations and approaches to the study of care in the past. In Powell L, editor. *Care in the Past: Archaeological and Interdisciplinary Perspectives*. Oxbow Books. Pp. 1–20.

Steinbock RT (1976) *Paleopathological Diagnosis and Interpretation: Bone Diseases in Ancient Human Populations*. C.C. Thomas.

Stodder ALW (2012) Data and data analysis issues in paleopathology. In Grauer AL, editor. *A Companion to Paleopathology*. Wiley-Blackwell. Pp. 339–356.

Stodder ALW (2016) Quantifying morbidity in prehispanic southwestern villages. In Herhahn C and Ramenofsky AF, editors. *Causation and Explanation: Historical Ecology, Demography, and Movement in the Prehistoric Southwest*. University Press of Colorado. Pp. 121–135.

Stodder ALW (2017) Quantifying impairment and disability in bioarchaeological assemblages. In Byrnes JF and Muller JL, editors. *Bioarchaeology of Impairment and Disability: Theoretical, Ethnohistorical, and Methodological Perspectives*. Springer. Pp. 183–200.

Stodder ALW and Palkovich AM, editors (2012) *The Bioarchaeology of Individuals*. University Press of Florida.

Stojanowski CM and Duncan WN, editors (2017) *Studies in Forensic Biohistory: Anthropological Perspectives*. Cambridge University Press.

Swain J, French S, Barnes C, and Thomas C, editors (2014) *Disabling Barriers – Enabling Environments*, 3rd edition. Sage.

Thompson JL, Alfonso-Durruty MP, and Crandall JJ, editors (2014) *Tracing Childhood: Bioarchaeological Investigations of Early Lives in Antiquity*. University Press of Florida.

Thorpe N (2016) The palaeolithic compassion debate: alternative projections of modern-day disability into the distant past. In Powell L, editor. *Care in the Past: Archaeological and Interdisciplinary Perspectives*. Oxbow Books. Pp. 93–109.

Tilley L (2015) *Theory and Practice in the Bioarchaeology of Care*. Springer.

Tilley L and Cameron T (2014) Introducing the index of care: a web-based application supporting archaeological research in health-related care. *International Journal of Paleopathology* 6:5–9.

Tilley L and Oxenham M (2011) Survival against the odds: modeling the social implications of care provision to seriously disabled individuals. *International Journal of Paleopathology* 1(1):35–42.

Tilley L and Schrenk A, editors (2017) *New Developments in the Bioarchaeology of Care: Further Case Studies and Expanded Theory*. Springer.

Tremblay LA and Schrenk A (2018) New perspectives on past healthcare: challenges and opportunities for bioarchaeological analyses of population level healthcare in the past. *American Journal of Physical Anthropology* 165(66S):77.

Trinkaus E and Zimmerman MR (1982) Trauma among the Shanidar Neanderthals. *American Journal of Physical Anthropology* 57(1):61–76.

van Duijvenbode A, Herschensohn OJ, and Morgan ME (2015) A severe case of congenital aural atresia in pre-Columbian Venezuela. *International Journal of Paleopathology* 9:15–19.

Watson N, Roulstone A, and Thomas C (2012) *Routledge Handbook of Disability Studies*. Routledge.

Wesp JK (2017) Caring for bodies or simply saving souls: the emergence of institutional care in Spanish Colonial America. In Tilley L and Schrenk A, editors. *New Developments in the Bioarchaeology of Care*. Springer. Pp. 253–276.

Willett A and Harrod RP (2017) Caring for outcasts: a case for continuous care in the Precontact Southwest. In Tilley L and Schrenk A, editors. *New Developments in the Bioarchaeology of Care*. Springer. Pp. 65–84.

Wilson AS, Brown EL, Villa C, et al. (2013) Archaeological, radiological, and biological evidence offer insight into Inca child sacrifice. *Proceedings of the National Academy of Sciences* 110 (333):13322–13327.

World Health Organization (1980) *ICIDH: International Classification of Impairments, Disabilities and Handicaps: A Manual of Classification Relating to the Consequences of Disease*. World Health Organization.

World Health Organization (2001) *International Classification of Functioning. Disability and Health*. World Health Organization.

World Health Organization (2013) How to use the ICF: a practical manual for using the International Classification of Functioning, Disability and Health (ICF). Exposure draft for comment. www.who.int/classifications/drafticfpracticalmanual2.pdf?ua=1.

Worne H (2017a) Bioarchaeological analysis of disability and caregiving from a nineteenth-century institution in central Kentucky. *Bioarchaeology International* 1(3–4):116–130.

Worne H (2017b) Inferring disability and care provision in Late Prehistoric Tennessee. In Tilley L and Schrenk A, editors. *New Developments in the Bioarchaeology of Care*. Springer. Pp. 85–100.

Young JL and Lemaire ED (2014) Linking bone changes in the distal femur to functional deficits. *International Journal of Osteoarchaeology* 24(6):709–721.

Young JL and Lemaire ED (2017) Using population health constructs to explore impairment and disability in knee osteoarthritis. In Byrnes JF and Muller JL, editors. *Bioarchaeology of Impairment and Disability: Theoretical, Ethnohistorical, and Methodological Perspectives*. Springer. Pp. 159–182.

Zuckerman MK, Turner BL, and Armelagos GJ (2012) Evolutionary thought in paleopathology and the rise of the biocultural approach. In Grauer AL, editor. *A Companion to Paleopathology*. Wiley-Blackwell. Pp. 34–57.

7 Parsing the Paradox

Examining Heterogeneous Frailty in Bioarchaeological Assemblages

Sharon N. DeWitte

It has been over 25 years since Wood and colleagues published their seminal paper describing the Osteological Paradox (Wood et al. 1992). The Osteological Paradox encompasses a set of phenomena that impede straightforward interpretations of demography and, particularly, health in past populations using data derived from human skeletal assemblages. Wood and colleagues' seemingly daunting critiques of paleopathology and paleoepidemiology (as conventionally practiced) have not been universally accepted (see, for example: Cohen 1994; Goodman 1993). However, for many scholars in the field, recognition of the Osteological Paradox has inspired a search for creative approaches to skeletal data collection, analysis, and interpretation that will enable us to avoid making unjustified or incorrect inferences from the imperfect data available to us. Many researchers who wish to directly address the issues associated with the Osteological Paradox have been stymied by a lack of clarity or consensus regarding how to do so. This chapter briefly summarizes the Osteological Paradox and presents one possible way to engage with it, while simultaneously addressing socioeconomic differentials in morbidity, a topic of broad interest to anthropologists, human biologists, economists, and public health practitioners.

It must be acknowledged that the use of the term "health" in bioarchaeology is problematic (Reitsema and McIlvaine 2014; Temple and Goodman 2014). Health is notoriously difficult to define, even for living people (Jadad and O'Grady 2008). Definitions of health widely applied in studies of living people include such criteria as the absence of disease or infirmity, the ability to engage in self-care and interpersonal activities, and mental coherence (Brüssow 2013; Huber et al. 2011; Prüss-Üstün et al. 2003). These are phenomena that can be difficult to operationalize and assess among people whose activities and physiological status can be directly observed and who can be interviewed. What we can typically observe in human skeletal remains are demographic and pathological data (and in some cases biogeochemical data such as ancient DNA and isotopic signatures of diet and mobility). These data are not equivalent to the range of (admittedly imperfect) variables that can be observed for the living, which raises questions about the extent to which we truly can assess health itself in past populations. Though there is almost certainly a relationship of some kind between skeletal data and health status, I attempt to be conservative with terminology in this chapter and do not equate the two. I primarily interpret the presence of periosteal new bone formation as an indicator of exposure to some factor that perturbs the body from its normal condition (a physiological stressor). Such physiological disturbances might be associated with ill health, but I do not, in general, make that assumption here. I certainly do not want to imply that my analyses assess health directly, but the results might reflect something about underlying health patterns, and I use the term "health" in the discussion to describe how the results of this study might be interpreted in common bioarchaeological parlance.

The Osteological Paradox

The ultimate paradox that we confront in bioarchaeology is that we are trying to reconstruct the characteristics of living people in the past using samples of the skeletal remains of deceased people. As the products of multiple selection processes, these samples are simply not very good representations of living populations, and, in fact, they are often not even very good representations of the dead. The biased nature of skeletal samples begins, obviously, with the death of individuals, which typically reflects the interaction of heterogeneous frailty and selective mortality (which are described in detail in this chapter). Thereafter, samples typically become increasingly and varyingly biased because of the following factors: the fact that not everyone is buried in the same place or same manner and thus might not all be recovered during an excavation; variation in preservation conditions within a burial location (e.g., because of spatial differences in soil pH); differences among individuals in the likelihood of preservation irrespective of burial conditions (because of bone size and robusticity); and incomplete excavation of sites as a result of financial or other constraints.

Wood and colleagues (1992) emphasized the phenomena of heterogeneous frailty and selective mortality and how these structure samples of human skeletal remains in ways that complicate reconstruction of life in the past. Other selection processes (e.g., incomplete excavation and variable preservation conditions), though problematic, are not unique to bioarchaeology. For example, they also plague archaeologists interested in material culture, faunal remains, or botanical material. Following Wood and colleagues, the primary focus of this chapter, with respect to biased samples, is to evaluate strategies for addressing heterogeneous frailty and selective mortality.

Frailty is defined in bioarchaeology and human biology as an individual's risk of death relative to other members of the population (Vaupel et al. 1979). Frailty varies within a population (i.e., there is heterogeneity in frailty) because of differences in genetics, epigenetics, hormones, nutritional status, proclivity for risk-taking behavior, socioeconomic status, exposure to disease vectors, environmental contaminants, and other factors and their interactions. Selective mortality refers to the fact that mortality tends to target those people with the highest frailty at any particular age. Because of selective mortality, skeletal assemblages do not provide representative samples of all individuals who were once alive at any particular age. Instead, they are generally biased toward those people who were at highest risk of death (i.e., those who had the highest frailty) at each age. There are exceptions to this generalization, such as accidental causes of death, which are assumed to kill irrespective of frailty, but in general we expect mortality to be selective with respect to frailty. This is true even under catastrophic conditions, as has been observed, for example, during the medieval Black Death (DeWitte 2010; DeWitte and Wood 2008) and during modern natural disasters such as floods, landslides, and earthquakes (Chou et al. 2004; Salvati et al. 2018). Together, heterogeneous frailty and selective mortality make it difficult to make direct inferences about the health of once-living people from their skeletal remains. This difficulty is exacerbated because much of the variation that exists in frailty is produced by unobservable factors – i.e., what Wood and colleagues (1992:344) describe as "hidden heterogeneity" in frailty. There are some potential sources of heterogeneity that can be assessed from people's skeletons or their burial contexts, such as sex, socioeconomic status, or diet. But there are many factors that we simply cannot observe in skeletal samples, and thus their effects cannot be determined nor controlled for.

In light of the issues of heterogeneous frailty and selective mortality, Wood and colleagues (1992), following Ortner (1991), question the straightforward interpretations of skeletal lesions that are often made in bioarchaeology. Most often, the presence of skeletal lesions is interpreted as an indicator of poor health, and the absence thereof is viewed as a sign of good health. However, Wood and colleagues argue that the absence of a lesion might mean an individual was so frail that she/he died before a skeletal lesion formed in response to a stressor, whereas someone with a lesion might have been less frail and thus able to survive a stressor long enough for a skeletal lesion to form. In light of this suggestion, the Osteological Paradox is often summarized simply as "skeletal lesions = good health." However, this interpretation does not accurately reflect the argument made by Wood and colleagues, and they refuted it at the time of publication (1992:365). Viewing skeletal lesions as markers of good health is just as much an oversimplification and as un-nuanced as assuming they always indicate poor health (DeWitte and Stojanowski 2015; Wood et al. 1992). Wood and colleagues did not offer a strict directive about how to interpret skeletal lesions, but rather advised bioarchaeologists to be cautious and consider all equally plausible inferences from the data at hand.

In the years since Wood and colleagues published their paper, little work has been done directly addressing the Osteological Paradox (as summarized recently by DeWitte and Stojanowski [2015]). Though the Wood et al. (1992) paper has been cited hundreds of times, relatively few of the citing scholars explicitly address heterogeneous frailty and selective mortality in their research. Some scholars have argued that Wood and colleagues exaggerate the importance and potential impact of the Osteological Paradox on bioarchaeological interpretations of health (Cohen 1994). Some have championed the use of multiple stress indicators and careful attention to the archaeological or historical context in order to mitigate the potential effects of heterogeneous frailty and selective mortality on reconstructions of health (Cohen 1992; Goodman 1993). For some areas of research, the Osteological Paradox is unambiguously irrelevant; for example, case studies of specific diseases are generally unlikely to be substantially affected by ignoring the potential effects of frailty (DeWitte and Stojanowski 2015).

However, there are many scholars who acknowledge the possible effects of the Osteological Paradox and who might want to structure their research in ways that accommodate it. The target audience of this chapter, thus, is those scholars who recognize the relevance of the Osteological Paradox but for whom conventional approaches present an unsatisfactory resolution of the issues – i.e., for researchers who might have avoided grappling with the Osteological Paradox because there is a general lack of direction regarding how to assess frailty and selective mortality in samples of human skeletal remains.

This chapter presents one possible way to examine frailty and thus directly engage with the Osteological Paradox. The approach I describe here abandons a familiar bioarchaeological approach and adopts a relatively strange approach to interpreting skeletal pathology (in honor of the Familiar Strange theme of the 2015 American Anthropological Association meeting, at which this research was first presented). The "familiar" approach in this case refers to viewing skeletal stress markers as unambiguous, direct indicators of poor health and thus inferring that a (sub)population with a higher frequency of skeletal stress markers is unhealthy relative to another (sub)population that completely lacks or has fewer of those stress markers. The "strange" approach taken here abandons the assumption that skeletal stress markers indicate poor health, considers that they might instead reflect positive outcomes, and engages in a deeper examination of patterns that goes beyond the relatively simple frequentist analysis of presence *versus* absence that is common in the field of bioarchaeology. I take this approach by leveraging existing evidence about the effect of a particular skeletal stress marker (periosteal new bone formation) on survivorship in a specific sociocultural and temporal context (medieval London). Ultimately, I hope to demonstrate that incorporating observable skeletal markers of heterogeneous frailty into analyses can improve interpretive frameworks in bioarchaeology.

Another general goal of this chapter is to assess the relationship between physiological stress and socioeconomic status in medieval London in order to improve our understanding, in general, of the variable ways in which status affected the health of people in past populations. Numerous studies have revealed the negative effects that low status can have on health and survival in living populations. In many contexts, people of lower status face higher risks of mortality, experience shorter life expectancies, and are disproportionately or more severely affected by a variety of chronic and infectious diseases compared to higher-status people (Aartsen et al. 2017; Cavigelli and Chaudhry 2012; Olvera Alvarez et al. 2018; Phelan et al. 2010; Robertson et al. 2013). These disparities can result from a variety of risk factors associated with low socioeconomic status, such as insufficient access to quality healthcare, poor nutritional status, exposure to pollutants at home and work, inadequate access to clean water, elevated glucocorticoid production in response to physiological stress, and health behaviors such as smoking, heavy drinking, and physical inactivity (Chen and Miller 2013; Darmon and Drewnowski 2008; Evans and Kantrowitz 2002; Shaw et al. 2014). The associations between status and health observed in some studies are not, however, consistent across all diseases, and they may not be consistent across all subpopulations (e.g., racial or ethnic groups or gender) (Adler and Ostrove 1999).

Many bioarchaeological studies have similarly assessed the association between social status and mortality, survivorship, or skeletal markers of (presumed) health in past populations (Bigoni et al. 2013; Cucina and İşcan 1997; DeWitte et al. 2016; Hatch and Willey 1974; Hughes-Morey 2016; Nakayama 2016; Newman and Gowland 2017; Peck 2013; Redfern and DeWitte 2011; Robb et al. 2001; Sparacello et al. 2017; Trautmann et al. 2017; Vercellotti et al. 2011; Watts 2015). As with studies of living populations, many of these bioarchaeological analyses reveal evidence of the beneficial effects of higher status. However, the associations are not always straightforward or in the direction expected. For example, Newman and Gowland's (2017) analysis of children and adolescents (ages 0–17) in Industrial-era London revealed that the prevalence of pathology and rate of infant mortality were highest in a low-status cemetery. However, high-status children did not entirely escape negative outcomes; poor growth values were estimated for the high-status cemetery, and these likely reflect adherence to fashionable childcare practices such as artificial feeding of infants and keeping children indoors. Rickets has similarly been found to be more common in higher-status children compared to lower-status children in sixteenth- to eighteenth-century Douai, France (Schattmann et al. 2016). DeWitte and colleagues (2016) found that in Industrial-era London, low-status children suffered elevated risks of mortality compared to their high-status age-peers, but that status had no discernible effect on risks of mortality for adults. These results might reflect the buffering effects of high status during childhood and the disproportionate mortality of frail, low-status children; i.e., the survival of frail high-status individuals, but not of frail low-status individuals, to adulthood might have reduced differences in adult mortality between the social strata. Hughes-Morey (2016) found variable estimated effects of short stature on adult risks of mortality across sex and status in Industrial-era London; these patterns might reflect the long-term outcomes of disproportionately high mortality for frail, low-status children, and the protective effects of high status in childhood (for females) or throughout the lifespan (for males). Bigoni and colleagues (2013) assessed fluctuating asymmetry (a marker of developmental stress) in a sample from medieval Czech Republic and found that while there were no significant differences among males, higher-status females, surprisingly, had higher levels of fluctuating asymmetry compared to lower-status females.

The lack of consistent results across these studies suggests further examination of the phenomenon in more contexts is warranted in order to fully understand how and why the relationship between status and health varies. Research on this relationship in past populations is also crucial, given the debate regarding the antiquity of disparities in health and mortality based on wealth (Antonovsky 1967; Bengtsson and van Poppel 2011; Marmot 2004; Phelan et al. 2004).

Medieval England provides a particularly interesting context in which to examine variation in health by social status. During the medieval period, England was characterized by a strict social hierarchy, with multiple axes of social inequality (Coss 2006; Rigby 1995, 2006), as codified, for example, in the 1379 parliamentary schedule of rates of contribution to the graded poll tax (Dyer 1989:20). However, this was also a period of tumultuous changes in standards of living, such as those precipitated by the Black Death in the fourteenth century. The Black Death killed an estimated 30–60 percent of affected populations, and the massive depopulation in England resulted in a severe labor shortage and thus increases in wages and decreases in prices for food, goods, and housing (Bailey 1996; Dyer 1989). In general, there were improvements in standards of living for people lower in the social hierarchy (such as peasants, laborers, and servants) after the Black Death. For example, in the fifteenth century, most tenants apparently paid rents that were at least 20 percent lower than was the case prior to the epidemic; tenants also benefitted financially from new opportunities to migrate in the aftermath of the Black Death by refusing to pay fines due to lords and threatening to leave their holdings if payment was enforced (Dyer 1989:147). In the fourteenth and fifteenth centuries, peasant diets in England changed in three important ways: consumption of wheat, ale, and meat increased (Dyer 1989). According to Dyer, these dietary changes certainly positively affected the psychological well-being of people, and the rectification of the shortage of animal protein that had been characteristic of the pre-Black Death diet might have improved the nutritional quality of post-epidemic diets.

These changes threatened the status quo, and motivated people of higher social ranks to enact laws preventing working people from taking advantage of increased economic opportunities (Maddern 2006). In England, laws such as the Ordinance of Labourers (1349) and the Statute of Labourers (1351) were passed after the Black Death to restrict labor mobility, require all physically fit adults below the age of 60 to accept work if it was offered, and to cap wages at relatively low pre-Black Death levels and maintain rents at relatively high levels (Coss 2006; Rexroth 2007; Rigby 1995). A sumptuary law was passed in 1363 to regulate expenditures (e.g., on high-quality clothing and jewelry) by lower-status people (Cohn 2007; Dyer 1989). According to Maddern (2006), this legislation was not entirely successful. The passage of the new labor laws might have had the effect of stimulating higher rates of migration, as some people might have migrated as an expression of resistance against the restrictions imposed by those laws (Dyer 2005). In the aftermath of the epidemic, while many large towns in England experienced population decline and the loss of commerce and industry, London maintained its prosperity and attracted migrants (Britnell 2006; Dyer 1989). In general, then, this was a time of newly found freedoms of mobility across the landscape and improved access by the masses to resources that potentially improved health. But it remains unclear whether improvements in standards of living and other changes following the Black Death resulted in reduced differences in health between higher- and lower-status individuals.

In summary, the goals of this chapter are to use well-contextualized skeletal samples from medieval London in order to: (1) assess differences in frailty between higher and lower socioeconomic status individuals in medieval London; and (2) demonstrate whether including or excluding data on skeletal lesion activity (i.e., whether skeletal lesions were active or healed at the time of death) during analysis affects the interpretations that are made about variation in exposure to physiological stress and, by careful inference, health differentials in the past.

Materials and Methods

Skeletal Sample

The sample for this study comes from the site of St. Mary Graces, London (c.1350–1538, n = 191). The Cistercian Abbey of St. Mary Graces was established in London in 1350, soon after the Black Death ended in the city, and it was in use until the Reformation in 1538 (Grainger and Hawkins 1988; Grainger et al. 2008). St. Mary Graces was excavated in the 1980s as part of a larger site (Royal Mint, MIN86) that included the underlying East Smithfield Black Death burial ground, which was established explicitly for and used only during the epidemic, c.1349–1350. Burials in St. Mary Graces include individuals of all ages, both sexes, both high- and low-status individuals, and monks (Grainger and Phillpotts 2011).

Burial location within St. Mary Graces indicates socioeconomic status; a cemetery associated with the Abbey of St. Mary Graces was used for burial of members of the general population and represents lower socioeconomic status, while monks and important lay people (i.e., higher socioeconomic status individuals) were buried within the Abbey's church and chapels. The lay cemetery also contains victims of a fourteenth-century plague outbreak subsequent to the Black Death (the plague of 1361 or a later outbreak) in an area spatially distinct from the rest of the St. Mary Graces burials. These putative 1361 plague burials are close to the Black Death burials in the underlying East Smithfield cemetery and far from the Abbey, whereas the non-plague burials are clustered close to or are within the Abbey (Gilchrist and Sloane 2005; Grainger and Phillpotts 2011; Sloane 2011). An unusually high proportion of people (49 percent) in the 1361 plague burials were buried in coffins; this high proportion is similar to that observed in East Smithfield, but more than twice that observed in the non-plague burials in St. Mary Graces and in other non-epidemic medieval cemeteries in England. During medieval plague epidemics, many cities ordered the use of coffins to prevent corruption from rotting plague victims (Creighton 1891), and the high use of coffins in East Smithfield and the St. Mary Graces plague burials is consistent with these ancient public health measures. Ancient DNA analyses have revealed the presence of *Yersinia pestis* in an individual buried in the plague area of St. Mary Graces, thus confirming that individuals buried there were affected by bubonic plague (Bos et al. 2016).

To verify whether the findings of this study reflect non-epidemic mortality patterns, the analyses were done with the total sample of 191 individuals as well as a subsample of 80 individuals that excludes the fourteenth-century plague victims (though note the lack of effect produced by including medieval plague victims in a previous study of periosteal new bone formation described in the next section). These samples include all of the excavated individuals from St. Mary Graces that were preserved well enough to provide data on periosteal new bone formation using the scoring method described in the next section.

Periosteal New Bone Formation

Periosteal new bone formation (also described in the paleopathological literature as periosteal lesions or periostitis) is an abnormal growth of bone that forms in response to a variety of causes, such as trauma, local or systemic infection, malnutrition, and neoplastic disease (Chen et al. 2012; Geber and Murphy 2012; Huss-Ashmore et al. 1982; Larsen 2015; Ortner 2003; Paine and Brenton 2006; Roberts and Manchester 2005; Weston 2008). Because there are so many possible etiologies of periosteal new bone formation, and given the difficulty or impossibility of differentiating those various causes in dry bone, this pathology is frequently used as a nonspecific skeletal indicator of stress in bioarchaeological research (Larsen 2015). Using periosteal new bone formation in this way, rather than attempting to diagnose specific etiologies, ignores potentially important variation in morbidity and mortality associated with the pathology (Powell 1988; Weston 2012). Incorporation of data on the activity of periosteal new bone formation might provide a way to uncover some of that variation while avoiding the limitations imposed by the low specificity of the pathology.

Periosteal new bone formation can be scored as active, healed, or a combination of the two. Active periosteal new bone formation (also described as woven bone) has an unremodeled appearance and is indicative of active disease or inflammatory responses at the time of death. Healed lesions (also described as sclerotic or lamellar bone) have a remodeled appearance, are indicative of healing by the time the individual died, and in some cases might reflect chronic disease processes (Buikstra and Ubelaker 1994). The activity of skeletal lesions in general (including, but not limited to periosteal new bone formation) might be informative about underlying differences in health or heterogeneity in frailty. That is, an individual who died with active lesions might have done so because of poor general health and thus a reduced ability to recover from the associated cause. Healed lesions might reflect relatively good health (or low frailty) as they indicate survival of an individual beyond the occurrence of disease or other physiological disturbance (Wood et al. 1992). Numerous bioarchaeological studies have assessed the age distributions of active *versus* healed skeletal lesions, such as periosteal new bone formation, cribra orbitalia, porotic hyperostosis, and manifestations of rickets (Brickley et al. 2018; Grauer 1993; Ives 2017; Mittler and Van Gerven 1994; Novak and Šlaus 2010; Pinhasi et al. 2014; Rose 1985; Shuler 2011; Watts and Valme 2018). Many of these studies suggest that there are survival or health advantages associated with the presence of healed skeletal lesions (but see, for example, Shuler 2011).

My previous research using data from medieval London cemeteries has yielded information that informs the application and interpretation of periosteal new bone formation data in the St. Mary Graces sample. Hazards analysis of the effect of periosteal lesion presence (with no distinction made between active and healed lesions) on a baseline, parametric model of mortality, using a sample from the East Smithfield Black Death cemetery in London, suggests that periosteal lesions, in general, were associated with elevated risks of mortality during the epidemic

(DeWitte and Wood 2008). People who exhibited periosteal lesions (some of whom, with healed lesions, had been exposed to, but survived, some associated physiological stressor prior to the epidemic, and others, with active lesions, who were experiencing the stressor when infected with plague) apparently faced elevated risks of mortality during the Black Death compared to their age-peers who lacked the lesion. These results are similar in nature to those estimated for a pre-Black Death normal mortality sample from medieval Denmark. This suggests that the results from the London Black Death sample are not reflective solely of catastrophic mortality patterns, and that the presence of periosteal lesions might be a good indicator of frailty under a variety of mortality conditions.

As indicated above, this previous analysis of the effect of periosteal new bone formation on risks of mortality used pooled data on active and healed, thus raising the question of whether the relationship between this pathology and demographic outcomes varies across the spectrum of activity. Subsequent Kaplan–Meier survival analyses using additional samples from medieval London (including many of the individuals from the St. Mary Graces cemetery used in the study reported here) reveal significant variation in survivorship based on the activity of periosteal new bone formation (DeWitte 2014a). Analyses were performed using a sample of individuals of all ages and a sample that included just those people above the age of 15 years to verify that any observed differences in survival were not an artifact of incorrectly scoring porosity associated with normal growth as active lesions; both sets of analyses reveal similar results. Furthermore, the results of analyses that excluded Black Death victims buried in the East Smithfield cemetery are similar to the results obtained using the larger sample, which indicates that inclusion of epidemic victims did not strongly affect the patterns observed in that study. Individuals with active periosteal new bone formation had the lowest estimated survivorship compared to all other categories (absent, healed, and mixed lesions), and thus active lesions might most accurately reflect high frailty. Individuals with healed periosteal lesions had higher estimated survivorship compared to both those with active lesions and those without any lesions at all.

These results suggest that healed periosteal lesions, in general, are reflective of the ability to survive the associated stressors long enough for the lesions to form and thus indicate relatively low frailty. The (perhaps surprising) lower estimated survivorship of those without any periosteal lesions, compared to those with healed lesions, might reflect heterogeneity in frailty among those lacking lesions. That is, the group of individuals without lesions might include both (1) people with high frailty and thus reduced ability to survive stressors long enough for lesions to form, and (2) those with low frailty who were either never exposed to lesion-producing stressors and thus did not suffer increased frailty as a result thereof or those who were intrinsically robust and able to respond successfully to stressors before lesions formed in response. The results for the mixed lesion category were more ambiguous, as there was overlap between the 95 percent confidence intervals for mean survivorship of individuals with mixed lesions and those of people both without lesions and with healed lesions. Together, these results suggest that the presence of periosteal new bone formation by itself might not provide the resolution necessary to examine patterns of frailty and, by inference, health in the past and that lesion activity data should ideally be incorporated into analyses of this particular pathology.

This study uses data on both the presence and activity (i.e., active, healed, or mixed) of periosteal lesions on the right tibia. Periosteal lesions were scored on the tibia because this bone is usually preserved relatively well and because previous research has demonstrated that it is affected by periosteal lesions at a relatively high frequency (Eisenberg 1991; Galloway et al. 1997; Larsen 1997; Roberts and Manchester 2005; Stojanowski et al. 2002; Willey et al. 1997). The right tibia was selected because it provided the largest sample sizes for analysis. As mentioned above, periosteal lesions can have infectious or traumatic causes. Infectious etiologies are more likely to produce bilateral lesions, whereas trauma more often produces unilateral lesions (Larsen 2015; Weston 2012). By including scores only from the right tibia, it is possible that the lesions observed in this study were produced both by trauma and infection (which presumably is more closely associated with underlying immune competence and thus frailty). However, preliminary analyses for my previous study (DeWitte 2014a) revealed that analyses of unilateral periosteal lesion data yielded results similar to those produced by analyses of bilateral data. For this chapter, I used unilateral data in order to maximize sample sizes for analysis given that the sample was subdivided into high- and low-status groups. The possible inclusion of people with traumatic injuries might mask associations in lesion patterns resulting from differences in frailty.

Periosteal new bone formation was scored only on the anterior surfaces of the tibial diaphysis in order to avoid incorrectly scoring soft tissue attachments on the posterior surfaces and along the margins of articular surfaces as pathological. Furthermore, in order to avoid scoring the porosity that is associated with normal growth as periosteal new bone formation, I only evaluated diaphyseal surfaces at least 1 cm away from the epiphyseal growth plates when scoring for periosteal lesions in non-adults (normal cortical porosity rarely extends beyond a centimeter from the growing end of the metaphysis [Ortner et al. 2001]). Bone surfaces were evaluated macroscopically under good lighting. Periosteal new bone formation was scored as present if an individual had at least one distinct patch, of any size, of woven or sclerotic bone laid down on the surface of the diaphysis. The periosteal lesions were scored as active if the patch of bone appeared porous and had sharp, unremodeled edges. Lesions were scored as healed if the patch of bone had rounded, remodeled edges (Weston 2008). Only those tibiae with diaphyseal surfaces that were free of both periosteal new bone formation and postmortem damage were assigned a score of "absent" with respect to new bone formation. Tibiae without observable lesions but with postmortem damage that prevented visual assessment of the entire anterior surface of the bone were assigned a score of "unobservable" with respect to periosteal new bone formation and thus excluded from analysis. This conservative approach reduces the likelihood of including false negatives for periosteal new bone formation in the sample.

Statistical Analysis

I compared the presence and activity of periosteal new bone formation between the high- and low-status individuals from St. Mary Graces using chi-square analysis or, when limited by sample size, Fisher's exact tests. In general, I would not recommend this analytical approach in isolation because it does not, by itself, allow one to control for age. This is a crucial limitation in analyses of skeletal lesions that are known or suspected to be associated with age. It is important to control for age in analyses of periosteal lesions as some studies have revealed positive associations between periosteal lesions and adult age (DeWitte 2014b; Grauer 1993; Rose and Hartnady 1991), and thus significant differences between two groups in frequencies of periosteal lesions, as indicated by chi-square tests, might be an artifact of differences in age-at-death distributions between those groups. However, import- antly for this study, previous research in the context of medieval London has revealed significant effects of periosteal lesion activity on survival, and this means that a chi-square test of the association between lesions and status is potentially informative about underlying differences in exposure to physiological stress between two groups.

In order to rule out the possibility that the results of this study are affected by the inclusion of fourteenth-century plague victims, analyses were done both including and excluding individuals in the putative 1361 plague burials from St. Mary Graces.

Results

As shown in Table 7.1, when all categories of periosteal new bone formation (i.e., active, healed, and mixed lesions) are pooled into a single "presence" score, analysis reveals a higher frequency of periosteal lesions in general among the high-status people compared to the low-status people from St. Mary Graces. This is true regard- less of whether the 1361 plague burials are included in the analyses, though the results are statistically significant only for the sample that includes the plague burials. However, closer examination of variation in patterns of periosteal new bone formation activity (Table 7.2) reveals a higher proportion of *healed* lesions in the high-status sample compared to the low-status sample. In the sample that includes the 1361 plague burials, of those individuals scored for periosteal new bone forma- tion (i.e., including those who had no observable lesions), 56.9 percent of high-status people have healed lesions compared to only 24.1 percent of low-status people. As a proportion of just those individuals with observable periosteal lesions (i.e., excluding those who had no observable lesions), 78.6 percent of high-status people with lesions have healed periosteal new bone formation compared to 57.1 percent of low-status people. This general pattern holds true regardless of whether 1361 plague burials are included in the analyses, though again the results are significant only when the plague burials are included. The lack of statistically significant results for the analyses that exclude the 1361 plague burials might be an artifact of reduced sample sizes, as discussed in more detail in the next section.

Table 7.1 Frequencies of periosteal new bone formation in low- and high-status burials

Periosteal new bone formation	Low-status burials (including plague)	High-status burials (including plague)	Low-status burials (excluding plague)	High-status burials (excluding plague)
Absent	77 (57.9%)	16 (27.6%)	11 (40.7%)	14 (26.4%)
Present	56 (42.1%)	42 (72.4%)	16 (59.3%)	39 (73.6%)
Chi-square	$p < 0.001$		$p = 0.19$	

Table 7.2 Frequencies of active, healed, and mixed periosteal new bone formation in low- and high-status burials

Periosteal new bone formation	Low-status burials (including plague)	High-status burials (including plague)	Low-status burials (excluding plague)	High-status burials (excluding plague)
Active	5 (8.93%)	4 (9.5%)	1 (6.25%)	4 (10.25%)
Healed	32 (57.14%)	33 (78.6%)	10 (62.5%)	31 (79.5%)
Mixed	19 (33.93%)	5 (11.9%)	5 (31.25%)	4 (10.25%)
Chi-square (or *Fisher's exact)	$p = 0.04$		*$p = 0.16$	

Note: this only includes individuals with periosteal new bone formation.

Discussion

If we examine only the presence versus absence of periosteal new bone formation in St. Mary Graces and apply the "familiar" approach to bioarchaeological interpretations of health (i.e., viewing skeletal stress markers as direct indicators of health), the higher frequency of these lesions in high-status people would suggest poorer general health for those individuals compared to lower-status people in medieval London. However, adherence to the warnings raised by Wood and colleagues (1992) means considering the equally plausible interpretation that higher-status people in London were, compared to lower-status people, better able to survive the stressors associated with periosteal new bone formation long enough to produce those lesions. From this relatively "strange" perspective, the higher frequency of lesions in the high-status sample would suggest they were in better general health compared to the low-status individuals. Looking only at the presence versus absence of periosteal new bone formation leaves us in a quandary: how do we decide between two possible, contradictory interpretations of these findings?

Making use of information about lesion activity, and thus examination of trends with somewhat finer resolution, produces a clearer picture of the relationship between status and physiological stress in this population and lends support in favor of the seemingly paradoxical interpretation. As detailed above, previous research using medieval London skeletal samples (including many of the same individuals from St. Mary Graces included in the current study) suggests that individuals in this context with active periosteal new bone formation had the lowest survivorship, whereas those with healed periosteal lesions had the highest survivorship. These results suggest that healed periosteal lesions reflect superior abilities to survive physiological stressors and thus indicate relatively low frailty. The higher proportion of high-status people with healed lesions compared to their lower-status peers is, thus, likely indicative of better general health for the higher-status group. It is possible that the high proportion (nearly 58 percent) of low-status individuals without any lesions at all might mean that this group contains a relatively high number of very frail people who died from the associated stressors before lesions could form. However, the absence of pathological lesions can also reflect a lack of exposure to stressors that cause periosteal new bone formation, so any interpretation regarding the health status of individuals without lesions must remain tentative.

Relatively few bioarchaeological studies (including much of my own work) use data on pathological lesion activity, even when it is available. Pooling data on lesion activity provides sample sizes that are inherently larger compared to the samples available following subdivision of a dataset into activity categories. Thus, analyses of presence versus absence will often have higher statistical power compared to those using the active/healed distinction, and they are more likely to fulfill the criteria of statistical tests. For example, as seen in Table 7.2, when I excluded plague burials from the analysis and subdivided my samples into lesion activity categories, I was faced with small cell counts, which precluded chi-square analysis. Use of larger sample sizes might reveal patterns that are otherwise undiscernible. While it is understandable why we might not always take advantage of lesion activity data, not doing so means we might risk a high degree of ambiguity when making inferences about patterns of health (or more conservatively, exposure to some anatomical or physiological disturbance) in past populations. In this case, focusing on just presence/absence data produces results suggesting either that lower-status medieval Londoners experienced better general health than high-status people, or that lesion presence by itself might be indicative of relatively low frailty. Incorporation of lesion activity data and leveraging information about the demographic patterns attendant to lesion activity in medieval London, however, yields results strongly suggestive of better health among high-status people. This, in turn, furthers our understanding of the antiquity of health differentials based on wealth and perhaps lends support to the argument that such differentials have existed for a very long time (the fundamental social-causes model or the constancy hypothesis) (Bengtsson and van Poppel 2011; Marmot 2004; Phelan et al. 2004) and are not solely a consequence of industrialization (see Antonovsky 1967).

As mentioned above, significant differences between the higher- and lower-status samples from St. Mary Graces were found only for the analyses that included the 1361 plague burials, the vast majority of whom were buried in the lower-status lay cemetery. This raises the question of whether the observed distribution of lesions in the sample that includes the plague burials reflects plague mortality patterns rather

Table 7.3 Frequencies of periosteal new bone formation in low-status and 1361 plague burials

Periosteal new bone formation	Low-status burials (excluding plague)	1361 plague burials	Chi-square
Absent	11 (40.74%)	66 (62.2%)	
Active	1 (3.7%)	4 (3.8%)	$p = 0.16$
Healed	10 (37.04%)	22 (20.8%)	
Mixed	5 (18.52%)	14 (13.2%)	

than status differentials. As shown in Table 7.3, there is a higher proportion of individuals in the 1361 plague burials without periosteal new bone formation compared to low-status, non-plague burials (62 percent versus 40.7 percent). Of those with lesions, 55 percent of 1361 plague burials have healed lesions compared to 62.5 percent of low-status, non-plague burials. However, these are not significantly different. Furthermore, previous studies have yielded evidence that the Black Death and the plague of 1361 were selective with respect to frailty, specifically that individuals with periosteal new bone formation were more likely to die during these epidemics compared to their age-peers without lesions (DeWitte and Kowaleski 2017; DeWitte and Wood 2008). This suggests that we should not necessarily expect lesion frequencies in plague and non-plague burials to be substantially different from one another. The results of this study, therefore, likely reflect the effects of status rather than the effects of medieval plague on observed patterns of periosteal new bone formation.

The inference that high status buffered individuals not from exposure to the physiological stressors sufficient to cause periosteal new bone formation but, rather, enabled them to avoid dying as a result of such exposures has been suggested previously by Grauer (1989) for another medieval English population. Analysis of skeletal samples from St. Helen-on-the-Walls, York revealed no significant differences in survival between higher- and lower-status non-adults, but an apparent survival advantage for higher-status adult males. Analysis of porotic hyperostosis and periosteal new bone formation revealed an association between healed lesions and age, suggesting that higher status did not shield people from exposure to physiological stressors, but instead improved their chances of surviving those stressors.

As mentioned above, the samples used in this study date to a period (c. 1350–1540) characterized by dramatic changes in standards of living, such as improvements in diet across social strata, that occurred as a consequence of the Black Death. However, the results of this study suggest that despite improvements in standards of living and decreasing social inequalities in diet, there were still differences in exposure to physiological stress or survival thereof between higher- and lower-status individuals in medieval London. The differences observed here raise the question: To what extent did the post-Black Death changes in diet and other standards of living truly affect health outcomes? Further, assuming that these changes produced substantial positive effects, did all people enjoy those benefits equally, or was there variation within the population (for example, by sex)? Future bioarchaeological research, which avoids treating lower-status individuals as members of a homogeneous group and incorporates data on sex, status, diet, survivorship, and physiological stress markers, might clarify this issue.

Despite the insights that lesion activity data provide for examining health differentials in this context, I do not advocate assuming that the relationship between periosteal new bone formation and survivorship estimated for medieval London is necessarily generalizable. The association between the activity of this particular pathological lesion or other lesions of interest should ideally be evaluated before applying the approach described in this chapter in other contexts. As has been strongly argued by scholars such as Cohen (1992) and Larsen (2015), attention to context is a crucial component of any bioarchaeological analysis. However, regardless of the generalizability of the relationship between periosteal new bone formation activity and survivorship, the results of this study suggest that going beyond the use of just dichotomous categories of lesions allows us to engage with the Osteological Paradox in a relatively simple but still informative way.

Acknowledgments

I thank Drs. Sang-Hee Lee and Cathy Willermet for inviting me to present this research as part of their session, "Scientific Approaches to Biological Anthropology: The Strange and Familiar," at the American Anthropological Association meeting in 2015. I am grateful to Ms. Jelena Bekvalac and Dr. Rebecca Redfern at the Museum of London Centre for Human Bioarchaeology for providing access to the skeletal samples used in this study and for generously providing the physical facilities for this work. I also thank the three reviewers of an earlier version of this chapter for their helpful comments and suggestions. Data for this study were collected as part of projects funded by the NSF (BCS-1261682), the Wenner Gren Foundation (#8247), and the American Association of Physical Anthropologists (Professional Development Grant).

References

Aartsen M, Veenstra M, and Hansen T (2017) Social pathways to health: on the mediating role of the social network in the relation between socio-economic position and health. *SSM: Population Health* 3:419–426.

Adler NE and Ostrove JM (1999) Socioeconomic status and health: what we know and what we don't. *Annals of the New York Academy of Sciences* 896:3–15.

Antonovsky A (1967) Social class, life expectancy and overall mortality. *The Milbank Memorial Fund Quarterly* 45(2):31–73.

Bailey M (1996) T. S. Ashton Prize: Joint Winning Essay. Demographic decline in late medieval England: some thoughts on recent research. *The Economic History Review* 49(1):1–19.

Bengtsson T and van Poppel F (2011) Socioeconomic inequalities in death from past to present: an introduction. *Explorations in Economic History* 48(3):343–356.

Bigoni L, Krajíček V, Sládek V, Velemínský P, and Velemínská J (2013) Skull shape asymmetry and the socioeconomic structure of an early medieval Central European society. *American Journal of Physical Anthropology* 150(3):349–364.

Bos KI, Herbig A, Sahl J, et al. (2016) Eighteenth century *Yersinia pestis* genomes reveal the long-term persistence of an historical plague focus. *eLife* 5:e12994.

Brickley MB, Mays S, George M, and Prowse TL (2018) Analysis of patterning in the occurrence of skeletal lesions used as indicators of vitamin D deficiency in subadult and adult skeletal remains. *International Journal of Paleopathology* 23:43–53.

Britnell R (2006) Town life. In Horrox R and Ormond WM, editors. *A Social History of England 1200–1500.* Cambridge University Press. Pp. 134–178.

Brüssow H (2013) What is health? *Microbial Biotechnology* 6(4):341–348.

Buikstra JE and Ubelaker DH, editors (1994) *Standards for Data Collection from Human Skeletal Remains: Proceedings of a Seminar at the Field Museum of Natural History.* Arkansas Archeological Survey Press.

Cavigelli SA and Chaudhry HS (2012) Social status, glucocorticoids, immune function, and health: can animal studies help us understand human socioeconomic-status-related health disparities? *Hormones and Behavior* 62(3):295–313.

Chen E and Miller GE (2013) Socioeconomic status and health: mediating and moderating factors. *Annual Review of Clinical Psychology* 9:723–749.

Chen EM, Masih S, Chow K, Matcuk G, and Patel D (2012) Periosteal reaction: review of various patterns associated with specific pathology. *Contemporary Diagnostic Radiology* 35 (17):6.

Chou Y-J, Huang N, Lee C-H, et al. (2004) Who is at risk of death in an earthquake? *American Journal of Epidemiology* 160(7):688–695.

Cohen MN (1992) Comment on: "The Osteological Paradox," by J.W. Wood et al. *Current Anthropology* 33(4):358–359.

Cohen MN (1994) The Osteological Paradox reconsidered. *Current Anthropology* 35(5):629–631.

Cohn S (2007) After the Black Death: labour legislation and attitudes towards labour in late-medieval western Europe. *The Economic History Review* 60(3):457–485.

Coss P (2006) An age of deference. In Horrox R and Ormond WM, editors. *A Social History of England 1200–1500.* Cambridge University Press. Pp. 31–73.

Creighton C (1891) *A History of Epidemics in Britain. Vol. 1: From AD 664 to the Extinction of Plague.* Cambridge University Press.

Cucina A and İşcan MY (1997) Assessment of enamel hypoplasia in a high status burial site. *American Journal of Human Biology* 9(2):213–222.

Darmon N and Drewnowski A (2008) Does social class predict diet quality? *The American Journal of Clinical Nutrition* 87(5):1107–1117.

DeWitte SN (2010) Age patterns of mortality during the Black Death in London, AD 1349–1350. *Journal of Archaeological Science* 37(12):3394–3400.

DeWitte SN (2014a) Differential survival among individuals with active and healed periosteal new bone formation. *International Journal of Paleopathology* 7:38–44.

DeWitte SN (2014b) Health in post-Black Death London (1350–1538): age patterns of periosteal new bone formation in a post-epidemic population. *American Journal of Physical Anthropology* 155 (2):260–267.

DeWitte SN and Kowaleski M (2017) Black death bodies. *Fragments: Interdisciplinary Approaches to the Study of Ancient and Medieval Pasts* 6:1–37.

DeWitte SN and Stojanowski CM (2015) The Osteological Paradox 20 years later: past perspectives, future directions. *Journal of Archaeological Research* 23(4):397–450.

DeWitte SN and Wood JW (2008) Selectivity of Black Death mortality with respect to preexisting health. *Proceedings of the National Academy of Sciences of the United States of America* 105 (5):1436–1441.

DeWitte SN, Hughes-Morey G, Bekvalac J, and Karsten J (2016) Wealth, health and frailty in Industrial-era London. *Annals of Human Biology* 43(3):241–254.

Dyer C (1989) *Standards of Living in the Later Middle Ages: Social Change in England c. 1200–1520.* Cambridge University Press.

Dyer C (2005) *An Age of Transition? Economy and Society in England in the Later Middle Ages.* Oxford University Press.

Eisenberg LE (1991) Mississippian cultural terminations in Middle Tennessee: what the bioarcheological evidence can tell us. In Powell ML, Bridges PS, and Mires AM, editors. *What Mean These Bones?* University of Alabama Press. Pp. 70–88.

Evans GW and Kantrowitz E (2002) Socioeconomic status and health: the potential role of environmental risk exposure. *Annual Review of Public Health* 23(1):303–331.

Galloway A, Willey P, and Snyder L (1997) Human bone mineral densities and survival of bone elements: a contemporary sample. In Haglund WD and Sorg MH, editors. *Forensic Taphonomy: The Postmortem Fate of Human Remains.* CRC Press. Pp. 295–317.

Geber J and Murphy E (2012) Scurvy in the Great Irish Famine: evidence of vitamin C deficiency from a mid-19th century skeletal population. *American Journal of Physical Anthropology* 148(4):512–524.

Gilchrist R and Sloane B (2005) *Requiem: The Medieval Monastic Cemetery in Britain.* Museum of London Archaeology Service.

Goodman AH (1993) On the interpretation of health from skeletal remains. *Current Anthropology* 34(3):281–288.

Grainger I and Hawkins D (1988) Excavations at the Royal Mint site 1986–1988. *The London Archaeologist* 5:429–436.

Grainger I and Phillpotts C (2011) *The Cistercian Abbey of St Mary Graces, East Smithfield, London.* Museum of London Archaeology.

Grainger I, Hawkins D, Cowal L, and Mikulski R (2008) *The Black Death cemetery, East Smithfield, London.* Museum of London Archaeology Service.

Grauer AL (1989) *Health, Disease and Status in Medieval York* (PhD Thesis). University of Massachusetts at Amherst.

Grauer AL (1993) Patterns of anemia and infection from medieval York, England. *American Journal of Physical Anthropology* 91(2):203–213.

Hatch J and Willey P (1974) Stature and status in Dallas society. *Tennessee Archaeology* 30:107–131.

Huber M, Knottnerus JA, Green L, et al. (2011) Health: how should we define it? *British Medical Journal* 343(7817):235–237.

Hughes-Morey G (2016) Interpreting adult stature in Industrial London. *American Journal of Physical Anthropology* 159(1):126–134.

Huss-Ashmore R, Goodman AH, and Armelagos GJ (1982) Nutritional inference from paleopathology. *Advances in Archaeological Method and Theory* 5:395–474.

Ives R (2017) Rare paleopathological insights into vitamin D deficiency rickets, co-occurring illnesses, and documented cause of death in mid-19th century London, UK. *International Journal of Paleopathology* 23:76–87.

Jadad AR and O'Grady L (2008) How should health be defined? *British Medical Journal* 337(7683):1363–1364.

Larsen CS (1997) *Bioarchaeology: Interpreting Behavior from the Human Skeleton.* Cambridge University Press.

Larsen CS (2015) *Bioarchaeology: Interpreting Behavior from the Human Skeleton,* 2nd edition. Cambridge University Press.

Maddern PC (2006) Social mobility. In Horrox R and Ormond WM, editors. *A Social History of England 1200–1500.* Cambridge University Press. Pp. 113–133.

Marmot M (2004) *The Status Syndrome: How Social Standing Affects Our Health and Longevity.* Bloomsbury Publishing.

Mittler DM and Van Gerven DP (1994) Developmental, diachronic, and demographic analysis of cribra orbitalia in the medieval Christian populations of Kulubnarti. *American Journal of Physical Anthropology* 93(3):287–297.

Nakayama N (2016) The relationship between linear enamel hypoplasia and social status in 18th to 19th Century Edo, Japan. *International Journal of Osteoarchaeology* 26(6):1034–1044.

Newman SL and Gowland RL (2017) Dedicated followers of fashion? Bioarchaeological perspectives on socio-economic status, inequality, and health in urban children from the Industrial Revolution (18th–19th C), England. *International Journal of Osteoarchaeology* 27(2):217–229.

Novak M and Šlaus M (2010) Health and disease in a Roman walled city: an example of Colonia Iulia Iader. *Journal of Anthropological Sciences* 88:189–206.

Olvera Alvarez HA, Appleton AA, Fuller CH, Belcourt A, and Kubzansky LD (2018) An integrated socio-environmental model of health and well-being: a conceptual framework exploring the joint contribution of environmental and social exposures to health and disease over the life span. *Current Environmental Health Reports* 5(2):233–243.

Ortner DJ (1991) Theoretical and methodological issues in paleopathology. In Ortner DJ and Aufderheide AC, editors. *Human Paleopathology: Current Syntheses and Future Options.* Smithsonian Institution Press. Pp. 5–11.

Ortner DJ (2003) *Identification of Pathological Conditions in Human Skeletal Remains*, 2nd edition. Academic Press.

Ortner DJ, Butler W, Cafarella J, and Milligan L (2001) Evidence of probable scurvy in subadults from archeological sites in North America. *American Journal of Physical Anthropology* 114(4):343–351.

Paine RR and Brenton BP (2006) The paleopathology of pellagra: investigating the impact of prehistoric and historical dietary transitions to maize. *Journal of Anthropological Sciences* 84(2006):125–135.

Peck JJ (2013) Status, health, and lifestyle in Middle Iron Age Britain: a bioarcheological study of elites and non-elites from East Yorkshire, Northern England. *International Journal of Paleopathology* 3(2):83–94.

Phelan JC, Link BG, Diez-Roux A, Kawachi I, and Levin B (2004) "Fundamental causes" of social inequalities in mortality: a test of the theory. *Journal of Health and Social Behavior* 45(3):265–285.

Phelan JC, Link BG, and Tchranifar P (2010) Social conditions as fundamental causes of health inequalities: theory, evidence, and policy implications. *Journal of Health and Social Behavior* 51(Suppl.):S28–S40.

Pinhasi R, Timpson A, Thomas M, and Šlaus M (2014) Bone growth, limb proportions and non-specific stress in archaeological populations from Croatia. *Annals of Human Biology* 41(2):127–137.

Powell ML (1988) *Status and Health in Prehistory: A Case Study of the Moundville Chiefdom.* Smithsonian Institution Press.

Prüss-Üstün A, Mathers C, Corvalán C, and Woodward A (2003) *Introduction and Methods: Assessing the Environmental Burden of Disease at National and Local Levels.* World Health Organization.

Redfern RC and DeWitte SN (2011) Status and health in Roman Dorset: the effect of status on risk of mortality in post-conquest populations. *American Journal of Physical Anthropology* 146(2):197–208.

Reitsema LJ and McIlvaine BK (2014) Reconciling "stress" and "health" in physical anthropology: what can bioarchaeologists learn from the other subdisciplines? *American Journal of Physical Anthropology* 155(2):181–185.

Rexroth F (2007) *Deviance and Power in Late Medieval London.* Cambridge University Press.

Rigby SH (1995) *English Society in the Later Middle Ages: Class, Status and Gender.* Palgrave.

Rigby SH (2006) Introduction: social structure and economic change in late medieval England. In Horrox R and Ormond WM, editors. *A Social History of England 1200–1500.* Cambridge University Press. Pp. 1–30.

Robb J, Bigazzi R, Lazzarini L, Scarsini C, and Sonego F (2001) Social "status" and biological "status": a comparison of grave goods and skeletal indicators from Pontecagnano. *American Journal of Physical Anthropology* 115(3):213–222.

Roberts CA and Manchester K (2005) *The Archaeology of Disease.* Cornell University Press.

Robertson T, Batty GD, Der G, et al. (2013) Is socioeconomic status associated with biological aging as measured by telomere length? *Epidemiologic Reviews* 35(1):98–111.

Rose JC, editor (1985) *Gone to a Better Land.* Arkansas Archeological Survey.

Rose JC and Hartnady P (1991) Interpretation of infectious skeletal lesions from a historic Afro-American cemetery. In Ortner DJ and Aufderheide AC, editors. *Human Paleopathology: Current Syntheses and Future Options.* Smithsonian Institution Press. Pp. 119–127.

Salvati P, Petrucci O, Rossi M, et al. (2018) Gender, age and circumstances analysis of flood and landslide fatalities in Italy. *The Science of the Total Environment* 610–611:867–879.

Schattmann A, Bertrand B, Vatteoni S, and Brickley M (2016) Approaches to co-occurrence: scurvy and rickets in infants and young children of 16–18th century Douai, France. *International Journal of Paleopathology* 12:63–75.

Shaw BA, McGeever K, Vasquez E, Agahi N, and Fors S (2014) Socioeconomic inequalities in health after age 50: are health risk behaviors to blame? *Social Science and Medicine* 101:52–60.

Shuler KA (2011) Life and death on a Barbadian sugar plantation: historic and bioarchaeological views of infection and mortality at Newton Plantation. *International Journal of Osteoarchaeology* 21(1):66–81.

Sloane B (2011) *The Black Death in London.* The History Press.

Sparacello VS, Vercellotti G, d'Ercole V, and Coppa A (2017) Social reorganization and biological change: an examination of stature variation among Iron Age Samnites from Abruzzo, Central Italy. *International Journal of Paleopathology* 18:9–20.

Stojanowski CM, Seidemann RM, and Doran GH (2002) Differential skeletal preservation at Wind-over Pond: causes and consequences. *American Journal of Physical Anthropology* 119(1):15–26.

Temple DH and Goodman AH (2014) Bioarcheology has a "health" problem: conceptualizing "stress" and "health" in bioarcheological research. *American Journal of Physical Anthropology* 155(2):186–191.

Trautmann B, Wißing C, Bonilla MD-Z, Bis-Worch C, and Bocherens H (2017) Reconstruction of socioeconomic status in the medieval (14th–15th century) population of Grevenmacher (Luxembourg) based on growth, development and diet. *International Journal of Osteoarchaeology* 27(6):947–957.

Vaupel JW, Manton KG, and Stallard E (1979) The impact of heterogeneity in individual frailty on the dynamics of mortality. *Demography* 16(3):439–454.

Vercellotti G, Stout SD, Boano R, and Sciulli PW (2011) Intrapopulation variation in stature and body proportions: social status and sex differences in an Italian medieval population (Trino Vercellese, Vc). *American Journal of Physical Anthropology* 145(2):203–214.

Watts R (2015) The long-term impact of developmental stress: evidence from later medieval and post-medieval London (AD 1117–1853). *American Journal of Physical Anthropology* 158(4):569–580.

Watts R and Valme S-R (2018) Osteological evidence for juvenile vitamin D deficiency in a 19th century suburban population from Surrey, England. *International Journal of Paleopathology* 23:60–68.

Weston DA (2008) Investigating the specificity of periosteal reactions in pathology museum specimens. *American Journal of Physical Anthropology* 137(1):48–59.

Weston DA (2012) Nonspecific infection in paleopathology: interpreting periosteal reactions. In Grauer AL, editor. *A Companion to Paleopathology.* Wiley-Blackwell. Pp. 492–512.

Willey P, Galloway A, and Snyder L (1997) Bone mineral density and survival of elements and element portions in the bones of the Crow Creek Massacre victims. *American Journal of Physical Anthropology* 104(4):513–528.

Wood JW, Milner GR, Harpending HC, and Weiss KM (1992) The Osteological Paradox: problems of inferring prehistoric health from skeletal samples. *Current Anthropology* 33(4):343–370.

8 Seeing RED

A Novel Solution to a Familiar Categorical Data Problem

Cathy Willermet, John Daniels, Heather J. H. Edgar, and Joseph McKean

Biological anthropologists interested in population interactions compare biological relationships among living populations, among past populations, and between living and past populations. To do this, we utilize datasets that can be compared equivalently across space and time. One such source of data comes from dental morphological traits, nonmetric characteristics observable on the crown surfaces of teeth. Tooth morphology is largely under genetic control and less affected by environmental factors than many other tissue systems (Hillson 1996; Larsen and Kelley 1991; Scott et al. 2018), and therefore presents an effective dataset with which to trace intrapopulation variation, interpopulation relationships, and microevolution.

While the exact mode of inheritance for these dental morphological traits is not well understood, it appears that many of them do not follow a single gene model (Goose and Lee 1971; Harris 1977; Nichol 1989). Despite advances in our understanding of dental development (Jernvall and Jung 2000; Townsend et al. 2012), genetics (Kimura et al. 2009; Thesleff 2006), and heritability (Paul and Stojanowski 2017; Stojanowski et al. 2017, 2018), much is still unknown about the genetics of dental morphological traits. Many of these traits, if present, are continuous in their expression, which suggests that the mode of inheritance may be polygenic or have epigenetic influences (Harris 1977; Mielke et al. 2006; Nichol 1989). Under this model, while the underlying distribution may be unknown or unobservable, the observable pattern of trait expression is quasicontinuous (Scott et al. 2018; Sofaer 1969). That is, the trait can be considered either not observed (absent) or observed (present); if present, it can vary continuously in degree of expression. The point at which the trait is considered "present" is called the trait threshold (Berry 1968; Falconer 1960; Sofaer 1970). In some cases, quasicontinuous traits may be influenced by multiple environmental and genetic factors with additive effects (as in Ossenberg 1970); however, dental morphological traits are thought to be relatively free from environmental influences (Scott et al. 2018).

The Arizona State University Dental Anthropology System standardizes nonmetric dental morphological characteristics observable from crown surfaces of teeth (Scott and Turner 1988; Turner et al. 1991). Some traits, such as cusp number, provide count data. Other variables, for example distosagittal ridge, record presence or absence of a trait. However, for most dental nonmetric traits, such as incisor shoveling and Carabelli's trait, expression has been partitioned into ordinal grade standards. Ordinal data are categorical, and are organized into a logical ordering, such as from small to large. In the Arizona State University Dental Anthropology

System, they represent grades reflecting an increasingly pronounced expression of a trait. By collecting ordinal grade data, researchers can capture patterning of trait expression in a given population. This system is designed to allow researchers to observe the range of expression of a trait, reduce inter- and intra-observer error, and to compare datasets (Buikstra and Ubelaker 1994; Turner et al. 1991). Some misclassification error is inevitable in any system designed to partition a continuously variable trait into grades of expression. While there are situations in which researchers can reasonably disagree regarding an individual's degree of expression, disagreements of one grade may simply represent a difference in how two researchers score an individual whose expression of a trait is intermediate between two grades (Nichol and Turner 1986).

Dental morphological traits indirectly reflect genetic data; as such, they can be used successfully to calculate biological distance between populations. The commonly used statistics mean measure of divergence (MMD) and pseudo-Mahalanobis D^2 (pD^2) both require dichotomization of the ordinal-scale data into trait frequencies. An estimation of Mahalanobis distance can be determined for samples with a combination of continuous and discrete (ordinal) data (Bedrick et al. 2000), but this approach is not applicable for data that are exclusively ordinal. Two areas of concern exist when analyzing dental morphological traits using these statistics. To dichotomize ordinal data, a grade level is identified for each trait as the putative trait threshold (or breakpoint); individual scores below this grade are considered "absent," and those above are considered "present." Ideally, this threshold represents the underlying genetic threshold. Unfortunately, dichotomization significantly compresses the data, when more than two levels of expression have been scored, as is the case for most dental morphological traits. Additional limits include that MMD is sensitive to inter-trait correlation, but somewhat insulated from effects from missing data, as its analyses are based on sample frequencies, and pD^2 is insulated from inter-trait correlations because of the inclusion of a correction term (tetrachoric correlation; see the next section), but it is sensitive to the effects of missing data, as individual-level data points are included in its calculation of trait-by-trait comparisons. So MMD is more sensitive to correlation but less to missing data; pD^2 is more sensitive to missing data and less so for inter-trait correlation.

Data Analysis Issues

Problem 1: Data Compression

Dental anthropologists routinely dichotomize morphological trait data, and then calculate the frequency of a trait's coding as "present." They then use frequencies to calculate biological distance (or biodistance) statistics to compare populations using MMD, pD^2, or both (Bulbeck 2013; Edgar 2002; Haeussler and Turner 1992; Hanihara 1967; Haydenblit 1996; Hubbard et al. 2015; Irish 1993; Irish and Konigsberg 2007; Irish and Turner 1990; Khamis et al. 2006; Lauer 2015; McIlvaine et al. 2014; Passalacqua 2015; Ragsdale 2015; Ragsdale and Edgar 2018; Sofaer et al.

1972; Sutter 2006; Sutter and Sharratt 2010; Taylor and Creel 2012; Thompson et al. 2015; Willermet and Edgar 2009; Willermet et al. 2013). It is a standard practice to dichotomize trait expression utilizing a trait breakpoint to calculate these trait frequencies between populations. While the trait may have an underlying inherited continuity, usually assumed to be normally distributed (Falconer 1960), researchers generally consider the breakpoint as a threshold that imposes some observable discontinuity on the phenotypic expression (Falconer 1981). Ideally, the genetic threshold point is chosen as the breakpoint (Scott et al. 2018), but in reality these thresholds are not known. Unfortunately, the trait breakpoint and the trait threshold do not always match, and we cannot know whether they do. Researchers may choose to use breakpoints used by previous researchers, so that their work may be comparable. As standards for breakpoints have never been agreed upon, a challenge is met when numerous breakpoints can be found for the same trait (Edgar 2017). Alternatively, a researcher may use a breakpoint that more clearly discriminates between the populations under study, even if those individuals subsequently coded as "absent" actually present a clearly observable expression of the trait. While this practice can aid in discrimination between populations (an important and desired result), it could also suggest a greater biological distance than is warranted by the trait expression.

Operationally, all grades above the threshold point are collapsed into "present," and the richness of the collected data is not retained for biodistance analysis. This data compression could mask important biological relationships among and between populations, particularly if two populations are closely related in space or time. For example, at a breakpoint of grade 3, any potentially meaningful differences among the samples in the relative frequencies of higher grades (one group has a relatively high frequency of grade 6 shoveling, while another has mostly grade 3) will not be visible in the analysis. The inconsistency with which researchers apply the breakpoint across their own analyses or those of others makes the data of different studies difficult to compare.

Scott (2008) argues that for quasicontinuous traits, total trait frequencies are the best way to characterize a population; he states: "this one number specifies the entire continuous and normal distribution of the genotypic variation underlying trait expression" (Scott 2008:271). But, he continues, when comparing populations, either total trait frequencies or breakpoint frequencies "are equally useful parameters for characterizing the genetic variation underlying trait expression in a particular group" (Scott 2008:271). He goes on to say: "Although some quantitative method to take all ranks into account might provide information above and beyond total trait frequency … quasicontinuous traits are best characterized by a single frequency as this specifies the nature of the entire normal distribution" (Scott 2008:271).

However, Falconer argues that, "[i]t is possible to assign arbitrary values, 0 and 1, to the two phenotypic classes of a threshold character … to do this is like using the phenotypic expression as a very coarsely graduated instrument … an instrument, in fact, with only one graduation mark. This introduces a large amount of measurement error" (Falconer 1981:275). Some researchers prefer dichotomous categories, arguing that by coding traits as merely present or absent, misclassifications are more rare, particularly when traits are difficult to score (Khamis et al. 2006; Palomino et al. 1977). When a grade system is converted to presence/absence, a one-grade scoring difference can become significant if it occurs at the breakpoint. Misclassification errors around the threshold point are particularly influential, as the difference in one grade can shift an individual's grade from, say, "presence" to "absence." Scott states that "the dividing line between present and absent is always 'fuzzy'" (Scott 2008:284). Nichol and Turner (1986) report that fully one-third of all scoring differences in both their intra- and inter-observer error studies occurred at the breakpoint threshold.

Whatever the motivation, dichotomization does not allow the researcher to capture the variation of trait expression present in a population (Harris 2008). We argue that while threshold frequencies can provide information that can compare populations, the drawbacks to data compression are real. What we lose is the ability to compare populations on the range of variation of the expression of the feature's presence, which might provide additional useful information not held in the threshold point alone.

Problem 2: Data Reduction and Missing Data

Small sample sizes and missing data are inherent problems in bioarchaeological research, which is necessarily limited by preservation and recovery. If an individual can only be used for analysis if data is present for all variables, samples will usually be very small. Missing data therefore can limit the number of usable individuals in a data sample. Small samples due to missing data, then, reduce the amount of statistical assurance that researchers can have in the validity of their results (Irish and Konigsberg 2007; McIlvaine et al. 2014; Stojanowski and Johnson 2015; Ware et al. 2012). Using the pD^2, analyses run on samples with a great deal of missing data will often fail to provide any results, as tetrachoric correlations, which are a component of the pD^2 equation used to adjust for pairwise correlations between characteristics (Konigsberg 1990), cannot be determined if there are zero denominators. As a correction, one might consider imputation or case deletion. Imputation allows replacement of missing data with probability-based data substitutions. Imputing allows calculation of statistics that are not calculable with missing data points. However, any significant proportion of imputed data risks biasing the entire dataset (Barnard and Meng 1999). Case deletion can be done in two ways: omitting individuals missing information for a large number of variables, or omitting variables with many missing values or individuals (Altman and Bland 2007). Case deletion, which is probably more common than imputation, eliminates potentially useful information and results in a weaker statistical model. Data remaining after case deletion may be less representative of the sample as a whole (Irish 2010; Little and Rubin 1987). It also leads to smaller sample sizes in a dataset that is already not large, bringing its own statistical concerns (see Van Arsdale, Chapter 9, this volume).

Another issue with dental morphological data that results in data reduction is inter-trait correlation. Some correlations may be expected, such as the expression of shovel shape on teeth in the same developmental field, such as the maxillary central and lateral incisors and maxillary canines. However, other correlations that are less obvious are often found, such as between Carabelli's cusp on the second maxillary molar and anterior fovea on the first mandibular molar (Edgar 2004). While the biological meanings of such correlations are unclear, statistically, they can inappropriately inflate some distance results while reducing others. Assumptions necessary for the calculation of MMD and pD^2 both affect which traits should be included in any analysis. MMD assumes that traits are uncorrelated; while it is usually desirable to use as many traits as possible in an analysis (Sjøvold 1977), a test of correlation will often result in trait elimination for MMD (Edgar 2004; Irish et al. 2014; Sutter 2006). However, there is no standard for how correlated is too correlated to violate the statistic's assumptions or return poor results (Harris and Sjøvold 2004; Sjøvold 1977). On the other hand, pD^2 makes use of traits that are at least minimally correlated, but cannot be calculated if correlations are too low or too high. If correlations are too low, the matrices can be singular and therefore cannot be rotated. These inter-trait correlations are adjusted in the tetrachoric correlation matrix that is part of the statistic's equation (Edgar 2004; Konigsberg 1990).

Solution: Rank Estimator of Grade Differences (RED)

Here we propose rank estimator of grade differences (RED), an alternative method that solves the limitations discussed above. The motivation for this technique can be found in rank-based inference methods, extending back to the early work by Frank Wilcoxon (1945). A detailed explanation of rank-based estimators is beyond the scope of this chapter, but a recent work by Hettmansperger and McKean (2011) has been adapted to this context (see also the applied text on rank-based analysis by Kloke and McKean [2014]). There is a continued history of development of rank-based methods, but the reader is referred to the recent R packages *Rfit* (Kloke and McKean 2015) and *mvrfit* (Kloke and McKean 2016). These methods are well suited to the analysis of dental morphological traits, and have desired advantages as discussed in the next section. For a more detailed discussion of rank-based methods within this context, see the Appendix.

In essence, RED is an extension of a rank-based multivariate analysis of variance (MANOVA), with an R-written imputation algorithm (AMELIA) at the front end. A rank-based MANOVA allows for trait intercorrelations (Finch and French 2013). The program calculates a distance matrix, from which cluster analysis, principal components, and/or principal coordinates analysis (PCoA) can be performed just like the other conventional methods such as MMD and pD^2.

Advantages of RED. There are four methodological advantages in using RED. First, RED does not suffer from the data compression issues previously mentioned since it compares the grades as ordinal variables and not dichotomized based on arbitrarily selected breakpoints. Second, as it is nonparametric, the distribution requirements are relaxed in that the distribution of the errors may be skewed as well as symmetric and may be heavy-tailed as well as light-tailed. In this chapter, RED uses the default Wilcoxon scores but the analysis can be optimized by prudent score selection. Third, the use of the R imputation algorithm AMELIA can assist with increasing statistical power. Using other methods, if a single observation for a particular subject is missing, the entire row is deleted for analysis. Using AMELIA, important ordinal information is retained without introducing bias into the estimates. Finally, RED is naturally robust to outliers in Y-space, which can actually occur even within an ordinal context. The AMELIA algorithm alerts the user to highly correlated traits and, in extreme cases (less than full-column rank or an unstable-response matrix), the offending variable(s) can be removed before the analysis even begins.

Methods and Materials

Samples

Test 1: Simulated dataset. Simulated data, for which known relationships among populations can be constructed, can be used to evaluate and compare the performance of differing statistical methods (Barbiero and Ferrari 2014; Burton et al. 2006; Nikita 2015). Our simulated dataset was generated using the method outlined by Nikita (2015), who generated simulated observations created from a variance–covariance matrix from a real-world dataset dichotomized from continuous variables. We generated a total of 17,000 multivariate normal observations for three populations using a variance–covariance matrix based on real data from a previous research project that compared pre-European contact Maya, Aztec, and Totonac samples (Willermet et al. 2013). Twelve dental morphological trait variables were generated, with ranges of variation corresponding to the number of grades for that variable. For each trait variable, we examined the percentiles to create the ordinal results (Nikita 2015). We then dichotomized the ordinal data using the breakpoints listed in Table 8.1.

To make the simulated dataset more typical of those we encounter in bioarchaeological analyses, we randomly chose 20 percent of the observations to be missing. This level of missing data is a common outcome in studies using real data. Next, a stratified random sample of $n = 170$ was selected from this population. Resampling was performed 1000 times and the percentage total variation for principal components PC1 and PC2 was recorded. Finally, the mean percentages and standard deviation for PC1 and PC2 using both RED and MMD were calculated and compared. Based on numerous references for previous cultural, historical, and archaeological research (Berdan 2008; Cowgill 2003; Davies 1987; Hicks 2008; Jones 1997; Schroeder 2010; Stark and Arnold 1997), we expected that distance relationships from the simulated data would indicate a closer relationship between the Aztecs and the Totonacs than between the Aztecs and the Maya (Willermet et al. 2013). As pD^2 is sensitive to missing data, we could not calculate it for the simulated dataset.

Table 8.1 Variables used in each analysis, with breakpoints used in MMD and pD^2

Variable	Test 1 MMD, RED	Test 2 MMD, RED	Test 2 pD^2	Absent	Present
Labial curvature, UI1	x		x	0–1	2–4
Shoveling, UI1	x	x	x	0	1–7
Double shoveling, UI1		x		0	1–6
Interruption groove, UI2		x		0	1–4
Distal accessory ridge, UC	x		x	0–1	2–5
Carabelli's trait, UM1	x	x	x	0	1–7
Cusp 5, UM1		x		0	1–5
Hypocone, UM1	x		x	0–1	2–6
Metacone, UM1	x	x	x	0–5	6
Hypocone, UM2		x		0–1	2–6
Metacone, UM2		x		0–5	6
Deflecting wrinkle, LM1	x		x	0–1	2–3
Cusp 5, LM1	x			0–3	4–5
Cusp 6, LM1	x		x	0	1–5
Cusp 7, LM1	x	x	x	0	1–4
Protostylid, LM1	x	x	x	0	1–7
Trigonid crest, LM1		x		0	1
Protostylid, LM2		x		0	1–7

U = maxillary; L = mandibular; I = incisor; C = canine; M = molar

Test 2: American Orthodontic dataset. Edgar collected this dataset from several sources (see Table 8.2; this table also provides group codes for the subsequent tables and figures). All collections were contemporary orthodontic collections. The treating orthodontist recorded population affiliations[1] based on his or her personal knowledge of the patient. Three samples listed group affiliation as African American ($n = 232$), three samples were European American ($n = 190$), and four samples were Hispanic American ($n = 455$). The total sample contained $n = 877$ individuals. A total of 53 traits across several different teeth were collected for this analysis (see Table 8.3). We expected samples from the same putative ancestral group to cluster together, reflecting less biological distance among these samples than between samples from different putative ancestral groups due to their shared migration and population history.

[1] Edgar explained to the treating orthodontists that the topic under study was patterns of local variation, and asked them to describe their patients using whatever words they normally would. The treating orthodontists then provided patient sex, age, and a term that described the patient with words we often use to describe socially ascribed group memberships, such as race, ethnicity, or geographic origin.

Table 8.2 Samples used in Test 2: American orthodontic dataset (*n* = 877)

Collection	Group affiliation	Group source	Group code	Sample *n*
University of Southern California	African American	California	CA AA	65
New York University	African American	New York	NY AA	67
University of Tennessee	African American	Tennessee	TN AA	100
New York University	European American	New York	NY EA	35
Bolton Brush	European American	Ohio	OH EA	54
University of Tennessee	European American	Tennessee	TN EA	101
University of Southern California	Hispanic American	California	CA HA	82
Nova Southeastern	Hispanic American	South Florida	SF HA	202
Economides/Maxwell Museum of Anthropology	Hispanic American	New Mexico	NM HA	91
New York University	Hispanic American	New York	NY HA	80
			TOTAL	877

Table 8.3 Test 2: American orthodontic dataset; list of 53 traits used in the RED analysis

Trait name		
Winging, UI1	Distal sagittal ridge, UP3	Premolar complexity, LP4
Labial curvature, UI1	Tricuspid premolar, UP3	Anterior fovea, LM1
Shoveling, UI1	Tricuspid premolar, UP4	Groove pattern, LM1
Shoveling, UI2	Metacone, UM1	Groove pattern, LM2
Shoveling, UC	Metacone, UM2	Cusp number, LM1
Double shoveling, UI1	Hypocone, UM1	Cusp number, LM2
Double shoveling, UI2	Hypocone, UM2	Deflecting wrinkle, LM1
Peg incisor, UI2	Cusp number, UM1	Protostylid, LM1
Congenital absence, UI2	Cusp number, UM2	Protostylid, LM2
Interruption groove, UI1	Carabelli's trait, UM1	Trigonid crest, LM1
Interruption groove, UI2	Carabelli's trait, UM2	Trigonid crest, LM2
Tuberculum dentale, UI1	Parastyle, UM1	Cusp 5, LM1
Tuberculum dentale, UI2	Parastyle, UM2	Cusp 5, LM2
Tuberculum dentale, UC	Shoveling, LI1	Cusp 6, LM1
Mesial accessory ridge, UC	Shoveling, LI2	Cusp 6, LM2
Distal accessory ridge, UC	Congenital absence, LI1	Cusp 7, LM1
Accessory cusps, UP3	Distal accessory ridge, LC	Cusp 7, LM2
Accessory cusps, UP4	Premolar complexity, LP3	

U = maxillary; L = mandibular; I = incisor; C = canine; P = premolar; M = molar

Determination of Trait Breakpoints and Correlation Tolerances

Both MMD and pD^2 are calculated using frequencies of trait presence. Dental trait frequencies must be converted from multiple ordinal graded categories to dichotomized presence/absence format. We initially examined the raw data for evidence of clear breaks in expression frequency in each trait, and used those scores as breakpoints as noted. Additional breakpoints were drawn primarily from Scott and Turner (1997), with additional reference to Haeussler et al. (1989), Irish (1993), Irish and Turner (1990), and Turner (1987). Table 8.1 shows the breakpoints used in each of the two tests.

In order to meet the assumptions of the MMD, we used a Spearman rank correlation coefficient to discover which traits were over $|0.3|$ correlated; we then removed those traits from the analysis. In order to allow tetrachoric correlations to be calculated, we removed traits from pD^2 if they were less than $|0.05|$ or greater than $|0.95|$ correlated. The pD^2 statistic returns unreliable results when there are too many uncorrelated trait pairs; additionally, traits with correlations too close to 1 or −1 provide redundant information that artificially inflates or deflates intergroup relationships (Edgar 2002).

Statistical Methods

Analytical method: mean measure of divergence (MMD). The MMD statistic is a phenetic dissimilarity measure that anthropologists have used to analyze nonmetric traits for some time (Berry and Berry 1972; Harris and Sjøvold 2004; Irish 2010; Turner 1984). To calculate the MMD, the data are first dichotomized into presence/absence. Then, a count is made of all individuals scored as having the trait, from all individuals in the sample. In this way, the MMD converts dichotomous trait frequencies into a numerical value that estimates biological distance between pairs of samples and quantifies the dissimilarity (Harris and Sjøvold 2004). Care must be taken that traits are not correlated, as this will affect weighting of the underlying dimensions. MMD works best when trait frequencies are mostly between 0.5 and 0.95 (de Souza and Houghton 1977). A major benefit of the MMD is that it can be calculated despite missing data. However, missing data do limit the reliability of results (Irish and Konigsberg 2007; McIlvaine et al. 2014; Stojanowski and Johnson 2015; Ware et al. 2012). After removing traits with lots of missing data, a small subset of the traits remained to be used in MMD analyses (listed in Table 8.1).

We calculated MMD with the Freeman–Tukey correction to test for between-group distances among the samples using the R package AnthropMMD, version 3.1.3 (Santos 2014). While MMD does not have a test of significance, many people use the rule of thumb that significance can be estimated using two-sided Z-scores as MMD/SD, assuming normality (Sołtysiak 2011). We computed Ward's cluster analysis and PCoA of the distances using PAST (Hammer et al. 2001) to visualize results.

Analytical method: Pseudo-Mahalanobis D². The pseudo-Mahalanobis D^2 (pD^2) statistic is another measure of intersample phenetic dissimilarity. It extends the squared Mahalanobis distance for use with dichotomized data by using a tetrachoric correlation matrix. This method converts the individual dichotomized scores into correlations by sample group for use in the Mahalanobis distance statistic. The correlations are pooled by sample size to calculate the weighted average correlation (Irish 2010; Irish and Konigsberg 2007; Konigsberg 1990). Although pD^2 is sensitive to correlated traits, the pD^2 variation adjusts the matrix to minimize over-weighting correlated traits (Irish 2010). As with the MMD, traits with a large amount of missing data could not be analyzed with this method. Traits were removed for that reason and because of very high or low inter-trait correlations, leaving 10 traits to be used in the pD^2 analysis (listed in Table 8.1).

We calculated pD^2 as a statistical measure of distance using an IML program executed through SAS 9.2 (SAS Institute 2009). We then computed Ward's cluster analysis and PCoA of the distances using PAST (Hammer et al. 2001) to create a graphic representation of the results. There is no test of significance associated with pD^2.

Analytical method: rank estimator of grade differences (RED). RED allows for missing data, avoids data compression due to dichotomizing data, and is essentially nonparametric. A RED analysis requires no assumptions regarding the correlation structure of the data. It simply allows the data to be expressed independently, as ordinal data, without any adjustments for a covariance component. The design matrix in Equation 8.2 in the Appendix is an incident matrix and, hence, is bounded. So the rank-based estimates and, subsequently RED, are robust procedures.

We ran the RED analysis on Test 2 (orthodontic dataset) twice: once with the same 11-trait sample as used in the MMD analyses, and once with the full dataset of 53 traits, including traits that were removed from MMD and pD^2 analyses due to inter-trait correlation or missing data points (Table 8.1). The RED program was completed using the *agnes* (agglomerative nesting) function (package: cluster) developed for R version 3.2.5 (R Development Core Team 2015). The script is available at http://pcoplc.cst.cmich.edu/danie1je. We computed PCoA of the distances using Equation 8.2, and then completed the PCoA by calculating the percentage of total variance explained by PC1 and PC2.

Results

Test 1: Simulated Dataset

Analytical method: RED. Figure 8.1 provides the mean PCoA results for the RED analysis of the simulated data with three groups. We expected to see a smaller distance between the Aztecs and the Totonacs than between the Aztecs and the Maya. The first component, PC1, which explains a similar percentage (76.4 percent) and lower standard deviation (11.07 percent), separates the Aztecs from the Maya, with the Totonacs in between. On PC2 (23.6 percent of the variance) the Totonacs are separated from the Aztecs and Maya. This outcome is also supported by the RED distance matrix (Table 8.4), which reports the Aztec–Totonac distance as the smallest distance. Ward's cluster analysis of the RED results (Figure 8.2) reports an agglomerative coefficient of 0.11.

Table 8.4 Test 1: Simulated dataset; comparison of mean PCoA results from resampling

	RED analysis		
	Aztec	Totonac	Maya
Aztec	0	6.338	7.758
Totonac	6.338	0	6.800
Maya	7.758	6.800	0
	MMD analysis		
	Aztec	Totonac	Maya
Aztec	0	0.086	0.066
Totonac	0.086	0	0.078
Maya	0.066	0.078	0

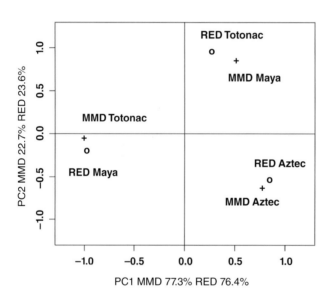

Figure 8.1 Test 1: Simulated dataset. MMD and RED principal coordinate analysis results.

Analytical method: MMD. Figure 8.1 also provides the mean PCoA results for the MMD analysis of the simulated data with three groups. Our expectation, based on the simulated dataset, was to see a closer relationship between the Aztecs and the Totonacs than between the Aztecs and the Maya. The first component, PC1 (77.3 percent of the variance), separates the Totonac population from the Aztec and Maya populations. On PC2 (22.7 percent of the variance), the Aztecs are separated from the Maya, with the Totonac population in between. The standard deviation for averaged PCoA values is 12.09 percent. The mean distance matrix (Table 8.4) reports that the Aztec–Totonac distance is the largest. Ward's cluster analysis of the MMD results (Figure 8.3) reports an agglomerative coefficient of 0.57. This finding deviates from our expectation that the Aztec–Totonac distance would be the smallest.

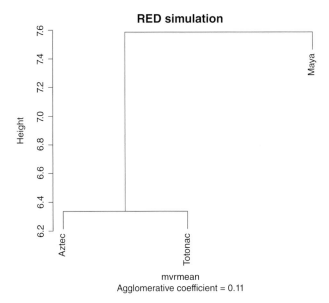

Figure 8.2 Test 1: Simulated dataset. Cluster analysis of RED results.

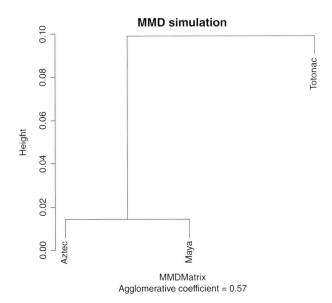

Figure 8.3 Test 1: Simulated dataset. Cluster analysis of MMD results.

Test 2: American Orthodontic Dataset

Analytical method: RED. Table 8.5 provides the dissimilarity matrix from the RED application to the restricted sample of 12 traits. There are values of 0, essentially no differences, between several pairs: California African Americans and New York African Americans; Ohio European Americans and New York European Americans;

Table 8.5 Test 2: American orthodontic dataset; RED results for 12 traits

	NY AA	CA AA	TN AA	OH EA	NY EA	TN EA	CA HA	NY HA	NM HA	SF HA
NY AA	0	0	627.390	85.340	85.300	651.960	52.470	132.740	52.470	52.470
CA AA	0	0	627.390	85.340	85.300	651.970	52.470	132.740	52.470	52.470
TN AA	627.390	627.390	0	598.680	598.650	18.660	688.190	660.330	688.190	688.190
OH EA	85.340	85.340	598.680	0	0	589.490	118.440	61.830	118.440	118.440
NY EA	85.300	85.300	598.650	0	0	589.510	118.410	61.790	118.410	118.410
TN EA	651.960	651.970	18.660	589.490	589.510	0	703.430	679.160	703.430	703.430
CA HA	52.470	52.470	688.190	118.440	118.410	703.430	0	70.240	0	0
NY HA	132.740	132.740	660.330	61.830	61.790	679.160	70.240	0	70.240	70.240
NM HA	52.470	52.470	688.190	118.440	118.410	703.430	0	70.240	0	0
SF HA	52.470	52.470	688.190	118.440	118.410	703.430	0	70.240	0	0

See Table 8.2 for group codes.

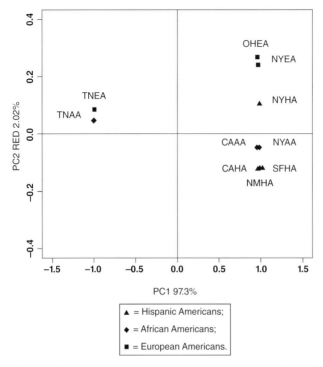

Figure 8.4 Test 2: American orthodontic dataset. Principal coordinate analysis of RED results using 12 traits.

California Hispanic Americans and New Mexico Hispanic Americans; California Hispanic Americans and South Florida Hispanic Americans; and New Mexico Hispanic Americans and South Florida Hispanic Americans. The largest distance (703.430) is seen between Tennessee European Americans and Hispanic Americans from California, New Mexico, and San Francisco. As these three Hispanic groups have 0 distance among them (see above), they should share equal distances with other groups. Figure 8.4 provides the PCoA results for this matrix. The Tennessee samples are clearly separated from all other groups on PC1 (97.3 percent of the variance). On PC2 (2.02 percent of the variance), three of the Hispanic American groups appear on one end, African Americans in the center, and European Americans on the other end; New York Hispanic Americans are grouped with the Tennessee samples. Collectively the first two components account for 99 percent of the total variance. In addition, using a Bonferroni adjustment, pairwise comparisons using Equation 8.1 in the Appendix were calculated. The Ward's cluster analysis of the RED results for 12 traits (Figure 8.5) reports an agglomerative coefficient of 0.99.

Table 8.6 provides the dissimilarity matrix results for the analysis with all 53 traits. Here, the smallest distance is seen between California and New York Hispanic Americans (13.090) and the largest is between California Hispanic Americans and New York European Americans (1850.300). While the magnitude of the distance seems large, this is an artifact of analyzing all 53 traits. The RED analysis is

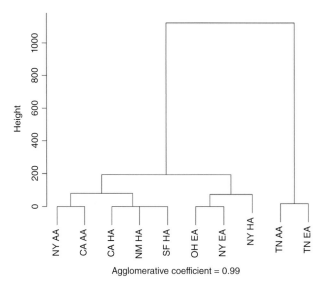

Figure 8.5 Test 2: American orthodontic dataset. Cluster analysis of RED results using 12 traits.

essentially reacting to the overparameterized model, which causes instability. Figure 8.6 provides the PCoA results for this matrix. The Tennessee samples are separated from the other samples on PC1 (53.5 percent of the variance); the remainder of the samples spread out with European Americans on the left, Hispanic Americans on the right, and African Americans between. On PC2 (40.2 percent of the variance), samples reflect three groups. The Hispanic Americans from all samples save California are separated from the rest, and the Tennessee samples are intermediate. Collectively, the first two components account for 93.7 percent of the total variance. The Ward's cluster analysis of the RED results for 53 traits (Figure 8.7) reports an agglomerative coefficient of 0.93. The Tennessee samples remain distinct here. African American and European American samples are grouped together, with the California Hispanic Americans between them. The other three Hispanic samples, from New Mexico, South Florida, and New York, cluster closely together.

Analytical method: MMD. Table 8.7 lists the results of the MMD analysis. The largest distance is between South Florida Hispanic Americans and Tennessee European Americans (0.217). There are several pairs of samples with negative MMD values, indicating that the samples do not come from discernibly different populations: California African Americans and New York African Americans; California Hispanic Americans and New Mexico Hispanic Americans; California Hispanic Americans and New York Hispanic Americans; New York Hispanic Americans and New York European Americans; and Ohio European Americans and New York European Americans. Figure 8.8 provides the PCoA results. Over half of the variance (52.2 percent) on PC1 tightly groups almost all of the Hispanic American groups with California African Americans and New York European Americans, and less closely groups them with Tennessee African Americans, and Ohio European Americans. Separately, New York African Americans, New York Hispanic Americans, and

Table 8.6 Test 2: American orthodontic dataset; RED results for 53 traits

	NY AA	CA AA	TN AA	OH EA	NY EA	TN EA	CA HA	NY HA	NM HA	SF HA
NY AA	0	1240.960	1183.500	958.560	183.340	1122.750	2117.480	2017.320	1420.090	1801.900
CA AA	1240.960	0	13.200	673.090	1279.930	277.060	966.400	949.130	178.660	881.100
TN AA	1183.500	13.200	0	705.750	1283.880	287.060	994.070	956.400	215.920	889.840
OH EA	958.560	673.090	705.750	0	720.280	404.880	1332.490	1336.170	614.670	1167.160
NY EA	183.340	1279.930	1283.880	720.280	0	971.210	1850.300	1819.880	1236.030	1731.450
TN EA	1122.750	277.060	287.060	404.880	971.210	0	991.110	964.730	268.260	825.180
CA HA	2117.480	966.400	994.070	1332.490	1850.300	991.110	0	13.090	842.290	170.000
NY HA	2017.320	949.130	956.400	1336.170	1819.880	964.730	13.090	0	851.020	151.860
NM HA	1420.090	178.660	215.920	614.670	1236.030	268.260	842.290	851.020	0	915.170
SF HA	1801.900	881.100	889.840	1167.160	1731.450	825.180	170.000	151.860	915.170	0

See Table 8.2 for group codes.

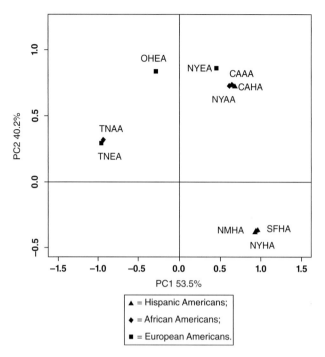

Figure 8.6 Test 2: American orthodontic dataset. Principal coordinate analysis of RED results using 53 traits.

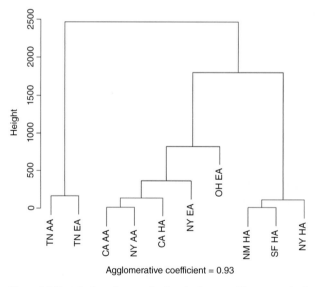

Figure 8.7 Test 2: American orthodontic dataset. Cluster analysis of RED results using 53 traits.

Tennessee European Americans are grouped together. On PC2 (31.9 percent of the variance), California African Americans and New York European Americans are separated from the rest of the samples. Together, the first two components account for 84.1 percent of the total variance. The Ward's cluster analysis of the MMD results (Figure 8.9) reports an agglomerative coefficient of 0.77. There are some unexpected

Table 8.7 Test 2: American orthodontic dataset; MMD results for 12 traits

	CA AA	CA HA	NM HA	NY AA	NY EA	NY HA	OH EA	SF HA	TN AA	TN EA
CA AA	0	0.066	0.112	-0.021	0.075	0.044	0.137	0.094	0.076	0.171
CA HA	0.066	0	-0.007	0.076	0.016	-0.014	0.085	0.076	0.023	0.084
NM HA	0.112	-0.007	0	0.098	-0.001	0.005	0.056	0.053	0.030	0.102
NY AA	-0.021	0.076	0.098	0	0.058	0.039	0.136	0.055	0.076	0.183
NY EA	0.075	0.016	-0.001	0.058	0	0.044	-0.029	0.059	0.064	0.014
NY HA	0.044	-0.014	0.005	0.039	0.044	0	0.125	0.054	0.009	0.125
OH EA	0.137	0.085	0.056	0.136	-0.029	0.125	0	0.110	0.094	0.032
SF HA	0.094	0.076	0.053	0.055	0.059	0.054	0.110	0	0.057	0.217
TN AA	0.076	0.023	0.030	0.076	0.064	0.009	0.094	0.057	0	0.118
TN EA	0.171	0.084	0.102	0.183	0.014	0.125	0.032	0.217	0.118	0

See Table 8.2 for group codes.

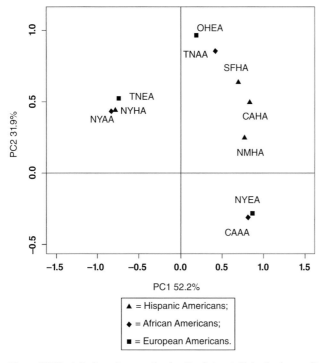

Figure 8.8 Test 2: American orthodontic dataset. Principal coordinate analysis of MMD results using 12 traits.

clusters, such as New York African Americans and Ohio European Americans, while other clusters are perhaps less surprising, such as the cluster of California Hispanic Americans and South Florida Hispanic Americans.

Analytical method: Pseudo-Mahalanobis D^2. Table 8.8 lists the results of the pseudo-Mahalanobis D^2 analysis. The smallest distance is between California and New Mexico Hispanic Americans (0.372); the largest distance is between New York European Americans and Tennessee African Americans (10.818). Figure 8.10 provides the PCoA results; PC1 (73.9 percent of the variance) groups all of the Hispanic

Table 8.8 Test 2: American orthodontic dataset; pseudo-Mahalanobis D^2 results for 10 traits

	CA AA	NY AA	TN AA	NY EA	OH EA	TN EA	CA HA	FL HA	NM HA	NY HA
CA AA	0	0.963	7.731	2.207	3.725	5.807	2.498	3.256	2.121	2.998
NY AA	0.963	0	5.670	3.839	4.252	5.461	3.567	2.034	3.037	3.075
TN AA	7.731	5.670	0	10.818	9.915	3.916	9.442	8.079	9.914	8.957
NY EA	2.207	3.839	10.818	0	1.670	6.426	2.375	2.616	2.225	4.377
OH EA	3.725	4.252	9.915	1.670	0	4.687	4.620	3.419	4.815	6.675
TN EA	5.807	5.461	3.916	6.426	4.687	0	6.475	7.827	7.126	6.614
CA HA	2.498	3.567	9.442	2.375	4.620	6.475	0	3.204	0.372	2.240
FL HA	3.256	2.034	8.079	2.616	3.419	7.827	3.204	0	3.042	4.587
NM HA	2.121	3.037	9.914	2.225	4.815	7.126	0.372	3.042	0	1.111
NY HA	2.998	3.075	8.957	4.377	6.675	6.614	2.240	4.587	1.111	0

See Table 8.2 for group codes.

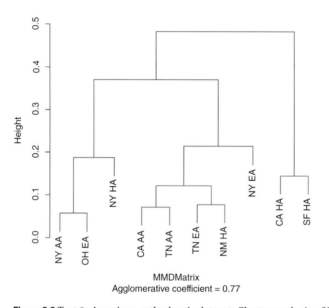

MMDMatrix
Agglomerative coefficient = 0.77

Figure 8.9 Test 2: American orthodontic dataset. Cluster analysis of MMD results using 12 traits.

American groups with California African Americans, Ohio European Americans, and New York African Americans and European Americans. The two groups from Tennessee form a widely spread group on the right. On PC2 (14.1 percent of the variance), the European Americans are separated from the Hispanic Americans; the African Americans fall in the middle of the Hispanic American range. The first two components account for 88 percent of the total variance. The Ward's cluster analysis of the pD^2 results (Figure 8.11) reports an agglomerative coefficient of 0.85, and reflects the two Tennessee groups as being quite different than all the other samples.

Discussion

In both tests, RED performed as well as or better than the traditional methods in reflecting the results expected from known relationships created by the simulated

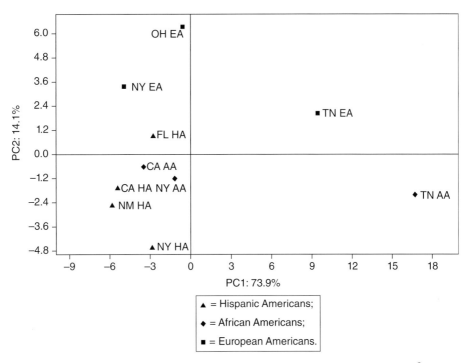

Figure 8.10 Test 2: American orthodontic dataset. Principal coordinate analysis of pD^2 results using 10 traits.

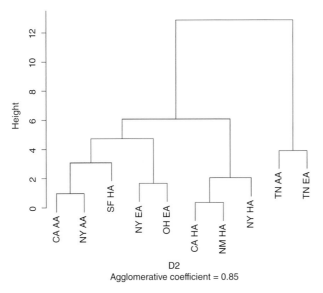

Figure 8.11 Test 2: American orthodontic dataset. Cluster analysis of pD^2 results using 10 traits.

dataset (Test 1) and those hypothesized based on historical and archaeological evidence (Test 2). In Test 1, the pattern of RED results shows the distance between the Aztec and the Totonac to be less than the distance between the Aztec and the Maya, meeting the expectation based on previous research. The MMD result indicates an unexpected relationship; the Maya are more similar to Aztec and Totonac samples than either of these is similar to the other. Additionally, RED results had a smaller standard deviation, and the first PC explained more of the variation, simplifying interpretation.

Considerable historical and archaeological evidence informs our hypotheses about putative biological relationships expected in Test 2. While all of the Test 2 analyses generally group the Hispanic American samples, regardless of their geographic origin, MMD conforms to these hypothesized relationships the least. These results are similar to previous analysis of these same samples (Edgar 2013). The relationship of the African Americans to the European American and Hispanic American samples is less clear. Overall, however, RED outperforms MMD and pD^2 in Test 2. The combined explanatory power of PC1 and PC2, which represents our accumulated knowledge of the sample variation, is greater for each of the RED plots than in the MMD or pD^2 plot. Both MMD and pD^2 fairly closely group Hispanic Americans, African Americans, and European Americans in a way that aggregates samples with similar population histories. The expected separation of the three ancestral groups can only be seen on PC2, particularly for pD^2 and RED using 12 traits, and less so for RED using 53 traits.

The RED analysis of 12 traits groups Hispanic Americans and coastal African Americans in a way that is unexpected, but does a good job of indicating expected differences between the three populations on PC2. However, the true value of RED is in the analysis of 53 traits, an analysis that is not possible with pD^2 or advisable with MMD. Results show European Americans, African Americans, and Hispanic Americans separated from left to right along PC1 (with the exception of Tennessee African Americans; the Tennessee samples are anomalous in all of the analyses). Further biodistance information is provided by PC2, which places California and New York African Americans at the top of the graph, separated from the non-California Hispanic Americans. We obtained these results using the full suite of traits, without data compression from dichotomization or data reduction to remove missing data.

Nonmetric traits are extensively used in paleoanthropology, bioarchaeology, and forensic anthropology as a way to capture the degree of variation in study samples, as representatives of larger populations. We are normally limited to MMD, pD^2, and other techniques that similarly require dichotomization to compare trait frequencies between these populations, which require trait dichotomization for analysis. When we compress data, we lose information about the variation within dichotomous categories. Using the RED technique, data are not compressed into dichotomous variables. A major benefit to these fields is an improvement in our ability to utilize multistate, rather than dichotomous, information about the variation in our population samples. If dental morphological traits are indeed polygenic, the variation of trait expression may provide important information on genetic relationships between populations. This complexity simply is not fully captured by dichotomous trait frequency data (Mayhall 1999).

In fact, Nikita (2015) raises similar points regarding the use of dichotomized distance statistics (MMD and different versions of Mahalanobis D^2). Her COMD (corrected ordinal Mahalanobis distance) also performs well with ordinal data. Bedrick and colleagues (2000) discuss difficulties with estimating distance using mixed continuous interval and categorical ordinal data. They point out that until their work there were "no standard approaches to measuring distance using data that are a mixture of quantitative and qualitative characteristics" (Bedrick et al. 2000:394). They suggest a modification of Mahalanobis distance for such a mixed-case scenario. In another approach, Cucina (2015) utilizes multistate ordinal data analysis techniques instead of dichotomizing data. For some traits, he defines several ranges of expression for a single trait, and analyzes them as separate variables. To understand population relationships, some researchers avoid biological distance statistics altogether, making use of such tools as unweighted pair group method with arithmetic mean (UPGMA) for comparing samples (Cucina 2015; Scott et al. 2013; Sokal and Michener 1958) or correspondence analysis (Lukacs and Kuswandari 2013; Sciulli 1990). Our results underscore the importance of exploring the use of all these new statistical methods, including RED, for our multivariate ordinal datasets.

Our new analytic technique, RED, provides a method that does not require data compression in the form of dichotomization or reduction of categories. It is robust without data reduction in the face of the kind of missing data common in bioarchaeology, paleoanthropology, and forensic anthropology. It is a valuable addition to our toolkit of biological distance statistics commonly used today. As it is a technique for analyzing ordinal data, it could be useful for analysis of paleopathological data on lesion severity, cranial nonmetrics, and other categorical data widely used in biological anthropology research.

Acknowledgments

Data on contemporary casts were collected from orthodontic collections housed at New York University, the University of Tennessee, the University of Southern California, Bolton Brush/Case Western Reserve University, Nova Southeastern University, and the University of New Mexico Maxwell Museum. Corey Ragsdale and Alexis O'Donnell provided statistical support. Data collection for Test 2 took place under several protocols approved at the University of New Mexico's Institutional Review Board. Grant sponsorship: University of Tennessee Forensic Sciences Center. We thank Marin Pilloud, Sharon DeWitte, and several anonymous reviewers for their insights and suggestions during the preparation of this manuscript. CW, JD, and HJHE designed the study, analyzed the data, and drafted the manuscript. HJHE collected the data. JD and JM wrote the RED program.

Appendix

Suppose we have k groups and within the jth group, $j = 1, \ldots, k$, we have a sample of size n_j. For each subject a d-dimensional vector of variables has been recorded. Let y_{ijl} represent the response for the ith subject in the jth group for the lth variable and let yij = $(y_{ij1}, \ldots, y_{ijl})^{\mathrm{T}}$ denote the vector of responses for the subject. First, consider the univariate cell means model,

$$y_{ij} = v_{j+}\varepsilon_{ij} \quad j = 1, \ldots k, i = 1, \ldots, n_k, \tag{8.1}$$

where ε_{ij} are independent and identically distributed. Now, let $Y_{n \times \mathrm{d}}$ represent the matrix of responses in which the y_{ij} are stacked sequentially by group and let ε be the corresponding $n \times d$ matrix of e_{ij}. Let $\Gamma = (\mu_1, \ldots, \mu_k)$ be the $k \times$ d matrix of parameters. We can then express this model as

$$\mathbf{Y} = \mathbf{W}\mathbf{\Gamma} + \mathbf{\varepsilon}, \tag{8.2}$$

where W is the incident matrix indicating group membership and Γ is the $k \times d$ matrix of regression parameters to be estimated. This is the full model and is the multivariate analog of the basic one-way design. It should also be noted that the parameters of this model are invariant to the choice of location functional. If μ_i is the mean of Y_{ij}, then this is the means model (Hocking 1985). If μ_i is the median of Y_{ij}, then it is the medians model. Once this model has been created and validated, any linear hypotheses of interest may be tested. For example, as discussed by Kloke and McKean (2016), a general hypothesis is given by

$$H_0 : \mathbf{M}\mathbf{\Gamma}\mathbf{K} = \mathbf{0} \text{ versus } H_A : \mathbf{M}\mathbf{\Gamma}\mathbf{K} \neq \mathbf{0}, \tag{8.3}$$

where M is q $\times$ k of rank r and K is a $d \times s$ matrix of rank s. The choice of M and K provides for a wide range of reduced model tests, including contrasts (pairwise comparisons of groups), significance of individual parameters, and the significance of any linear combination of either within-group and/or across-group parameters. This α level test has been shown to be an asymptotic χ^2 test and calculated by:

$$Q = \mathrm{tr}\left\{ \left[\mathbf{M}\hat{B}\mathbf{K}\right]^{\mathrm{T}} \left[\mathbf{M}(\mathbf{X}^{\mathrm{T}}\mathbf{X})^{-1}\mathbf{M}^{\mathrm{T}}\right]^{-1} \mathbf{M}\hat{B}\mathbf{K} \left[\mathbf{K}^{\mathrm{T}}\hat{T}\,\hat{\Sigma}\hat{T}\,\mathbf{K}\right]^{-1} \right\} \tag{8.4}$$

Reject H_0 in favor of H_A if $Q \geq \chi^2$ (α , qs), where $\hat{\beta}$ estimates Γ, $\hat{\Sigma}$ is the variance–covariance of ε, and $\hat{T}$ is the scale parameter. In a least squares based context, Equation 8.4 is similar to the traditional Lawley–Hotelling test.

In essence, RED is an extension of a rank-based multivariate analysis of variance (MANOVA), with an R-written imputation algorithm (AMELIA) at the front end. A rank-based MANOVA allows for trait intercorrelations (Finch and French 2013). In testing for simultaneous pairwise group relationships, a Bonferroni adjustment could be considered as part of the one-way MANOVA. Also, a natural distance matrix could be the equivalent of the conventional Mahalanobis distance. Let $\hat{\beta}$ represent the p $\times$ 1 vector of rank-based estimators of the MANOVA coefficients and *sigma* represent the variance–covariance matrix of the rank-based estimators. Then, we can define *diss(i,j)*, the distance between group *i* and group *j*, as:

$$diss(i,j) = beta^T(sigma)^{-1}beta. \tag{8.5}$$

From this distance matrix, cluster analysis and PCoA can be performed just like the other conventional methods (i.e., MMD and pD^2).

References

Altman DG and Bland JM (2007) Missing data. *British Medical Journal* 334(7590):424.

Barbiero A and Ferrari PA (2014) Simulating correlated ordinal and discrete variables with assigned marginal distributions. In Melas VB, Mignani S, Monari P, and Salmaso L, editors. *Topics in Statistical Simulation*. Springer Science & Business Media. Pp. 37–46.

Barnard J and Meng XL (1999) Applications of multiple imputation in medical studies: from AIDS to NHANES. *Statistical Methods in Medical Research* 8(1):17–36.

Bedrick EJ, Lapidus J, and Powell JF (2000) Estimating the Mahalanobis distance from mixed continuous and discrete data. *Biometrics* 56(2):394–401.

Berdan FF (2008) Concepts of ethnicity and class in Aztec-period Mexico. In Berdan FF, Chance JK, Sandstrom AR, et al., editors. *Ethnic Identity in Nahua Mesoamerica: The View from Archaeology, Art History, Ethnohistory, and Contemporary Ethnography*. The University of Utah Press. Pp. 105–132.

Berry AC and Berry RJ (1972) Origins and relationships of the ancient Egyptians: based on a study of non-metrical variations in the skull. *Journal of Human Evolution* 1(2):199–208.

Berry RJ (1968) The biology of non-metrical variation in mice and men. In Brothwell DR, editor. *Skeletal Biology of Earlier Human Populations*. Pergamon Press. Pp. 103–133.

Buikstra JE and Ubelaker DS, editors (1994) *Standards for Data Collection From Human Skeletal Remains*. Arkansas Archaeological Survey.

Bulbeck D (2013) Craniodental affinities of Southeast Asia's "Negritos" and the concordance with their genetic affinities. *Human Biology* 85(1–3):95–133.

Burton A, Altman DG, Royston P, and Holder RL (2006) The design of simulation studies in medical statistics. *Statistics in Medicine* 25:4279–4292.

Cowgill GL (2003) Teotihuacan and early Classic interaction: a perspective from outside the Maya region. In Braswell GE, editor. *The Maya and Teotihuacan: Reinterpreting Early Classic Interaction*. University of Texas Press. Pp. 315–335.

Cucina A (2015) Population dynamics during the Classic and Postclassic Maya in the northern Maya lowlands: the analysis of dental morphological traits. In Cucina A, editor. *Archaeology and Bioarchaeology of Population Movement among the Prehispanic Maya*. Springer. Pp. 71–83.

Davies N (1987) *The Toltecs: Until the Fall of Tula*. University of Oklahoma Press.

de Souza P and Houghton P (1977) The mean measure of divergence and the use of non-metric data in the estimation of biological distances. *Journal of Archaeological Science* 4(2):163–169.

Edgar HJH (2002) *Biological Distance and the African American Dentition* (PhD dissertation). The Ohio State University.

Edgar HJH (2004) Dentitions, distance, and difficulty: a comparison of two statistical techniques for dental morphological data. *Dental Anthropology Journal* 17(2):55–62.

Edgar HJH (2013) Estimation of ancestry using dental morphological characteristics. *Journal of Forensic Sciences* 58(s1):s3–s8.

Edgar HJH (2017) *Dental Morphology for Anthropology: An Illustrated Manual*. Routledge.

Falconer DS (1960) *Introduction to Quantitative Genetics*. The Ronald Press Company.

Falconer DS (1981) *Introduction to Quantitative Genetics*, 2nd edition. Longman.

Finch H and French B (2013) A Monte Carlo comparison of robust MANOVA test statistics. *Journal of Modern Applied Statistical Methods* 12(2):35–81.

Goose DH and Lee GTR (1971) The mode of inheritance of Carabelli's trait. *Human Biology* 43(1):64–69.

Haeussler AM and Turner CG II (1992) The dentition of Soviet central Asians and the quest for New World ancestors. *Culture, Ecology, and Dental Anthropology, Journal of Human Ecology* (Special Issue) 2:273–297.

Haeussler AM, Irish JD, Morris DH, and Turner CG II (1989) Morphological and metrical comparison of San and central Sotho dentition from southern Africa. *American Journal of Physical Anthropology* 78(1):115–122.

Hammer Ø, Harper DAT, and Ryan PD (2001) PAST: Paleontological statistics software package for education and data analysis. *Palaeontologica Electronica* 4(1):9. http://palaeo-electronica.org/2001_1/past/issue1_01.htm.

Hanihara K (1967) Racial characteristics in the dentition. *Journal of Dental Research* 46(5):923–926.

Harris EF (1977) *Anthropologic and Genetic Aspects of the Dental Morphology of Solomon Islanders, Melanesia* (PhD dissertation). Arizona State University.

Harris EF (2008) Statistical applications in dental anthropology. In Irish JD and Nelson GC, editors. *Technique and Application in Dental Anthropology.* Cambridge University Press. Pp. 35–67.

Harris EF and Sjøvold T (2004) Calculation of Smith's mean measure of divergence for intergroup comparisons using nonmetric data. *Dental Anthropology Journal* 17(3):83–96.

Haydenblit R (1996) Dental variation among four prehispanic Mexican populations. *American Journal of Physical Anthropology* 100(2):225–246.

Hettmansperger TP and McKean JW (2011) *Robust Nonparametric Statistical Methods*, 2nd edition. Chapman-Hall.

Hicks F (2008) Mexica political history. In Brumfiel EM and Feinman GM, editors. *The Aztec World.* Abrams Press. Pp. 5–21.

Hillson S (1996) *Dental Anthropology.* Cambridge University Press.

Hocking R (1985) *The Analysis of Linear Models.* Brooks/Cole.

Hubbard AR, Guatelli-Steinberg D, and Irish JD (2015) Do nuclear DNA and dental nonmetric data produce similar reconstructions of regional population history? An example from modern coastal Kenya. *American Journal of Physical Anthropology* 157(2):295–304.

Irish JD (1993) *Biological Affinities of Late Pleistocene Through Modern African Aboriginal Populations: The Dental Evidence.* PhD dissertation. Arizona State University.

Irish JD (2010) The mean measure of divergence: its utility in model-free and model-bound analyses relative to the Mahalanobis D^2 distance for nonmetric traits. *American Journal of Human Biology* 22(3):378–395.

Irish JD and Konigsberg L (2007) The ancient inhabitants of Jebel Moya redux: measures of population affinity based on dental morphology. *International Journal of Osteoarcheology* 17(2):138–156.

Irish JD and Turner CG II (1990) West African dental affinity of late Pleistocene Nubians: peopling of the Eurafrican–South Asian triangle II. *HOMO: Journal of Comparative Human Biology* 41(1):42–53.

Irish JD, Black W, Sealy J, and Rogers Ackermann R (2014) Questions of Khoesan continuity: dental affinities among the indigenous Holocene peoples of South Africa. *American Journal of Physical Anthropology* 155(1):33–44.

Jernvall J and Jung H-S (2000) Genotype, phenotype, and developmental biology of molar tooth characters. *Yearbook of Physical Anthropology* 43:171–190.

Jones L (1997) Conquests of the imagination: Maya–Mexican polarity and the story of Chichén Itzá. *American Anthropologist* 99(2):275–290.

Khamis MF, Taylor JA, Samsudin AR, and Townsend GC (2006) Variation in dental crown morphology in Malaysian populations. *Dental Anthropology Journal* 19(2):49–60.

Kimura R, Yamaguchi T, Takeda M, et al. (2009) A common variation in EDAR is a genetic determinant of shovel-shaped incisors. *American Journal of Human Genetics* 85(4):528–535.

Kloke J and McKean J (2014) *Nonparametric Statistical Methods using R.* Chapman-Hall.

Kloke J and McKean J (2015) Rfit: rank estimation for linear models. *The R Journal* 4:10.32614/RJ-2012-014.

Kloke J and McKean J (2016) Working manual for Mvrfit. http://people.cst.cmich.edu/daniel1je.

Konigsberg LW (1990) Analysis of prehistoric biological variation under a model of isolation by geographic and temporal distance. *Human Biology* 62(1):49–70.

Larsen CS and Kelley MA (1991) Introduction. In Kelley MA and Larsen CS, editors. *Advances in Dental Anthropology.* Wiley-Liss. Pp. 1–7.

Lauer A (2015) *Biological Relationships Across the Taiwan Strait: Evidence from Skulls and Teeth* (PhD dissertation). University of Hawai'i.

Little RJA and Rubin DB (1987) *Statistical Analysis with Missing Data.* Wiley.

Lukacs JR and Kuswandari S (2013) Crown morphology of Malay deciduous teeth: trait frequencies and biological affinities. In Scott GR and Irish JD, editors. *Anthropological Perspectives on Tooth Morphology: Genetics, Evolution, Variation.* Cambridge University Press. Pp. 453–478.

Mayhall JT (1999) Dichotomy in human dental morphology: a plea for complexity. In Mayhall JT and Heikkenen T, editors. *Dental Morphology 98.* Oulu University Press. Pp. 43–47.

McIlvaine BK, Schepartz LA, Larsen CS, and Sciulli PW (2014) Evidence for long-term migration on the Balkan Peninsula using dental and cranial nonmetric data: early interaction between Corinth (Greece) and its colony at Apollonia (Albania). *American Journal of Physical Anthropology* 153(2):236–248.

Mielke JH, Konigsberg LW, and Relethford JH, editors (2006) *Human Biological Variation.* Oxford University Press.

Nichol CR (1989) Complex segregation analysis of dental morphological variants. *American Journal of Physical Anthropology* 78(1):37–59.

Nichol CR and Turner CG II (1986) Intra- and inter-observer concordance in classifying dental morphology. *American Journal of Physical Anthropology* 69(3):299–315.

Nikita E (2015) A critical review of the mean measure of divergence and Mahalanobis distances using artificial data and new approaches to the estimations of biodistances employing nonmetric traits. *American Journal of Physical Anthropology* 157(2):284–294.

Ossenberg NS (1970) The influence of artificial cranial deformation on discontinuous morphological traits. *American Journal of Physical Anthropology* 33(3):357–371.

Palomino H, Chakraborty R, and Rothhammer F (1977) Dental morphology and population diversity. *Human Biology* 49(1):61–70.

Passalacqua KZ (2015) *An Investigation of Late Woodland and Mississippian Biological Relationships Using Odontometric and Dental Non-Metric Trait Analyses* (PhD dissertation). Indiana University.

Paul K and Stojanowski CM (2017). Comparative performance of deciduous and permanent dental morphology in detecting biological relatives. *American Journal of Physical Anthropology* 164(1):97–116.

Ragsdale CS (2015) *Cultural Interaction and Biological Distance among Postclassic Mexican Populations* (PhD dissertation). University of New Mexico.

Ragsdale CS and Edgar HJH (2018) Population continuity and replacement in the pre-contact valley of Mexico. In Willermet C and Cucina A, editors. *Bioarchaeology of Pre-Columbian Mesoamerica: An Interdisciplinary Approach.* University Press of Florida. Pp. 39–69.

R Development Core Team (2015) *A Language and Environment for Statistical Computing.* R Foundation for Statistical Computing. www.R-project.org.

Santos F (2014) Package "AnthropMMD": a GUI for mean measures of divergence. http://cran.r-project.org.

SAS Institute (2009) SAS® 9.2 software. http://support.sas.com/software/92.

Schroeder S (2010) The Mexico that Spain encountered. In Beezley WH and Meyer MC, editors. *The Oxford History of Mexico.* Oxford University Press. Pp. 45–72.

Sciulli PW (1990) Deciduous dentition of a Late Archaic population of Ohio. *Human Biology* 62(2):221–245.

Scott GR (2008) Dental morphology. In Katzenberg MA and Saunders SR, editors. *Biological Anthropology of the Human Skeleton,* 2nd edition. Wiley. Pp. 265–298.

Scott GR and Turner CG II (1988) Dental anthropology. *Annual Review of Anthropology* 17:99–126.

Scott GR and Turner CG II (1997) *The Anthropology of Modern Human Teeth: Dental Morphology and its Variation in Recent Human Populations.* Cambridge University Press.

Scott GR, Anta A, Schomberg R, and de la Rúa C (2013) Basque dental morphology and the "Eurodont" dental pattern. In Scott GR and Irish JD, editors. *Anthropological Perspectives on Tooth Morphology: Genetics, Evolution, Variation.* Cambridge University Press. Pp. 296–318.

Scott GR, Turner CG II, Townsend Grant C, and Martinón-Torres, M (2018) *The Anthropology of Modern Human Teeth: Dental Morphology and Its Variation in Recent and Fossil Homo sapiens,* 2nd edition. Cambridge University Press.

Sjøvold T (1977) Non-metric divergence between skeletal populations. *Ossa* 4(1):1–133.

Sofaer JA (1969) Aspects of tabby-crinkled-downless syndrome: I. The development of tabby teeth. *Journal of Embryology and Experimental Morphology* 22(2):181–205.

Sofaer JA (1970) Dental morphological variation and the Hardy–Weinberg law. *Journal of Dental Research* 49(6):1505–1508.

Sofaer JA, Niswander JD, MacLean CJ, and Workman PL (1972) Population studies on Southwestern Indian tribes: V. Tooth morphology as an indicator of biological distance. *American Journal of Physical Anthropology* 37(3):357–366.

Sokal R and Michener C (1958) A statistical method for evaluating systematic relationships. *University of Kansas Scientific Bulletin* 38(2):1409–1438.

Sołtysiak A (2011) Technical note: an R script for Smith's mean measure of divergence. *Bioarchaeology of the Near East* 5:41–44.

Stark BL and Arnold PJ III (1997) Introduction to the archaeology of the Gulf lowlands. In Stark BL and Arnold PJ III, editors. *Olmec to Aztec: Settlement Patterns in the Ancient Gulf Lowlands.* The University of Arizona Press. Pp. 3–32.

Stojanowski CM and Johnson KM (2015) Observer error, dental wear, and the inference of New World Sundadonty. *American Journal of Physical Anthropology* 156(3):349–362.

Stojanowski CM, Paul KS, Seidel AC, Duncan WN, and Guatelli-Steinberg D (2017) Heritability and genetic integration of tooth size in the South Carolina Gullah. *American Journal of Physical Anthropology* 164(3):505–521.

Stojanowski CM, Paul KS, Seidel AC, Duncan WN, and Guatelli-Steinberg D (2018) Heritability and genetic integration of anterior tooth crown variants in the South Carolina Gullah. *American Journal of Physical Anthropology* 167(1):124–143.

Sutter RC (2006) The test of competing models for the prehistoric peopling of the Azapa Valley, northern Chile, using matrix correlations. *Chungara: Revista de Antropologia Chilena* 38 (1):63–82.

Sutter RC and Sharratt N (2010) Continuity and transformation during the terminal Middle Horizon (AD 950–1150): a bioarchaeological assessment of Tumilaca origins within the middle Moquegua Valley, Peru. *Latin American Antiquity* 21(1):67–86.

Taylor M and Creel D (2012) Biological relationships between foragers and farmers of south-central North America: nonmetric dental traits. *American Antiquity* 77(1):99–114.

Thesleff I (2006) The genetic basis of tooth development and dental defects. *American Journal of Medical Genetics* 140A(23):2530–2535.

Thompson AR, Hedman KM, and Slater PA (2015) New dental and isotope evidence of biological distance and place of origin for mass burial groups at Cahokia's mound 72. *American Journal of Physical Anthropology* 158(2):341–357.

Townsend GC, Bockmann M, Hughes T, and Brook A (2012) Genetic, environmental and epigenetic influences on variation in human tooth number, size and shape. *Odontology* 100(1):1–9.

Turner CG II (1984) Advances in the dental search for Native American origins. *Acta Anthropogenetica* 8(1–2):23–78.

Turner CG II (1987) Late Pleistocene and Holocene population history of East Asia based on dental variation. *American Journal of Physical Anthropology* 73(3):305–322.

Turner CG II, Nichol CR, and Scott GR (1991) Scoring procedures for key morphological traits of the permanent dentition: the Arizona State University dental anthropology system. In Kelley M and Larsen CS, editors. *Advances in Dental Anthropology.* Wiley-Liss. Pp. 13–31.

Ware JH, Harrington D, Hunter DJ, and D'Agostino RB (2012) Missing data. *New England Journal of Medicine* 367(14):1353–1354.

Wilcoxon F (1945) Individual comparisons by ranking methods. *Biometrics Bulletin* 1(6):80–83.

Willermet CM and Edgar HJH (2009) Dental morphology and ancestry in Albuquerque, New Mexico Hispanics. *HOMO: Journal of Comparative Human Biology* 60(3):207–224.

Willermet CM, Edgar HJH, Ragsdale C, and Aubry BS (2013) Biodistances among Mexica, Maya, Toltec, and Totonac groups of central and coastal Mexico. *Chungara: Revista de Antropología Chilena* 45(3):447–459.

9 Paleoanthropology and Analytical Bias

Citation Practices, Analytical Choice, and Prioritizing Quality over Quantity

Adam P. Van Arsdale

Since the nineteenth century, studies of the human fossil record and human skeletal variation have made scientific rigor a valued goal. In the nineteenth and early twentieth centuries, this manifested itself in the creation of objective standards of measurement and observation (Boas 1899; Hrdlička 1919). More recent attempts have been made to further address the challenges of gathering standardized data from skeletal or fossil samples deriving from different populations, contexts, or taphonomic conditions (Buikstra and Ubelaker 1994). By the early twentieth century, the growth of available metric data required greater attention to the use of quantitative data in formal statistical analyses, often with the aim of explicit hypothesis testing (Morant 1939). Since the 1960s, multivariate statistical approaches have increasingly dominated the quantitative literature in evolutionary studies, accommodating ever-increasing data availability and increased computer processing capabilities (Howells 1969; Sokal and Rohlf 1981).

The advances in analytical approaches to evolutionary and morphological issues raise a set of epistemological questions regarding methodology. Many of these questions revolve around the issue, expressed broadly, of quality versus quantity in paleoanthropological data. This is true for fossil-based studies of morphological evolution, but could also be extended to evolutionary questions that depend on secondary data gathered from fossils (e.g., isotopic analyses). More concretely, the advances in analytical techniques, specifically in multidimensional approaches, demand higher-quality input data: larger sample sizes, fewer missing data, and greater consistency across sample observations. While the fossil record itself has expanded at an ever-increasing rate over the past century, the expansion in hominin evolution observational data available to researchers has not provided researchers with orders of magnitude of new data. Furthermore, new fossils do not necessarily mean better preserved fossils, or fossils that more adequately represent sample or locality variation. Improvement in field excavation techniques and best practices have improved the overall quality of fossil finds, but they have not fundamentally changed the nature of the fossil data sources available to researchers. Put simply, these changes, while important, have not fundamentally changed the epistemological challenges of working with fossil-based data sources.

This raises the important methodological question of prioritizing sample breadth or sample quality. At its root, this is a question about whether researchers should prioritize the methodological approach toward developing knowledge or maximizing the number and type of observations available to address such a question. Embedded within this question and these choices are assumptions about how evolutionary information is bound up with the fossils themselves, and how that information is translated into scientific knowledge about the fossil record through analytical approaches. This chapter attempts to examine the choices researchers have made regarding this question over almost the past three decades by looking at the rate at which hominin fossils of differing preservation status have been incorporated into published papers.

Specifically, this chapter tests the hypothesis that the rise of rigorous multivariate analytical techniques over the past three decades has significantly shifted the representation of fossils in published research, leading to an increase in studies of highly preserved specimens and a decrease in more poorly preserved specimens.

Methods and Materials

This hypothesis is addressed with a two-part approach. First, 102 hominin cranial fossils available for study prior to 1988 were classified on the basis of their degree of preservation (Table 9.1). In order to achieve this, a "fragmentation index" (FI) was calculated for each specimen on the basis of its state of cranial preservation and the available standardized measurements observable on each specimen. Second, the frequency with which these fossils were mentioned in published texts was recorded by digitally surveying issues of the *American Journal of Physical Anthropology* and the *Journal of Human Evolution* for the 28-year time period of 1988–2015. Crania were chosen as a focus, given their disproportionate role in hominin taxonomic arguments (e.g., Baab 2018; Lahr 1996; Wood and Collard 1999). Crania were also chosen because fragmentation across crania are more easily comparable than fragmentation across diverse post-cranial elements. Whereas two cranial fragments might be reasonably compared on their degree of preservation, it is harder to compare the preservation between a radius and a pelvis alongside a femoral–scapula comparison.

This time period postdates the widespread adoption of multivariate techniques within the discipline, but also spans the initial emergence and subsequent spread of geometric morphometrics (GM; Figures 9.1 and 9.2). These visualizations are consistent with the introduction and adoption of multivariate techniques within paleoanthropology (e.g., Giles and Elliot 1963; Howells 1969; Sokal and Rohlf 1981), as well as the publication of critical texts in GM methods (Bookstein 1997; Rohlf and Bookstein 1990; Slice 2005; Zelditch et al. 2012). While just one of many multivariate approaches used in hominin studies, GM studies are a convenient stand-in for the question being addressed here because they typically demand high-quality fossil data. GM techniques attempt to control for allometric or related size-related features in an analysis by distinguishing size variables from shape variables (Rohlf and Bookstein 1990). Shape, the target of most GM studies, is a complex variable distributed across integrated morphological structures, and not well preserved in more fragmentary remains. Within GM approaches, techniques have been developed to deal with problems of "missing data" in the analysis of fossil samples (Weber and

Table 9.1 Fossil specimen list, sorted by fragmentation index (FI) category

5[a]	4	3	2	1
KNM-WT 15000	KNM-ER 1470	KNM-ER 3732	KNM-ER 1808	KNM-ER 2598
KNM-ER 3733	KNM-ER 3883	KNM-ER 1805	KNM-ER 1590	KNM-ER 3735
KNM-ER 1813	OH-24	KNM-ER 730	OH-7	KNM-ER 1478
Sts 5	Sangiran 2	OH-9	OH-12	KNM-ER 3892
Kabwe	Sangiran 17	Sangiran 4	OH-13	KNM-ER 2592
Bodo	Sts 71	Sts 52	OH-16	KNM-ER 3891
Petralona	Saccopastore 1	Stw 53	Sangiran 1	KNM-ER 417
Amud 1	Jebel Irhoud 1	ZKD E1	Sangiran 10	KNM-ER 2602
Skhul 5	Laetoli 18	ZKD L1	Sangiran 12	OH-6
	Qafzeh 6	ZKD L2	Sts 17	OH-14
	Qafzeh 9	ZKD L3	Sts 19	Sangiran 3
		Solo 1	Sts 22	Sangiran 20
		Ndutu	Sts 53	Sangiran 27
		Arago 21	Stw 252	Sangiran 31
		Saccopastore 2	Stw 505	Omo L894–1
		Steinheim	Gongwangling	Sts 12
		Krapina C	Trinil 2	ZKD G2
		Skhul 1	ZKD D1	ZKD I2
		Skhul 4	ZKD H3	ZKD J1
		Tabun 1	Solo 5	ZKD B2
			Solo 6	ZKD O1
			Solo 9	Solo 2
			Solo 10	Solo 3
			Solo 11	Solo 4
			Swanscombe	Solo 7
			Biache	Solo 8
			Krapina A	Arago 3
			Krapina D	Bilzingsleiben
			Krapina E	
			Jebel Irhoud 2	
			Qafzeh 3	
			Qafzeh 5	
			Qafzeh 7	
			Skhul 9	

[a] The most highly preserved specimens are in FI = 5, the most poorly preserved are in FI = 1.

Bookstein 2011), but such advances act more as localized patches than system fixes to problems of missing data in fossil analyses. As technologies for scanning fossil remains have become more accessible, and as such data has become more accessible (Boyer et al. 2016), shape-based analyses have become standard within paleoanthropological studies.

The complete list of 102 fossils and their fragmentation index is available in Table 9.1. Classification into the five categories of FI were based on the degree of

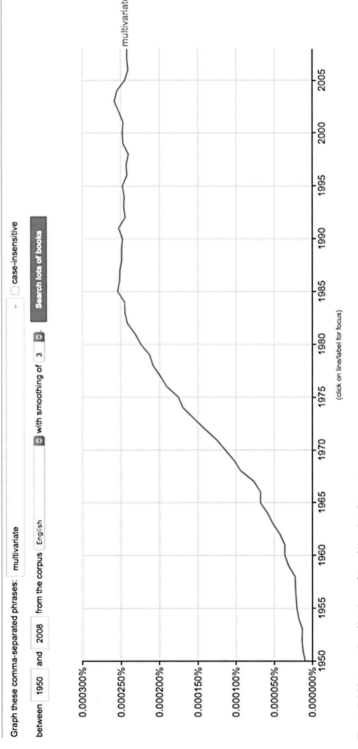

Figure 9.1 Ngram visualization of "multivariate" usage.

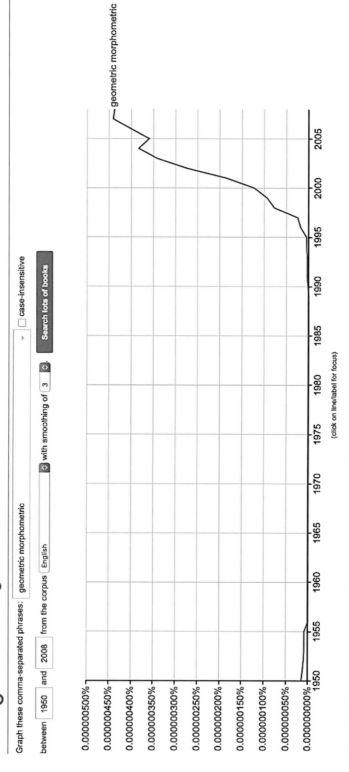

Figure 9.2 Ngram visualization of "geometric morphometric."

morphological preservation across the skull. Specimens preserving near-complete crania, allowing for measurement within and across all the anatomical regions of the crania, were grouped into FI category 5. Fossils were assigned to the intermediate categories, 2–4, based on the relative number of regions and preservation of those regions. For example, specimens that were, on the whole, well-preserved, but lacking one whole anatomical region were placed in category 4 (e.g., KNM-ER 3883). Fossils that preserve several regions well, but lack significant parts or the entirety of several others might end up in FI category 3 (e.g., OH 9, Krapina C). More fragmentary specimens, or specimens that only preserve one major anatomical region, are found in FI category 2 (e.g., Biache). The most poorly preserved, typically having only a small measurable fragment or two, can be found in FI category 1 (e.g., KNM-ER 3892). For specimens that appeared to fall on the border between any two categories, a comparison of the available number of standard cranial measurements was used to place specimens into the more or less preserved category (Howells 1973). The total distribution of specimens across the five FI categories can be seen in Table 9.1.

For each fossil, the number of citations that mention that fossil as well as the year of publication were recorded. The *Journal of Human Evolution* and *American Journal of Physical Anthropology* are taken to be representative of the paleoanthropological field as a whole, given their prominence as flagship journals within the field, particularly for fossil-related research. Citation lists were generated through digital searches of the journal, accounting for variant representation of specific fossil identifiers (e.g., Zhoukoudian, Choukoutien, ZKD).

It should be noted that one complication in the data is the inclusion of specimens that preserve both cranial and post-cranial remains. The bibliometric approach utilized here does not distinguish between papers that have a primary focus on cranial versus post-cranial material, or perhaps utilize both in their analyses. This may result in an over-representation of fossil individuals that preserve both cranial and post-cranial remains. The Nariokotome (KNM-WT-15000) individual is the most striking example of this phenomenon, as it is far and away the most-cited individual specimen in the record on the basis of this analysis (227 total citations). The inclusion of these specimens in the analysis, while it does create some degree of additional noise in the data, does not change the direction of the conclusions based on the analyses highlighted in the next section. This was determined by running the basic analyses with and without specimens that preserve post-cranial materials. Although the exact results differ, the direction and stepwise relationship between FI and citation frequency were unchanged. As such, to preserve as broad a representation of the fossil record as possible for this analysis, those specimens were kept within the final set of analyses.

Results

In total, the citation database compiled includes 2883 total citations. Consistent with expectations, fossils in the more highly preserved FI categories, particularly category 5, were more highly represented in the literature (Figure 9.3). A least squares

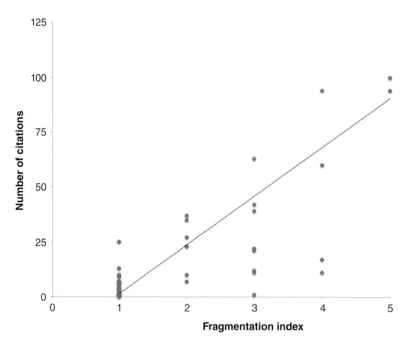

Figure 9.3 Citation frequency by fragmentation index (FI).

regression of fossil citation frequency against FI yields a highly significant R^2 value of 0.57. The average number of citations for the most highly preserved fossils are double that of even the category 4 fossils based on FI, with a linear decline in citation frequency beyond that (Figure 9.3).

This result is not surprising. Better-preserved fossils almost certainly lend themselves to a greater range of questions for analysis, in addition to simply garnering a greater amount of attention. What is striking, however, is what happens when the total time sample covered by this analysis (1988–2015) is broken down into smaller time intervals. Such an approach lends itself to more random bias, given the smaller time intervals being considered (i.e., edge effects associated with which fossils happen to be published within a given year), but also potentially provides a window into changing trends in current citation and research practices.

When the total 28-year time frame is divided into equal, 14-year windows (1988–2001, 2002–2015), it becomes clear that citation frequency increases across all FI categories (Figure 9.4). This is likely a result of an increase in the overall number of fossil-related publications, perhaps associated with more digital/online publications, or simply because of changes in the editorial practices of these journals which lend themselves to more fossil-based papers. In relation to the increase in overall publications, Ruff notes that between 2007 and 2013 there was a roughly 70 percent increase in the total yearly pages published in the *AJPA* (Ruff 2013). However, the uptick in publication rates between these two time periods is only significantly different for fossils falling into FI category 5, the most highly preserved, which sees a 67 percent increase in citation rate in the more recent time frame. This

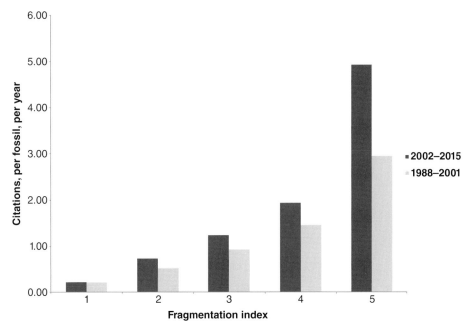

Figure 9.4 Fossil citation rate, 1988–2001 and 2002–2015.

comparison is based on a resampling analysis, within FI categories, across the two time periods. In other words, given the overall rate of citation for a given fossil, what is the likelihood of sampling the observed citation rates for time period one and time period two? This resampling was repeated 1000 times to generate a functional *p*-value to assess the significance of these resampled differences.

Further parsing the data, if only the most recent seven years of data are examined (2009–2015), a similar trend is visible. Relative to the citation rate across the entire temporal sample (citations per fossil per year), only those fossils in FI category 5 show a significant increase in publication rate (Figure 9.5), again using a resampling-based approach. Though not significant, the most poorly preserved fossils, those falling into FI category 1, actually show an overall decrease in publication rate over the most recent time period (Figure 9.5). Taken together, during the 1988–2001 period the most highly preserved fossils were cited about 13 times more frequently than the most poorly preserved fossils. In the 2009–2015 period, the most highly preserved fossils were cited 32 times more frequently than the most poorly preserved specimens.

Discussion

It is clear that the degree of preservation plays a significant role in the tendency of fossils to end up in published analyses in paleoanthropology. The data presented above suggests that this trend has been accelerating over the past three decades alongside the more widespread adoption of analytical approaches such as geometric morphometrics. This chapter is not sufficient to identify a direct causality between

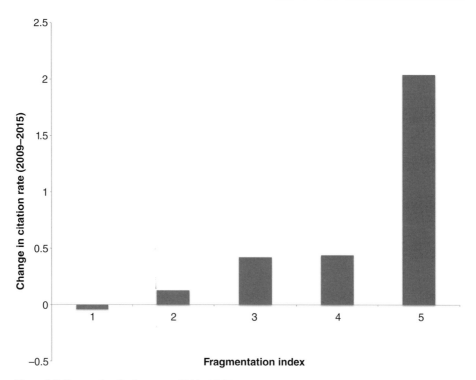

Figure 9.5 Change in citation rate, 2009–2015.

these observations, but it does suggest this is an issue that should be subject to more open conversation within the discipline. To be clear, the above observations do not necessarily identify a problem with how paleoanthropology is evolving as a discipline. What they do suggest is a potential area of bias that reflects implicit practices within the discipline that have pushed for greater analytical and statistical control over data. The result is an increasing emphasis on the quality of available data, rather than the quantity of such data.

Several additional inferences can be drawn from the above observation. One of the first related conclusions is that owing to taphonomic and geologic variability, the degree of preservation itself is not evenly (or even randomly) distributed across fossil localities. For example, when comparing cranial material from the Georgian Lower Pleistocene site of Dmanisi with Lower Pleistocene fossils from the Turkana Basin or Olduvai Gorge, clear differences exist in both the number of specimens available for study and their relative preservation. Although not included in this study because of the dates of discovery (1999–2005) and publication (2001–2013), the five cranial specimens from Dmanisi all fall within categories 4 and 5 for FI, giving the overall sample an average FI of 4.5. In contrast, the samples from the Turkana Basin ($n = 55$) and Olduvai Gorge ($n = 21$) are much more extensive, but also more fragmentary, with average FI values of 1.62 and 1.78, respectively.

This comparison provides an interesting contrast to how we might think about the fossil record. Which set of fossils is more important? Which has more evolutionary information? Which is more likely to influence how we understand the trajectory of human evolution? How will the significance of these fossils change as preferred methods of analysis change within the discipline? The answers to these questions are not straightforward, or even uniform across analyses. But they are influenced by the kinds of approaches we take to studying the fossil record.

The above questions can be considered in the context of several recent fossil discoveries and publications. Recent publications on the interpretation of the large collection of *Homo naledi* fossil specimens from the Rising Star Cave System, South Africa, have raised several of these questions. In this case, the fossils themselves are quite fragmentary, but the sheer numbers of them mean that many aspects of the anatomy – both cranial and post-cranial – are preserved in replicate (Berger et al. 2017). This has raised challenges for placing these specimens – and through them, *Homo naledi* – within existing phylogenetic interpretations within sub-Saharan Pleistocene Africa that consist mainly of isolated (and variably preserved) specimens (Berger et al. 2017; Dembo et al. 2016; Stringer 2015). The nearby locality of Malapa has also yielded hominin remains in the past decade (Berger et al. 2010). In this case, the specimens are less numerous, but represent multiple, well-preserved elements of associated individuals. Also within the Cradle of Humankind, the recovery of Stw 573 ("Little Foot") has finally been completed (Beaudet et al. 2019; Clarke 1998). This specimen, whose exact correlation with other Sterkfontein hominins is still debated, is a single, highly preserved individual (Bruxelles et al. 2014; Clarke and Tobias 1995; Walker et al. 2006). Across each of these sites, all within a close distance of one another, it is clear that taphonomic processes and recovery techniques have yielded specimens that preserve evolutionary information in a particular way that complicates how one might think of integrating these specimens into a broader comparative study. In these contexts, the choice of analytical approach is obviously not a neutral question, but one that interacts with the realities of the available evidence in ways that are both predictable (based on the degree of preservation) and potentially unpredictable (what evolutionary information is captured by the preserved specimens).

The second major issue this observation raises is the assumption made in the discipline about how evolutionary information is distributed within and between fossils. The trend is to place an ever-greater importance, as measured by citation frequency, on more highly preserved specimens. This may or may not be correct, in part depending on the specific question being asked. But it certainly assumes a specific relationship between fossil preservation and evolutionarily important information. In particular, it assumes a kind of "sum is greater than the parts" perspective, valuing the preservation within individuals of associated morphological elements. For questions of development and morphological integration, for example, it may indeed be the case that well-preserved fossils offer a clear and decisive advantage (Bastir 2008). Such an assumption may be problematic, however, when comparing across species or where uncertainty in covariance structures of the crania exist (Ackermann 2002; Mitteroecker and Bookstein 2008).

The above outlined trend simultaneously minimizes, by necessity, the problems of sample size within paleoanthropology. The fossil record itself represents a fundamental and limited constraint on what we can know. Anyone who has been involved with the discovery of hominin fossils or their analysis in museums or related institutions knows the tremendous value of each specimen. When addressing any given question, there is little a researcher can do to change the basic set of fossils available for study. This, perhaps, explains the preference for prioritizing analytical improvements in the discipline's recent history. However, the reality is that the hominin fossil samples available for any given analysis are overwhelmingly small, limiting the statistical power of any and all analytical approaches. The utter dearth of statistical power analyses – whether a given sample size is large enough to reliably reject/fail a given hypothesis – in paleoanthropological studies serves as a glaring testament to this reality.

The fact that, even as the known fossil record expands, certain fossils are falling out of the published literature due to their poor preservation (e.g., Skhul 9, Bilzingsleben), is at the very least an issue that should be the result of intentional and explicit decisions, rather than implicit byproducts of analytical choice. It is not the place of this chapter to identify what analytical approaches should be favored moving forward. But perhaps it is worth highlighting the value of a diversity of such approaches, including ones that encompass variation in the implicit values that go into the basic analytical approach. What this analysis does not reveal is the specific causality associated with changing fossil sample representation in the published literature. The broad trend identified in this chapter shows a correlation between increasing use of intensive multivariate methods, but a more nuanced examination of these publications, rather than the bibliometric approach pursued here, might reveal details about specific editorial practices, research groups, or training methods that are driving this trend. Or, alternatively, the discipline needs more detailed representations as to why methods that exclude relevant fossil material for a given question are preferential to approaches that are more inclusive of fragmentary specimens. Given the preciousness of any given hominin fossil find, it should be a striking observation that certain specimens are beginning to fall out of the published literature.

Obviously, issues of preservation and associated analytical bias are not the only biases in paleoanthropology, or even the most important. Basic access to fossil material and their associated data remain a fundamental and systematic source of bias in nearly all paleoanthropological analyses. Movements to continue improving data-sharing practices – by funding agencies, journals, and institutions – should remain a priority (Boyer et al. 2016; Delson et al. 2007). It remains the case today, even with now longstanding revisions to the funding agencies' data-sharing requirements (e.g., the National Science Foundation), that access to existing, relevant fossil data is a constraint on the basic scientific practices of paleoanthropology (Nelson 2009; Reed et al. 2015; Tenopir et al. 2011). Identifying clear solutions to the questions raised in this analysis is beyond the scope of this chapter, and there likely is no singular best practice approach. The intent of this chapter is mainly to raise the issue of the interaction between analytical technique and the diverse nature of the preserved fossil record. This point is under-represented in the current literature, and in most papers is present only in implicit ways. This issue should be made more explicit, and at the very least, the publication review process should support a variety of approaches to addressing questions in the fossil record, given the variation in the preserved fossil record and uncertainty in how evolutionarily relevant information is preserved in individual fossils and fossil samples.

References

Ackermann RR (2002) Patterns of covariation in the hominoid craniofacial skeleton: implications for paleoanthropological models. *Journal of Human Evolution* 43(2):167–187.

Baab KL (2018) Evolvability and craniofacial diversification in genus *Homo*. *Evolution* 72 (12):2781–2791.

Bastir M (2008) A systems-model for the morphological analysis of integration and modularity in human craniofacial evolution. *Journal of Anthropological Science* 86:37–58.

Beaudet A, Clarke RJ, de Jager EJ, et al. (2019) The endocast of StW 573 ("Little Foot") and hominin brain evolution. *Journal of Human Evolution* 126:112–123.

Berger LR, de Ruiter DJ, Churchill SE, et al. (2010) *Australopithecus sediba*: a new species of *Homo*-like australopith from South Africa. *Science* 328(5975):195–204.

Berger LR, Hawks J, Dirks PHGM, Elliott M, and Roberts EM (2017) *Homo naledi* and Pleistocene hominin evolution in subequatorial Africa. *Elife* 6:e24234.

Boas F (1899) Some recent criticisms of physical anthropology. *American Anthropologist* 1 (1):98–106.

Bookstein FL (1997) *Morphometric Tools for Landmark Data: Geometry and Biology*. Cambridge University Press.

Boyer DM, Gunnell GF, Kaufman S, and McGeary TM (2016) Morphosource: archiving and sharing 3-D digital specimen data. *The Paleontological Society Papers* 22:157–181.

Bruxelles L, Clarke RJ, Maire R, Ortega R, and Stratford D (2014) Stratigraphic analysis of the Sterkfontein StW 573 *Australopithecus* skeleton and implications for its age. *Journal of Human Evolution* 70:36–48.

Buikstra JE and Ubelaker DH (1994) *Standards for Data Collection From Human Skeletal Remains*. Arkansas Archaeological Survey.

Clarke RJ (1998) First ever discovery of a well-preserved skull and associated skeleton of *Australopithecus*. *South African Journal of Science* 94(10):460–463.

Clarke RJ and Tobias PV (1995) Sterkfontein Member 2 foot bones of the oldest South African hominid. *Science* 269(5223):521–524.

Delson E, Frost S, and Norris C (2007) Databases, data access, and data sharing in paleoanthropology: first steps. *Evolutionary Anthropology* 16(5):161–163.

Dembo M, Radovčic D, Garvin HM, et al. (2016) The evolutionary relationships and age of *Homo naledi*: an assessment using dated Bayesian phylogenetic methods. *Journal of Human Evolution* 97:17–26.

Giles E and Elliot O (1963) Sex determination by discriminant function analysis of crania. *American Journal of Physical Anthropology* 21(1):53–68.

Howells WW (1969) The use of multivariate techniques in the study of skeletal populations. *American Journal of Physical Anthropology* 31(3):311–314.

Howells WW (1973) *Cranial Variation in Man: A Study by Multivariate Analysis of Patterns of Difference among Recent Human Populations*. Peabody Museum of Archaeology and Ethnology, Harvard University Press.

Hrdlička A (1919) *Physical Anthropology, Its Scope and Aims: Its History and Present Status in the United States*. Wistar Institute of Anatomy and Biology.

Lahr MM (1996) *The Evolution of Modern Human Diversity: A Study of Cranial Variation*, Vol. 18. Cambridge University Press.

Mitteroecker P and Bookstein F (2008) The evolutionary role of modularity and integration in the hominoid cranium. *Evolution* 62(4):943–958.

Morant GM (1939) The use of statistical methods in the investigation of problems of classification in anthropology: Part I. The general nature of the material and the form of intraracial distributions of metrical characters. *Biometrika* 31(1–2):72–98.

Nelson B (2009) Data sharing: empty archives. *Nature News* 461(7261):160–163.

Reed D, Barr WA, McPherron SP, et al. (2015) Digital data collection in paleoanthropology. *Evolutionary Anthropology: Issues, News, and Reviews* 24(6):238–249.

Rohlf FJ and Bookstein FL (1990) *Proceedings of the Michigan Morphometrics Workshop.* University of Michigan Museum of Zoology.

Ruff C (2013) Change and continuity: reflections on editing the AJPA, 2007–2013. *American Journal of Physical Anthropology* 151(3):336–337.

Slice DE (2005) Modern morphometrics. In Slice DE, editor. *Modern Morphometrics in Physical Anthropology.* Springer. Pp. 1–45.

Sokal RR and Rohlf FJ (1981) *Biometry.* W.H. Freeman and Company.

Stringer C (2015) Human evolution: the many mysteries of *Homo naledi. Elife* 4:e10627.

Tenopir C, Allard S, Douglass K, et al. (2011) Data sharing by scientists: practices and perceptions. *PLoS One* 6(6):e21101.

Walker J, Cliff RA, and Latham AG (2006) U–Pb isotopic age of the StW 573 hominid from Sterkfontein, South Africa. *Science* 314(5805):1592–1594.

Weber GW and Bookstein FL (2011) *Virtual Anthropology: A Guide to a New Interdisciplinary Field.* Springer.

Wood B and Collard M (1999) The changing face of genus *Homo. Evolutionary Anthropology* 8 (6):195–207.

Zelditch ML, Swiderski DL, and Sheets HD (2012) *Geometric Morphometrics for Biologists: A Primer.* Academic Press.

10 (Re)Discovering Ancient Hominin Environments

How Stable Carbon Isotopes of Modern Chimpanzee Communities Can Inform Paleoenvironment Reconstruction

Melanie M. Beasley and Margaret J. Schoeninger

Since the 1980s, stable carbon isotopes (δ^{13}C) of pedogenic carbonates and fossil tooth enamel have been analyzed to contribute to paleoenvironment and dietary reconstructions of hominin habitats across Africa. Initial studies focused on documenting δ^{13}C values in paleosol and enamel carbonate to link the spreading of arid C_4 grasses with the habitat reconstructions of fossil fauna to interpret "open" versus "closed" canopies at fossil-bearing sites or the dietary differences between "grazers" versus "browsers." While habitat reconstructions of hominin-bearing sites are critical for our interpretations of human evolution, this is just one layer of (re)discovering ancient hominin environments that does not consider the difference between the entire habitat of a region versus the habitat primarily occupied by a species. What if early hominins procured food resources in particular microhabitats but ranged broadly throughout an environment for mating and sleeping? Would that change how we interpret the δ^{13}C values of pedogenic carbonates of a region compared to the δ^{13}C values of tooth enamel from fossil species occupying that region? This chapter provides a brief history of the increase in stable isotope geochemistry applied to paleoanthropology research, followed by a discussion of how we might "rediscover" hominin paleoenvironments by using extant chimpanzee data and observations.

Extensive stable isotope research in geology, paleoanthropology, and ecology have all contributed to our understanding of how we can use δ^{13}C values to reconstruct diet and environment. In paleoanthropology, researchers in South Africa, East Africa, and Europe focused on different material samples for the earliest applications of stable isotope research. In South Africa, where much of the hominin fossil-bearing sites are in cave systems, the earliest work focused on analysis of tooth enamel carbonate to compare δ^{13}C values of browsing and grazing faunal species (e.g., Lee-Thorp et al. 1989). In East Africa, the hominin fossil localities are mostly open-air sites; therefore the earliest efforts in stable isotope analysis of δ^{13}C and δ^{18}O values initially focused on pedogenic samples to characterize fluvial-lacustrine sequences and grassland versus woodland paleoenvironments (e.g., Cerling 1992; Cerling et al. 1988). While South and East Africa researchers focused on inorganic carbonate samples, the initial European studies highlighted the contributions of δ^{13}C and

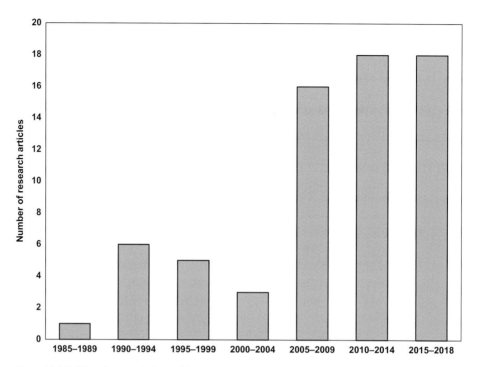

Figure 10.1 Publication trends in stable isotope research. Using the *Journal of Human Evolution*, the chart shows the trend in publication of original research articles published that utilize stable isotope research on pedogenic or biological samples to address questions about human evolution. Articles included in the count presented original stable isotope values (not just the mention of stable isotopes) from fossil localities, specifically prior to the Holocene, or used modern fauna stable isotope values to contextualize hominin site interpretations.

$\delta^{15}N$ values of the organic fraction of bone (collagen) from fossil vertebrates, including Neandertals, to reconstruct Upper Paleolithic diet (e.g., Bocherens et al. 1991).

To demonstrate the increase in stable isotope geochemistry applied to paleoanthropology research in South Africa, East Africa, and Europe, original research articles from *Journal of Human Evolution* were compiled to indicate the trend in publications from 1985 through 2018 (Figure 10.1). While paleoanthropology research is published in numerous academic journals, the *Journal of Human Evolution* was selected to demonstrate this trend in isotope research because it is a journal that concentrates on publishing the highest quality papers covering aspects of human evolution with a central focus on paleoanthropological research. There is a significant increase in stable isotope research articles published after 2005, which likely coincides with technological developments in mass spectrometry to decrease per-sample cost, such as improvements in gas extraction methods and use of autosamplers. For fossil tooth enamel stable isotope publications, early papers in the 1990s and early 2000s rarely exceeded a couple dozen samples, but after 2005 publications regularly included over 100 samples of fossil and/or modern fauna for comparison.

In modern and paleoenvironment reconstructions, $\delta^{13}C$ values have not only been used to identify the diet of an animal, but also the type of environment in which an animal is feeding (i.e., the canopy effect, amount of woody cover; Cerling et al. 2011b; van der Merwe and Medina 1991). It has been shown in Amazonian rainforest leaves (van der Merwe and Medina 1991), New World primate hair (Schoeninger et al. 1997, 1998), and from paleosol data from hominin-bearing fossil sites in East Africa (Cerling et al. 2011b), that animals feeding in more closed-canopy environments will have depleted $\delta^{13}C$ values relative to those from more open habitats. Additionally, C_3 plants will have higher $\delta^{13}C$ values under drought conditions, especially in more xeric environments like the modern Turkana Basin (Garten Jr. and Taylor Jr. 1992; Schoeninger et al. 1998). Today in East Africa, carbon can be used to distinguish between C_4 grazers and C_3 browsers because in the hot, arid climate of the Turkana Basin all the grasses are C_4 and all trees and shrubs are C_3 (Cerling et al. 2015; Schoeninger et al. 2003). Similar environmental observations of feeding position beneath a canopy and drought effects have been recorded in $\delta^{13}C_{enamel}$ values of ungulates from varying habitats (Cerling and Harris 1999), suggesting fossil fauna $\delta^{13}C_{enamel}$ values can be used for dietary and paleoenvironment reconstruction in conjunction with $\delta^{18}O_{enamel}$.

Case Study: (Re)discovering *Au. anamensis* Paleoenvironment in the Omo-Turkana Basin

Many important early hominin fossil sites that shape our understanding about the roots of our ancestral lineage occur in East Africa, which is currently one of the hottest regions in the world. The Omo-Turkana Basin has some of the oldest hominin fossil-bearing localities, including on the eastern shore of Lake Turkana at Allia Bay, Kenya (3.97 ± 0.03 million years ago) (Leakey et al. 1995; Wood and Leakey 2011) and southwest of the lake at Kanapoi, Kenya (4.17–4.07 million years ago) (Brown and McDougall 2011; Leakey et al. 1995, 1998). *Australopithecus anamensis*, the earliest confirmed obligate biped within the genus *Australopithecus*, has been recovered from these sites.

The ecological niche exploited by early hominins is assumed to have played an essential role in the origins of obligatory bipedalism, a distinguishing characteristic of hominins among mammals (see review in Domínguez-Rodrigo 2014). Therefore, reconstructing the paleoenvironment at early hominin sites is essential for understanding the selective forces that resulted in such a significant morphological change. A phylogenetic analysis supports the idea that *Au. anamensis* represents part of an anagenetically evolving lineage (i.e., a gradually evolving lineage), arising from a sudden transition out of the preceding *Ardipithecus* genus and giving rise to the later *Au. afarensis* species (Haile-Selassie et al. 2010; Kimbel et al. 2006; White et al. 2006). Kimbel et al. (2006) suggest that each site-sample captures a different point along the evolutionary trajectory of early hominins, so it is critical to reconstruct the paleoenvironment of each site to evaluate the interplay between habitat and human evolution.

Over the years, many hypotheses have suggested links among climate, the environment, and significant morphological adaptations in hominins, especially bipedalism (Behrensmeyer 2006; deMenocal 2004; Domínguez-Rodrigo 2014; Potts 1998). Unfortunately, paleoenvironmental reconstructions in East Africa often rely on surface-collected fossil fauna that combine multiple temporal and geographically dispersed components that are not *in situ*. As a result, global or regional trends are most often discussed. On a global scale, cooling in the Neogene period (23–2.6 million years ago) resulted in the aridification of Africa (deMenocal and Rind 1993; Tiedemann et al. 1994; Zachos et al. 2001), with arid-adapted C_4 plants spreading between eight and six million years ago (Cerling 1992; Cerling et al. 1997; Kingston et al. 1994; Morgan et al. 1994; Ségalen et al. 2007). Fossil faunal, floral, and paleosol assemblages suggest a general trend of increasingly open-arid environments with pulses of species turnover during the past four million years (Behrensmeyer et al. 1997; Bobe et al. 2002; Bonnefille 1995; Bonnefille and Mohammed 1994; Bonnefille et al. 2004; Cerling et al. 1988, 2015; Fernández and Vrba 2006; Passey et al. 2010; Reed 1997; Vrba 1985, 1988; Vrba et al. 1995). In the last four million years, paleosol data indicate that the dominant environment in East Africa was wooded grassland with significant areas of open habitat, represented by 10–40 percent woody canopy cover (Cerling et al. 2011a, 2011b). Generally, the Plio-Pleistocene environment in East Africa became more open with less continuous tree-cover compared to earlier periods and continued to shift toward the arid environment that is experienced today in modern East Africa.

The general nature of this framework, however, lacks the temporal-spatial resolution to develop causal links between evolution and the environment (Kingston 2007). In fact, at the West Turkana fossil localities, the mammalian assemblages indicate a sufficiently humid climate to support perennial rivers during the past four million years (Harris et al. 1988). Fossil mammal assemblages from localities surrounding Lake Turkana suggest that despite regional climatic shifts in the Turkana Basin, the local habitats surrounding the lake were distinct ecologically to the extent that differences in the nature and abundance of species were maintained (Harris et al. 1988). Outside of the Turkana Basin at fossil localities in the Kenya Rift Valley from the past four million years, a heterogeneous environment of mixed C_3 and C_4 plants persisted, with no evidence of a shift from closed to more open habitats (Kingston et al. 1994). Yet, carbon isotope data indicate a dependence by *Australopithecus bahrelghazali* from Chad on C_4 plant resources as early as three million years ago, suggesting that open habitat environments were critical for subsistence strategies of this early hominin (Lee-Thorp et al. 2012). Recent studies reviewed by Kingston (2007) highlight how short-term ecological changes might match or even exceed the influence of long-term changes on evolution; assuming this is correct, then it is no longer reasonable to frame human evolution within long-term global or regional trends, but instead the focus must be on smaller, more local sites and time scales.

This debate about the scale of ecological influence on human evolution is highlighted in the ongoing different interpretations of how wet or dry, and how tree-covered or open the environment was at the period in human evolution when early hominins shifted their mode of locomotion to bipedalism (Cerling et al. 2010; White et al. 2009a; WoldeGabriel et al. 2009). In the Turkana Basin, the prevailing assumption is that the region was continually hot during the past four million years as arid-adapted C_4 plants spread throughout Africa, with soil temperatures typically above 30°C year-round supporting an early opening of the habitat (Cerling 1992; Cerling et al. 1997, 2015; Passey et al. 2010). Recent analysis of the bulk enamel $\delta^{13}C$ by Cerling et al. (2015) suggests that in the Turkana Basin four million years ago there were more mixed feeding species compared to the more distinct C_3 browsers or C_4 grazers that occur today. Kanapoi, the earliest documented site of *Au. anamensis* and the type locality for the species, has a diverse mammalian fauna including cercopithecid, elephantid, rhinocerotid, suid, giraffid, and bovid species, which have been used in approximating the paleoenvironment of this early hominin species as dry, possibly open, wooded or bushland conditions (Harris and Leakey 2003; Leakey et al. 1995). Kanapoi has also been characterized as having an open arid to semi-arid climate based on paleosol carbon isotope data (Wynn 2000), supporting the interpretation of a continually hot arid climate in the Turkana Basin over the past four million years. However, recent re-evaluation of the fauna (Geraads et al. 2013) and ecological structure analysis (Harris and Leakey 2003) suggest that Kanapoi had a mosaic habitat of woodland and open grassland possibly closer to a closed woodland similar to the habitat proposed for *Ardipithecus ramidus* (Harris and Leakey 2003; White et al. 2009b).

In contrast to the continuously hot and arid reconstruction of the climate from paleosol data, an early pilot study at Allia Bay of the $\delta^{18}O$ and $\delta^{13}C$ values from fossil fauna tooth enamel suggested that the local paleoenvironment was more mesic (wetter) than today, with a habitat similar to modern Miombo woodlands (Schoeninger et al. 2003). A Miombo-like savanna woodland is an ecosystem dominated by *Brachystegia* spp., with approximately 25–75 percent canopy cover (Moore 1996). This is supported by the four paleosol samples from Allia Bay, three of which have the lowest $\delta^{13}C$ values of any samples from the Turkana Basin, indicative of significant woody cover (>40 percent) (Levin et al. 2011; Levin et al. 2015). Additionally, a proxy climate method using strontium isotope ratios of lacustrine fish fossil remains from the Koobi Fora region demonstrate that between ~2 and 1.85 million years ago the Turkana Basin remained well-watered and was possibly an aridity refugium for obligate drinking fauna when other basins in the East African Rift System were impacted by droughts (Joordens et al. 2011). These conflicting interpretations of paleoenvironments both at the local scale based on soils and fauna and the regional scale emphasize the need for multiple lines of evidence from fossil localities across the Turkana Basin to better understand the proximal and causal links impacting the selection for the defining morphological features of our ancestral lineage.

When considering the multiple lines of evidence accumulated from sites across East Africa, there is a general trend for fossil fauna assemblages and isotopic data generated from enamel (which reflects the environment recorded by a single individual) to point toward mixed mosaic mesic habitats compared to isotopic data from paleosols, which indicate more open xeric (drier) habitats with significantly less woody canopy cover. Perhaps this is the result of warm-season bias in carbonate formation, which would impact interpretations generated from paleosol carbonate data (Peters et al. 2013). The seemingly conflicting interpretations of soil and faunal data result in the term "mosaic" being associated with multiple interpretations of varied paleoenvironments (Reed et al. 2014). By invoking the term "mosaic" to define a variety of paleoenvironments, the specific differences in the composition of openness compared to more densely tree-covered areas can be overlooked but might be key in understanding the environmental variables that promoted selection for bipedalism. The question is, within a mosaic habitat, was *Au. anamensis* associated more specifically with one habitat, either densely tree-covered woodlands or more open grassland savannas, or were they occupying the fringe ecotones between woodlands and grasslands exploiting a variety of resources favoring a flexible ecological adaptation?

Modern Chimpanzee Communities as a Referential Model

Chimpanzees often act as a referential model for our early hominin ancestors (Moore 1996; Sponheimer et al. 2006). Isotopic applications of extant chimpanzee communities in the wild have addressed questions such as: dietary changes at different life stages (i.e., infant, subadult, adult; Smith et al. 2010); distinguishing between terrestrial feeding, arboreal fruit-eating, and arboreal leaf-eating (Nelson 2013); and evidence of meat eating and hunting specialization in adult male chimpanzees (Fahy et al. 2013). In each of these studies, arguments were proposed of how the extant chimpanzee data could inform paleoanthropological reconstructions of diet, behavior, and habitat in early hominins.

A recent study of modern chimpanzee habitats reconstructed from biological tissues (δ^{13}C in hair) indicate that modern environmental model expectations will not conform to known ecological habitats when individuals are living within a riverine gallery forest in a region of low rainfall (Schoeninger et al. 2016). This has serious implications for paleoenvironment reconstructions because when chimpanzees occupy a habitat with a variety of ecosystem types they have been shown to feed only in the more densely tree-covered ecological niches (Schoeninger et al. 2016). In this instance, recovered fauna might indicate a "mosaic" habitat, while to the chimpanzees there was only one habitat in which they were feeding. Perhaps early hominins similarly had narrow ecological niches with a specific feeding ecology or possibly early hominins overcame this and occupied areas with a variety of habitats to exploit multiple ecosystem types. It is possible that the key to the success of early hominins was their adaptive flexibility to exploit the variety of ecosystem types within a single geographic region (Potts 1998). Therefore, it is critical to understand the nature of a "mosaic" habitat at a local site scale.

While δ^{13}C values of non-hominin fauna and paleosols have been used extensively to reconstruct paleoenvironments of early hominins, here we explore what δ^{13}C values of modern chimpanzee communities might indicate about early hominin behavior in terms of how an environment is utilized. We use chimpanzees as a referential model for early hominins and how we might interpret what a "mosaic" habitat determination from stable isotope evidence means in terms of hominin evolution. Specifically, we expect this comparison to expand our information on the types of habitats that *Au. anamensis* inhabited and, quite possibly, highlight adaptive flexibility in a species that may have flourished in a wide variety of environments.

Materials and Methods

To investigate how modern chimpanzee stable carbon isotope data can refine early hominin habitat reconstructions, we use published mean $\delta^{13}C$ values of chimpanzee hair from nine modern chimpanzee sites across two different biome types in Africa (Schoeninger et al. 2016; Table 10.1). Carbon stable isotope ratios of chimpanzee hair values were converted to enamel values following Sponheimer et al. (2006) and corrected for the Suess effect for comparison with published *Au. anamensis* $\delta^{13}C$ enamel values from Kanapoi (Cerling et al. 2013). To convert hair to enamel values, +9.8‰ was added to the hair values (Sponheimer et al. 2006). When comparing fossil and modern $\delta^{13}C$ values, it is necessary to apply a Suess effect correction to account for changes in atmospheric CO_2 due to the admixture of CO_2 produced by the combustion of fossil fuels since the Industrial Revolution (Keeling 1979). While there are different methods for correcting for the Suess effect (i.e., a sliding scale difference accounting for the date of collection of biological samples versus a standard offset applied to all samples), here we use a standard offset correction for hair values. A uniform standard +1.5‰ correction was used to make "modern" samples comparable to "fossil" samples because hair samples were collected across different decades and collection dates were not always available.

Results

Schoeninger et al. (2016) showed a statistically significant negative correlation between $\delta^{13}C$ and the mean annual precipitation (MAP) (trendline: $y = -0.0021x$ -20.648; $R^2 = 0.56$; Figure 10.2). While MAP values can vary based on sampling protocol, Schoeninger et al. (2016) reported MAP values that were provided by the authors of the original stable isotope data. At fossil localities, paleoprecipitation, specifically MAP, can be estimated from the measured depth to the top of a soil's calcic horizon (Retallack 1994), and has been applied to 33 paleosols of the composite Turkana Basin record (Wynn 2004). At Kanapoi, a calcic horizon is present and paleosol data indicate a seasonal climate regime with paleoprecipitation estimated at approximately 620 $\pm$ 100 mm/year (1 SD; Wynn 2004).

Although it is common among stable isotope practitioners to correct values between different biological tissue types when needed, most corrections will have inherent biases. Some corrections are based on comparisons of tissue types in animals experimentally fed known diets, while other corrections consider directly the fractionation between a tissue type and diet. Inherent bias in these corrections

Table 10.1 Description of published samples

Site	Species	General habitat[a]	Mean annual precipitation (mm)	Sample type	$\delta^{13}C$ (‰)[b]			Source
					N	Mean	SD	
Kanapoi	*Au. anamensis*	Savanna	620	Enamel	17	-10.7	0.8	Cerling et al. 2013
Ishasha	*P. troglodytes*	Savanna	750	Hair	8	-23.1	0.2	Schoeninger et al. 1999
Fongoli	*P. troglodytes*	Savanna	950	Hair	36	-22.2	0.4	Sponheimer et al. 2006
Ugalla	*P. troglodytes*	Savanna	1050	Hair	12	-22.0	0.3	Schoeninger et al. 1999
Gombe	*P. troglodytes*	Savanna	1250	Hair[c]	13	-23.1	0.3	Schoeninger et al. 2016
Kibale	*P. troglodytes*	Forest	1500	Hair	15	-23.5	0.5	Carter 2001
Kibale	*P. troglodytes*	Forest	1500	Enamel	13	-14.5	1.0	Nelson 2013
Cameroon	*P. troglodytes*	Forest	1700	Hair	39	-24.9	0.9	Macho and Lee-Thorp 2014
Taï	*P. troglodytes*	Forest	1800	Hair	52	-24.9	0.5	Fahy et al. 2013
Ganta	*P. troglodytes*	Forest	1956	Hair[c]	36	-24.6	0.5	Harley 1939; Smith et al. 2010
Ganta	*P. troglodytes*	Forest	1956	Enamel	31	-16.2	0.9	Smith et al. 2010
Loango	*P. troglodytes*	Forest	2215	Hair	14	-24.6	0.5	Oelze et al. 2014

[a] General habitat designated by biome type from Schoeninger et al. (2016) and for Kanapoi described from Wynn (2004) and Geraads et al. (2013).
Savanna = savanna, grassland, shrubland; Forest = moist broadleaf forest.
[b] All $\delta^{13}C$ values are reported from original publications with no corrections applied.
[c] In Schoeninger et al. (2016) bone collagen values were converted to hair values.

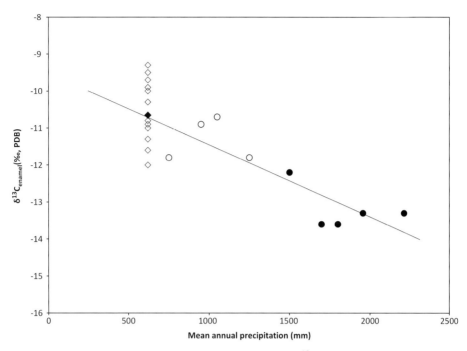

Figure 10.2 Plot of mean annual precipitation (MAP) versus $\delta^{13}C_{enamel}$; chimpanzee enamel values converted from published hair values. Carbon ($\delta^{13}C_{enamel}$) stable isotope ratios in chimpanzee enamel (Schoeninger et al. 2016; converted from hair values following Sponheimer et al. 2006 and corrected for the Suess effect, +1.5‰) and *Au. anamensis* enamel from Kanapoi (open diamond symbols, ◊, with the mean as a filled diamond, ◆; Cerling et al. 2013) plotted against MAP. Schoeninger et al. (2016) showed a statistically significant negative correlation between $\delta^{13}C$ and the MAP (trendline: $y = -0.0021x - 20.648$; $R^2 = 0.56$). Chimpanzee sites with an open circle symbol (○) are Ishasha, Fongoli, Ugalla, and Gombe (in order from lowest to highest MAP), classified as tropical and subtropical savanna, grassland, and shrubland (TSGSS) biomes. Chimpanzee sites with filled circle (●) are Kibale, Cameroon, Taï, Ganta, and Logango (in order from lowest to highest MAP), classified as tropical and subtropical moist broadleaf forest (TSMBF) biomes.

stems from the limitation of the animals, mostly pigs and rats, that have been experimentally fed known diets. In an attempt to confirm the use of corrected hair values for comparison to fossil enamel, two chimpanzee sites with published hair and enamel values available are compared to the trendline generated from corrected hair $\delta^{13}C$ values. The mean $\delta^{13}C$ hair values for Ganta (Smith et al. 2010) and Kibale (Nelson 2013) fall directly on the trendline generated by Schoeninger et al. (2016). When $\delta^{13}C$ enamel values are used from Ganta and Kibale there is a similar trend observed (trendline: $y = -0.0037x - 7.3631$; $R^2 = 0.44$), although the mean enamel values from the sites are more negative relative to the mean corrected hair values (Figure 10.3). As the trends are similar, the original trendline using hair converted to enamel values will be used for this comparison and following discussion.

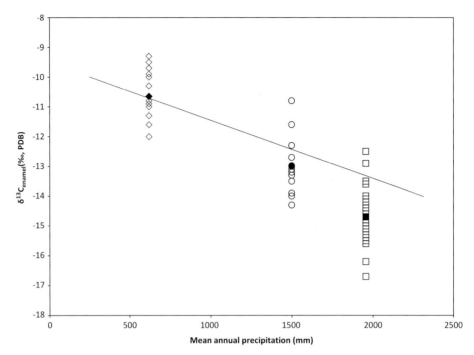

Figure 10.3 Plot of mean annual precipitation (MAP) versus $\delta^{13}C_{enamel}$ from Kibale, Ganta, and Kanapoi. Carbon ($\delta^{13}C_{enamel}$) stable isotope ratios in chimpanzee enamel from Kibale (open circle symbols, ○, with mean as a filled circle, ●; Nelson 2013), Ganta (open square symbols, □, with mean as a filled square, ■; Smith et al. 2010), and *Au. anamensis* enamel from Kanapoi (open diamond symbols, ◊, with the mean as a filled diamond, ♦; Cerling et al. 2013) plotted against MAP. The trendline is generated from hair values in Schoeninger et al. (2016) corrected to enamel values (trendline: $y = -0.0021x - 20.648$; $R^2 = 0.56$).

Discussion

It is important when reconstructing paleoenvironments to appreciate the potential biases of relying on one type of data over another. By looking at modern environmental reconstructions from animal data, we gain further appreciation for how inaccurate past ecosystem reconstructions might be if researchers relied on few lines of evidence. Schoeninger and colleagues found a strong correlation ($R^2 = 0.56$, $p < 0.001$) between MAP and the $\delta^{13}C$ values of chimpanzee hair, which confirmed that local site ecology influenced the source plant tissues consumed by chimpanzees (Schoeninger et al. 2016). However, two sites did not record the expected values in the hair. Ishasha chimpanzees recorded lower than expected $\delta^{13}C$ values for the predicted MAP and this is a habitat where the chimpanzees live and feed in a more humid gallery forest along a perennially flowing river (Schoeninger et al. 2016; Sept et al. 1992). Ugalla chimpanzees recorded higher than expected $\delta^{13}C$ values for the predicted MAP and this is a habitat of continuous leguminous trees with a very open canopy and enough light for C_4 grasses to grow, which possibly causes the MAP to be an unreliable indicator of canopy cover (Schoeninger et al. 2016). These examples highlight how, if biological isotopes alone were relied upon to reconstruct the paleoenvironments of hominins, it is possible that specific local site ecology or behavioral adaptations for exploiting particular niches within a larger mosaic habitat might not yield a complete picture of the past. In the East African Rift, transition between different biomes (for example, closed canopy forest transitioning into open grassland) can be sudden (Ward et al. 1999). During the fluvial phase that *Au. anamensis* occupied Allia Bay and Kanapoi, the Omo River could have dominated an otherwise arid environment to the extent that only narrow ecotones existed between desert and forest niches (Ward et al. 1999).

Currently, 12 individuals of *Au. anamensis* at Kanapoi have $\delta^{13}C_{enamel}$ and $\delta^{18}O_{enamel}$ values published (n = 17; Cerling et al. 2013) and unlike other later hominins they exhibit a narrow range of $\delta^{13}C_{enamel}$ values indicating a C_3-based diet similar to the earlier *Ar. ramidus* (White et al. 2009a). Using 620 mm as the estimated MAP for Kanapoi, the *Au. anamensis* $\delta^{13}C$ mean falls on the predicted trendline (Figure 10.2) for the local ecology of these early hominins similar to arid chimpanzee sites categorized as a tropical and subtropical savannas, grasslands, and shrublands (TSGSS) biome (Schoeninger et al. 2016), supporting the interpretation of Kanapoi as a semi-arid to arid paleoclimate. As an ecoregion, if Kanapoi had an arid climate with niches of denser woodland, then it is likely that within that mosaic habitat *Au. anamensis* was exploiting food resources primarily along a narrow riparian corridor (Cerling et al. 2013).

The noncalcic soil formation during the Allia Bay occupation suggests that the site experienced little seasonal precipitation or MAP values greater than 1000 mm (Wynn 2004). Previous interpretations of Allia Bay as a relatively well-watered site (Schoeninger et al. 2003) suggests that Allia Bay was more mesic compared to Kanapoi, suggesting MAP >620 mm, but other proxies are needed to characterize the amount of paleoprecipitation and level of seasonality. If Allia Bay *Au. anamensis* populations had a similar feeding ecology to Kanapoi hominins but a greater MAP, then it is possible that Allia Bay hominins would plot similar to the Ugalla chimpanzees (Figure 10.2). This would indicate that early hominins were occupying open Miombo woodlands similar to the environment at Ugalla (MAP = 1050 mm). The Allia Bay fauna isotope data clearly indicates a mosaic of habitats available to early hominins who could have been exploiting dietary resources from a more densely covered woodland along a riverine channel that was more mesic, situated in an ecoregion with areas that were arid with open grassland, as is observed from the Ugalla chimpanzees.

Conclusion

The value of considering what modern chimpanzee $\delta^{13}C$ values can contribute to paleoenvironment reconstructions of *Au. anamensis* sites in the Turkana Basin is in discussions of how adaptively flexible our early hominin species was in their feeding ecology and how they exploited a particular microhabitat. After applying correction factors (i.e., Suess effect, converting hair to enamel values) to the modern chimpanzee hair data, it is clear that we can move beyond using $\delta^{13}C$ values from fauna to solely characterize the diet or canopy cover in paleoenvironments. By using $\delta^{13}C$ values of modern chimpanzees, researchers can use the extensive observational data on feeding behavior and habitat use of modern chimpanzee communities to contribute more detailed reconstructions of the meaning of fossil hominin habitat data beyond an interpretation of mosaic. If we use chimpanzees as referential models for early hominin behavior, then *Au. anamensis* at Allia Bay and Kanapoi might have been feeding within limited mesic microhabitats within a larger xeric mosaic habitat. It is critical to evaluate multiple lines of evidence when reconstructing paleoenvironments of early hominins and each fossil locality should be considered at the local scale within a broader region.

References

Behrensmeyer AK (2006) Climate change and human evolution. *Science* 311(5760):476–478.

Behrensmeyer AK, Todd NE, Potts R, and McBrinn GE (1997) Late Pliocene faunal turnover in the Turkana Basin, Kenya and Ethiopia. *Science* 278(5343):1589–1594.

Bobe R, Behrensmeyer AK, and Chapman RE (2002) Faunal change, environmental variability and late Pliocene hominin evolution. *Journal of Human Evolution* 42(4):475–497.

Bocherens H, Fizet M, Mariotti A, et al. (1991) Isotopic biogeochemistry (13C, 15N) of fossil vertebrate collagen: application to the study of a past food web including Neandertal man. *Journal of Human Evolution* 20(6):481–492.

Bonnefille R (1995) A reassessment of the Plio-Pleistocene pollen record of East Africa. In Vrba E, Denton G, Partridge T, and Buckle LH, editors. *Paleoclimate and Evolution with Emphasis on Human Origins*. Yale University Press. Pp. 299–310.

Bonnefille R and Mohammed U (1994). Pollen-inferred climatic fluctuations in Ethiopia during the last 3000 years. *Palaeogeography, Palaeoclimatology, Palaeoecology* 109(2–4):331–343.

Bonnefille R, Potts R, Chalié F, Jolly D, and Peyron O (2004) High-resolution vegetation and climate change associated with Pliocene *Australopithecus afarensis*. *Proceedings of the National Academy of Sciences* 101(33):12125–12129.

Brown FH and McDougall I (2011) Geochronology of the Turkana depression of northern Kenya and southern Ethiopia. *Evolutionary Anthropology* 20(6):217–227.

Carter ML (2001) *Sensitivity of Stable Isotopes (^{13}C, ^{15}N, and ^{18}O) in Bone to Dietary Specialization and Niche Separation among Sympatric Primates in Kibale National Park, Uganda* (Doctoral dissertation). University of Chicago.

Cerling TE (1992) Development of grasslands and savannas in East Africa during the Neogene. *Palaeogeography, Palaeoclimatology, Palaeoecology* 97(3):241–247.

Cerling TE and Harris JM (1999) Carbon isotope fractionation between diet and bioapatite in ungulate mammals and implications for ecological and paleoecological studies. *Oecologia* 120:347–363.

Cerling TE, Bowman JR, and O'Neil JR (1988) An isotopic study of a fluvial-lacustrine sequence: the Plio-Pleistocene Koobi Fora sequence, East Africa. *Palaeogeography, Palaeoclimatology, Palaeoecology* 63(4):335–356.

Cerling TE, Harris JM, MacFadden BJ, et al. (1997) Global vegetation change through the Miocene/Pliocene boundary. *Nature* 389(6647):153–158.

Cerling TE, Levin NE, Quade J, et al. (2010) Comment on the paleoenvironment of *Ardipithecus ramidus*. *Science* 328(5982):1105.

Cerling TE, Levin NE, and Passey BH (2011a) Stable isotope ecology in the Omo-Turkana basin. *Evolutionary Anthropology* 20(6):228–237.

Cerling TE, Wynn JG, Andanje SA, et al. (2011b) Woody cover and hominin environments in the past 6 million years. *Nature* 476(7358):51–56.

Cerling TE, Manthi FK, Mbua EN, et al. (2013) Stable isotope-based diet reconstructions of Turkana Basin hominins. *Proceedings of the National Academy of Sciences* 110(26):10501–10506.

Cerling TE, Andanje SA, Blumenthal SA, et al. (2015) Dietary changes of large herbivores in the Turkana Basin, Kenya from 4 to 1 Ma. *Proceedings of the National Academy of Sciences* 112 (37):11467–11472.

deMenocal PB (2004) African climate change and faunal evolution during the Pliocene–Pleistocene. *Earth and Planetary Science Letters* 220(1–2):3–24.

deMenocal PB and Rind D (1993) Sensitivity of Asian and African climate to variations in seasonal insolation, glacial ice cover, sea surface temperature, and Asian orography. *Journal of Geophysical Research: Atmospheres* 98(D4):7265–7287.

Domínguez-Rodrigo M (2014) Is the "Savanna Hypothesis" a dead concept for explaining the emergence of the earliest hominins? *Current Anthropology* 55(1):59–81.

Fahy G, Richards MR, Riedel J, Hublin JJ, and Boesch C (2013) Stable isotope evidence of meat eating and hunting specialization in adult male chimpanzees. *Proceedings of the National Academy of Sciences* 110:5829–5833.

Fernández MH and Vrba ES (2006) Plio-Pleistocene climatic change in the Turkana Basin (East Africa): evidence from large mammal faunas. *Journal of Human Evolution* 50(6):595–626.

Garten Jr CT and Taylor Jr G (1992) Foliar $\delta^{13}C$ within a temperate deciduous forest: spatial, temporal, and species sources of variation. *Oecologia* 90(1):1–7.

Geraads D, Bobe R, and Manthi FK (2013) New ruminants (Mammalia) from the Pliocene of Kanapoi, Kenya, and a revision of previous collections, with a note on the Suidae. *Journal of African Earth Sciences* 85:53–61.

Haile-Selassie Y, Saylor BZ, Deino A, Alene M, and Latimer BM (2010) New hominid fossils from Woranso-Mille (Central Afar, Ethiopia) and taxonomy of early *Australopithecus*. *American Journal of Physical Anthropology* 141(3):406–417.

Harley GW (1939) Roads and trails in Liberia. *Geographical Review* 29:447–460.

Harris JM and Leakey M (2003) Introduction. In Harris J and Leakey M, editors. *Contributions in Science: Geology and Vertebrate Paleontology of the Early Pliocene Site of Kanapoi, Northern Kenya*. Natural History Museum of Los Angeles County. Pp. 1–7.

Harris JM, Brown F, Leakey M, Walker A, and Leakey R (1988) Pliocene and Pleistocene hominid-bearing sites from west of Lake Turkana, Kenya. *Science* 239(4835):27–33.

Joordens JC, Vonhof HB, Feibel CS, et al. (2011) An astronomically-tuned climate framework for hominins in the Turkana Basin. *Earth and Planetary Science Letters* 307(1):1–8.

Keeling CD (1979) The Suess effect: ^{13}carbon–^{14}carbon interrelations. *Environmental International* 2:229–300.

Kimbel WH, Lockwood CA, Ward CV, et al. (2006) Was *Australopithecus anamensis* ancestral to *A. afarensis*? A case of anagenesis in the hominin fossil record. *Journal of Human Evolution* 51(2):134–152.

Kingston JD (2007) Shifting adaptive landscapes: progress and challenges in reconstructing early hominid environments. *American Journal of Physical Anthropology* 134(S45):20–58.

Kingston JD, Marino BD, and Hill A (1994) Isotopic evidence for Neogene hominid paleoenvironments in the Kenya Rift Valley. *Science* 264(5161):955–958.

Leakey MG, Feibel CS, McDougall I, and Walker A (1995) New four-million-year-old hominid species from Kanapoi and Allia Bay, Kenya. *Nature* 376(6541):565–571.

Leakey MG, Feibel CS, McDougall I, Ward C, and Walker A (1998) New specimens and confirmation of an early age for *Australopithecus anamensis*. *Nature* 393(6680):62–66.

Lee-Thorp JA, van der Merwe NJ, and Brain CK (1989) Isotopic evidence for dietary differences between two extinct baboon species from Swartkrans. *Journal of Human Evolution* 18 (3):183–189.

Lee-Thorp JA, Likius A, Mackaye HT, et al. (2012) Isotopic evidence for an early shift to C_4 resources by Pliocene hominins in Chad. *Proceedings of the National Academy of Sciences* 109 (50):20369–20372.

Levin NE, Brown FH, Behrensmeyer AK, Bobe R, and Cerling TE (2011) Paleosol carbonates from the Omo Group: isotopic records of local and regional environmental change in East Africa. *Palaeogeography, Palaeoclimatology, Palaeoecology* 307(1):75–89.

Levin NE, Haile-Selassie Y, Frost SR, and Saylor BZ (2015) Dietary change among hominins and cercopithecids in Ethiopia during the early Pliocene. *Proceedings of the National Academy of Sciences* 112(40):12304–12309.

Macho GA and Lee-Thorp JA (2014) Niche partitioning in sympatric *Gorilla* and *Pan* from Cameroon: implications for life history strategies and for reconstructing the evolution of hominin life history. *PLoS One* 9:1–17.

Moore J (1996) Savanna chimpanzees, referential models and the last common ancestor. In McGrew WC, Marchant LF, and Nishida T, editors. *Great Ape Societies*. Cambridge University Press. Pp. 275–292.

Morgan ME, Kingston JD, and Marino BD (1994) Carbon isotopic evidence for the emergence of C_4 plants in the Neogene from Pakistan and Kenya. *Nature* 367(6459):162–165.

Nelson SV (2013) Chimpanzee fauna isotopes provide new interpretations of fossil ape and hominin ecologies. *Proceedings of the Royal Society B* 280(1773):1–6.

Oelze V, Head J, Robbins MM, Richards MP, and Boesch C (2014) Niche differentiation and dietary seasonality among sympatric gorillas and chimpanzees in Loango National Park (Gabon) revealed by stable isotope analysis. *Journal of Human Evolution* 66:95–106.

Passey BH, Levin NE, Cerling TE, Brown FH, and Eiler JM (2010) High-temperature environments of human evolution in East Africa based on bond ordering in paleosol carbonates. *Proceedings of the National Academy of Sciences* 107(25):11245–11249.

Peters NA, Huntington KW, and Hoke GD (2013) Hot or not? Impact of seasonally variable soil carbonate formation on paleotemperature and O-isotope records from clumped isotope thermometry. *Earth and Planetary Science Letters* 361:208–218.

Potts R (1998) Environmental hypotheses of hominin evolution. *American Journal of Physical Anthropology* 107(s27):93–136.

Reed KE (1997) Early hominid evolution and ecological change through the African Plio-Pleistocene. *Journal of Human Evolution* 32(2):289–322.

Reed KE, Rowan J, and Kamilar J (2014) African vegetation structure: modern analogs and hominin habitat reconstructions. *American Journal of Physical Anthropology* 153(S58):218.

Retallack G (1994) The environmental factor approach to the interpretation of paleosols. In Amundson R, Harden J, and Singer M, editors. *Factors of Soil Formation: A Fiftieth Anniversary Perspective*. Soil Science Society of America. Pp. 31–64.

Schoeninger MJ, Iwaniec UT, and Glander KE (1997) Stable isotope ratios indicate diet and habitat use in New World monkeys. *American Journal of Physical Anthropology* 103(1):69–83.

Schoeninger MJ, Iwaniec UT, and Nash LT (1998) Ecological attributes recorded in stable isotope ratios of arboreal prosimian hair. *Oecologia* 113(2):222–230.

Schoeninger MJ, Moore J, and Sept JM (1999) Subsistence strategies of two "savanna" chimpanzee populations: the stable isotope evidence. *American Journal of Primatology* 49:297–314.

Schoeninger MJ, Reeser H, and Hallin K (2003) Paleoenvironment of *Australopithecus anamensis* at Allia Bay, East Turkana, Kenya: evidence from mammalian herbivore enamel stable isotopes. *Journal of Anthropological Archaeology* 22(3):200–207.

Schoeninger MJ, Most CA, Moore JJ, and Somerville AD (2016) Environmental variables across *Pan troglodytes* study sites correspond with the carbon, but not the nitrogen, stable isotope ratios of chimpanzee hair. *American Journal of Primatology* 78(10):1055–1069.

Ségalen L, Lee-Thorp J, and Cerling T (2007) Timing of C_4 grass expansion across sub-Saharan Africa. *Journal of Human Evolution* 53:549–559.

Sept JM, King BJ, McGrew W, et al. (1992) Was there no place like home? A new perspective on early hominid archaeological sites from the mapping of chimpanzee nests [and comments and reply]. *Current Anthropology* 33(2):187–207.

Smith C, Morgan M, and Pilbeam D (2010) Isotopic ecology and dietary profiles of Liberian chimpanzees. *Journal of Human Evolution* 58:43–55.

Sponheimer M, Loudon J, Codron D, et al. (2006) Do "savanna" chimpanzees consume C_4 resources? *Journal of Human Evolution* 51(2):128–133.

Tiedemann R, Sarnthein M, and Shackleton NJ (1994) Astronomic timescale for the Pliocene Atlantic $\delta^{18}O$ and dust flux records of Ocean Drilling Program Site 659. *Paleoceanography* 9 (4):619–638.

van der Merwe NJ and Medina E (1991) The canopy effect, carbon isotope ratios and foodwebs in Amazonia. *Journal of Archaeological Science* 18:249–259.

Vrba ES (1985) Ecological and adaptive changes associated with early hominid evolution. In Delson E, editor. *Ancestors: The Hard Evidence.* Alan R. Liss. Pp. 63–71.

Vrba ES (1988) Late Pliocene climatic events and hominid evolution. In Grine F, editor. *Evolutionary History of the "Robust" Australopithecines.* Aldine de Gruyter. Pp. 405–426.

Vrba ES, Denton G, Partridge T, and Burckle L (1995) *Paleoclimate and Evolution with Emphasis on Human Origins.* Yale University Press.

Ward CV, Leakey M, and Walker A (1999) The new hominid species *Australopithecus anamensis. Evolutionary Anthropology* 7(6):197–205.

White TD, WoldeGabriel G, Asfaw B, et al. (2006) Asa Issie, Aramis and the origin of *Australopithecus. Nature* 440(7086):883–889.

White TD, Ambrose SH, Suwa G, et al. (2009a) Macrovertebrate paleontology and the Pliocene habitat of *Ardipithecus ramidus. Science* 326(5949):67–93.

White TD, Asfaw B, Beyene Y, et al. (2009b) *Ardipithecus ramidus* and the paleobiology of early hominids. *Science* 326(5949):64–86.

WoldeGabriel G, Ambrose SH, Barboni D, et al. (2009) The geological, isotopic, botanical, invertebrate, and lower vertebrate surroundings of *Ardipithecus ramidus. Science* 326(5949):65–65e5.

Wood B and Leakey M (2011) The Omo-Turkana Basin fossil hominins and their contribution to our understanding of human evolution in Africa. *Evolutionary Anthropology* 20(6):264–292.

Wynn JG (2000) Paleosols, stable carbon isotopes, and paleoenvironmental interpretation of Kanapoi, Northern Kenya. *Journal of Human Evolution* 39(4):411–432.

Wynn JG (2004) Influence of Plio-Pleistocene aridification on human evolution: evidence from paleosols of the Turkana Basin, Kenya. *American Journal of Physical Anthropology* 123 (2):106–118.

Zachos J, Pagani M, Sloan L, Thomas E, and Billups K (2001) Trends, rhythms, and aberrations in global climate 65 Ma to present. *Science* 292(5517):686–693.

11 Discussion and Conclusion

Move Forward, Critically

Cathy Willermet and Sang-Hee Lee

As far as I (Sang-Hee) was concerned, the attraction of biological anthropology was in its scientific approach. The lure of hypothesis testing using empirical data where the only bias to worry about was small sample size was such a powerful position for me, who had been on the humanities track until graduate school. During the 1990s in graduate school I was surprised to find out that the very premise of the scientific approach was questioned by my cohort in cultural anthropology. I quickly dismissed it without engaging in further discussion. Questioning the objectivity and the neutrality of research design was unthinkable.

While I (Cathy) found questions about humanity as addressed by anthropology intellectually satisfying, I also found the objective aspects of biological anthropology particularly appealing. I was most drawn to questions about patterning of biological variation, first in paleospecies and later with modern populations. However, the imprecision inherent in determining species boundaries, for me, became more troublesome the more I learned. This ultimately led me to question the boundaries themselves through fuzzy logic and fuzzy set theory (a legitimate scientific theory; see Zadeh 2015), one that was often misunderstood, and criticized, as vague, non-objective, non-scientific thinking.

The history of biological anthropology, in fact, parallels this psychology to a degree. The steadfast obsession with the scientific approach that characterized biological anthropology, like no other subfield in American anthropology, is in fact a response to mask the dark history surrounding its birth. Obsession with science, and in particular, a specific particular kind of science, the nomothetic, hypothetico-deductive kind, allowed us the privilege of assuming that the questions we ask and the data we employ to answer those questions stand alone, at a comfortable and safe distance from the political, historical contexts that generated the data (and the questions themselves).

The adherence to the scientific approach left unaddressed (rather, not addressed enough) the uncomfortable relationship between the field of biological anthropology and the scientific racism at the turn of the previous century. Now that a full century has passed, biological anthropology has been undergoing a fissure of identity – which way to go, biology or anthropology? In this volume, we anchor our discussion to explore biological anthropology as an integral part of anthropology. We are not the first to have raised this issue, nor to have thought of it. We are two of many similar voices calling to position biological anthropology squarely within anthropology (Aiello 2016; Calcagno 2003; Ellison 2017; Fuentes 2012; Fuentes and Weissner 2016; Marks 2009).

The fact is that biological anthropology *is* anthropology. It is the biology of ourselves. The pattern of variation in our species is a biological question, but in many ways a self-reflective one, larger than simply biological variation of a species. How does our biological variation impact our cultural beliefs? How do our cultural beliefs affect our biological variation? And how do we study this anthropologically, in keeping with our comparative, biocultural, and holistic roots?

The contributions in this volume interweave three different areas of growth in the field, pointing to the future of biological anthropology. First, we support critical and reflexive examination of our familiar thinking. Second, we advocate for creativity in evaluating our evidence and analytical techniques, and encourage the current trend toward opening the field to new perspectives and voices, including questioning our basic assumptions about our research questions. Finally, we recognize that we need to be better public advocates for anthropology.

The Strange Familiar, the Familiar Strange – Or, Giving Attention to the Unfamiliar

As we discussed in the introduction to this volume, "making the familiar strange" is a practice that can shake up one's thinking, giving room to new thoughts and ideas. Certain questions, certain methodologies, and certain data are considered more interesting and worthy to pursue. Are they more privileged than others? Contributions in this volume call out and unpack the research landscape in biological anthropology with a critical tool.

Dänae Khorasani and Sang-Hee Lee (Chapter 1) review the premise and the evidence of sexual division of labor in light of the Man the Hunter model, arguably one of the most influential models in human evolution research, and the Woman the Gatherer model, proposed as the response. Although the strange idea of gathering activity as woman's activity was made familiar, it also had the effect of conceding that the sexual division of labor is a human condition, rather than a development of historical particularity. Furthermore, the image of gathering women does not occupy equally important space in the public imagination of prehistoric humans compared to the image of men hunting. Khorasani and Lee analyzed images of prehistoric humans collected from a Google search, and found that hunting men (or men doing something) are still predominantly featured: Not much has changed since Gifford-Gonzalez's study that called out the "western"-gendered imagery in museum dioramas and textbook figures (Gifford-Gonzalez 1993).

Khorasani and Lee call for a different kind of making the strange familiar: women as hunters. Hunting as subsistence activity, on one hand, involves both men and women, as documented in ethnographic literature. Hunting as a sport, on the other hand, was historically a class-based rather than gender-based sport. It is only since the 1950s that "[t]he aftermath of World War II coincided with the creation of a new, aggressive construction of masculinity that sought to include the previously excluded working-class man" and hunting as a sport provided the means for "post-war formulations of homosocial middle-class masculinity" (Chapter 1). Man the Hunter is the familiar idea that should be strange, while woman the hunter is the strange to be made familiar.

Geographic region is another area where we should give attention to the unfamiliar. Michelle Glantz (Chapter 2) points out that the hegemonic narrative silences the others and the outsiders; the hegemonic narrative is the one that is familiar to us, and therefore needs to be made strange. Glantz asks, essentially, why is the west always controlling the models, the narratives? Perhaps evolution, like politics, is local? Central Asia is often overlooked in modern human origins research, as "the Out of Africa narrative of modern human origins . . . as well as the privileged position of the European paleoanthropological record . . . has created subordinate datasets" (Chapter 2). She argues that the peripheral areas of the Old World are marginalized in terms of research attention. Her review of the Central Asian data reveals that late Pleistocene refugia experienced less climatic fluctuation than in Western Europe, resulting in a predictable resource for hominins, and variation in both the archaeological and skeletal hominin record shows increased complexity and admixture compared to the dominant paradigm of Out of Africa replacement of local populations.

So why is Central Asia, and peripheries in general, given less attention? Glantz proffers several reasons for this. First, the hegemonic Eurocentric dominance of both research and researchers privileges certain perspectives over others, and points to a lack of reflexivity in paleoanthropology. Privileging the European and African data, reflecting the hegemony of the American research funding and Euro-American researchers, silences Asia data. She writes (Chapter 2), "high-status genomic research has now forced paleoanthropologists to add the caveat that archaic hominin displacement occurred with some admixture. However, this admission does not change the trajectory of the metanarrative; the expectation that the superior (biologically and/or culturally) always vanquishes the inferior, a colonial narrative so normalized in paleoanthropology that it often disguises itself as neo-Darwinism." Second, an emphasis on science, technology, and publication in English may play a role in prioritizing western work over that of local researchers, feeding into colonial structures of power, however unconsciously.

Marc Kissel (Chapter 3) calls out the racism, sexism, and colonialism that are in the substrate of popular science-writers who use human evolution research as supportive data. He points to several misunderstandings that appear in public discourse about science and biology. One such misunderstanding involves the oversimplification of the relationship between evolution, genetics, and human behavior, particularly as it relates to violence and sex. He critiques Steven Pinker's (2011, 2018) work in particular, challenging the data Pinker uses as the evidence for decrease in violence in human evolutionary history. The dataset showing decrease in violence includes certain behaviors while dismissing other acts that can be just as deadly: just because people are not getting killed in the same proportion does not mean they are not subject to death by violence. Are males naturally more violent? Some research on the MAOA gene suggests that low MAOA expression in males raised in abusive environments is associated with aggression and criminal behavior. In some cases, this study has been used to reduce jail time for violent crime (Feresin 2009).

Insects may have been a reliable food source for the majority of human evolutionary history, and the disgust response may be specific and limited to the western hegemonic cultures. Julie Lesnik (Chapter 4) asks: Why do some cultures, but not others, accept insects as food? Is this disgust simply a part of "western" culture, or are other factors at play? She confirms that there is a correlation between latitude and abundance of insects, and that latitude predicts insect consumption in 80 percent of the cases; populations living closer to the equator both have access to more insect abundance and eat them more often. Lesnik unpacks the idea that foraging in general, and insect eating in particular, is seen as inherently "uncivilized." Insects offer complete proteins, fats, and micronutrients, and are usually quite abundant, particularly in low-latitude areas. She argues that western Europeans, living in high-latitude areas, did not have the tradition of insect eating. Colonizers from these regions maintained their home food preferences in new environments and stigmatized this food source as part of primitive behavior in indigenous cultures. Moving past this "will contribute to decolonizing western culture and creating a more inclusive space for indigenous identities" (Chapter 4).

Data are not created equal; the bodies that make up our data are products of the particular history and politics. Robin Nelson (Chapter 5) tracks movement away from qualitative and descriptive methods within biological anthropology and toward hypothetico-deductive quantitative methods valued by the other biological sciences. She takes a historical approach, arguing that the shift stemmed from our desire to distance ourselves from the scientific racism inherent in typological race studies. More quantitative and objective methods would certainly shield us from biased results. One area of biological anthropology that lent itself well to quantitative methods was human reproduction and survivorship, nutrition, and growth. In fact, a mixed-methods approach that incorporates qualitative and quantitative research can be very powerful. She reviews research related to adaptation and reproduction, and states (Chapter 5), "[o]ur disciplinary emphasis on quantitative assessments of bodies has foregrounded and privileged these numerical data, while relegating the substantive and informative information regarding proximate decision-making, change, and quality of life to the footnotes." It is that qualitative research that contextualizes the numerical data and allows for a reasoned analysis of how decisions are actively made (Weissner 2016). A mixed-methods approach, then, can show a fuller picture.

Evaluating Evidence Critically

Methods matter. Research methods are (or should be) bound to the questions we ask, but they also signal how we see our science. Data are considered objective, and certain kinds of data are more respected. The field already recognized that the evaluation of data is always contextual, reflected in the saying, "Data do not speak for themselves." In the tradition of hypothesis testing with quantifiable data following statistical reasoning, this expression means that data alone cannot tell whether a hypothesis is true or false, it has to be put in a design that involves probabilistic statements. Statistics has held its central place as the singular barometer to assess the evidentiary weight of the data. And statistics give weight to datasets with a large enough size to assume a normal distribution, and to centroid values such as means and medians while overlooking outliers. We need to question our basic assumptions about our research. Authors in this volume call out such practices and call our attention to the kind of data that has taken a backseat.

Small or non-normal datasets have been considered less often, particularly in the history of paleopathological research, which was considered by some as being too focused on the individual. In this way, the integration of paleopathology into bioarchaeology as a whole can provide context for understanding illness and (dis) ability. Both familiar (median) and strange (outlier) individuals deserve attention for the information about life history events and care they bring. Stodder and Byrnes (Chapter 6) critique this practice through their questioning of the basic understanding of "disability." They point out that the category of disability was reified during the western Industrial era to characterize who was available to work. Disease or disability understood through a medical lens is different than through a social model, and may differ temporally and culturally. Someone "disabled" in one cultural community may not be so considered in another (Goodley 2014). Stodder and Byrnes (Chapter 6) point out that impairment and disability should not be conflated in bioarchaeology, stating "we are compelled to acknowledge and investigate the unfamiliar realms of cross-cultural health and the situationally complex perceptions and reactions to the differently abled and the 'other.'"

Analyzing our datasets in new ways makes the strange familiar. Sharon DeWitte (Chapter 7) highlights the importance of context as she points out that evidence of healing on periosteal lesions is critical to understanding status effects on health. A closer examination of data, differentiating between fresh periosteal lesions and healed periosteal lesions, paints a picture that is different from what would be inferred from a straightforward count of periosteal lesions. She explores how we can re-examine our skeletal lesion data in light of the Osteological Paradox: frailty, considered to be familiar evidence of ill health, can also be strange evidence of persistence. She turns on its head the conventional bioarchaeological approach of viewing the presence of skeletal lesions and stress markers as indicators of poor health. Generally, skeletal assemblages show a skewed sample toward people who are most frail, with the highest risk of death, regardless of age. DeWitte asks whether examining patterning in the degree of lesion healing can provide a more nuanced picture of health and frailty. Her population of study, the St. Mary Graces cemetery in fourteenth- to sixteenth-century London, contains both high socioeconomic status and low socioeconomic status individuals at a period marked by increasing standards of living in the wake of the Black Death. The high-status individuals have more lesions, which traditionally suggests poor health. However, when evidence of healing is considered, the high-status individuals show more evidence of healing. She states (Chapter 7), "Analysis of porotic hyperostosis and periosteal new bone formation revealed an association between healed lesions and age, suggesting that higher status did not shield people from exposure to physiological stressors, but, instead, improved their chances of surviving those stressors." During this period of improving diets and decreasing social inequalities, there is evidence for social status imparting more persistence and less frailty.

In conventional science, data are often placed in a hierarchy, and scalar data are privileged over ordinal and nonmetric data. We can also examine our nonmetric data in new ways. Cathy Willermet and Heather Edgar teamed with statisticians John Daniels and Joseph McKean to develop a new methodology for analyzing biological distance using ordinal data (Chapter 8). The data are dental morphological traits, bumps and grooves on the tooth surface whose development is genetically controlled. These nonmetric traits have a continuous expression that is parsed into grades or degree of expression. For biological distance analysis these grades are generally dichotomized into presence or absence; then the frequency of presence of features is compared among populations using biological distance analyses such as mean measure of divergence or pseudo-Mahalanobis D^2. Willermet and colleagues find a way to explore patterns of biological distance that does not require dichotomization – compressing sample variation from many grades to two can mask important, interesting differences between the samples. Also, the new technique should be robust with respect to missing data, a factor that can affect both MMD and pseudo-Mahalanobis D^2. They develop a new method, called rank estimator of grade differences, or RED (technically REGD, but that is a mouthful). The new method performs very well compared to the other methods with both a simulated dataset and an orthodontic one, without compressing the data. They write (Chapter 8), "[a] major benefit . . . is an improvement in our ability to utilize multistate, rather than dichotomous, information about the variation in our population samples. If dental morphological traits are indeed polygenic, the variation of trait expression may provide important information on genetic relationships between populations. This complexity simply is not fully captured by dichotomous trait frequency data." This method is a useful new tool in our statistical toolkit. But perhaps even more important, it helps us explore our familiar data in strange new ways.

New methodology opens new questions, but it also introduces a new kind of bias for more complete specimens while fragmentary specimens do not receive attention. With biases toward bigger data and more complete datasets, less complete datasets and critical details can be overlooked. Adam Van Arsdale (Chapter 9) recorded the frequency with which fossil crania were mentioned in articles published in the *American Journal of Physical Anthropology* and the *Journal of Human Evolution* from 1988 to 2015. He classified each of the 102 hominin fossils mentioned by degree of fragmentation (fragmentation index, or FI). He discovered, not surprisingly, that more complete fossils were cited more often. What was disturbing, however, was the degree to which highly complete fossils (FI category 5) were more highly represented – about twice that of the next highest category (Chapter 9; Figures 9.4, 9.5) and that bias seemed to increase over time (Chapter 9; Figure 9.4).

We could conduct a thought experiment based on Van Arsdale's selection of FI 5 and FI 4 data – what would be our dataset to understand human origins? How representative, how biased? His selection includes nine FI 5 specimens: a Neandertal

Table 11.1 Hominin fossils with fragmentation index 4 or 5, from Van Arsdale (this volume, Table 9.1), sorted by geographic area

FI[a]	Specimen name	Geographic area	Date range	Species name
5	Petralona	Greece	350–150 KYA[b]	*Homo heidelbergensis*
4	Saccopastore	Italy	130–100 KYA	*Homo neanderthalensis*[d]
4	Jebel Irhoud 1	Morocco	300 KYA	*Homo sapiens*
5	Amud	Israel	41 KYA	*Homo neanderthalensis*
4	Qafzeh 6	Israel	100 KYA	*Homo sapiens*
4	Qafzeh 9	Israel	100 KYA	*Homo sapiens*
5	Skhul 5	Israel	120–80 KYA	*Homo sapiens*
4	KNM-ER 1470	Kenya	1.9 MYA[c]	*Homo rudolfensis*
5	KNM-ER 1813	Kenya	1.9 MYA	*Homo habilis*
5	KNM-ER 3733	Kenya	1.78 MYA	*Homo erectus*
4	KNM-ER 3883	Kenya	1.6 MYA	*Homo erectus*
5	KNM-WT 15000	Kenya	1.6 MYA	*Homo erectus*
5	Bodo	Ethiopia	600 KYA	*Homo heidelbergensis*
4	Laetoli 18	Tanzania	120 KYA	*Homo sapiens*
4	OH-24	Tanzania	1.8 MYA	*Homo habilis*
5	Kabwe	Zambia	300–125 KYA	*Homo heidelbergensis*
5	STS 5	South Africa	2.5–2.1 MYA	*Australopithecus africanus*
4	STS 71	South Africa	2.8–2.4 MYA	*Australopithecus africanus*
4	Sangiran 17	Indonesia	1.3–1.0 MYA	*Homo erectus*
4	Sangiran 2	Indonesia	>1 MYA	*Homo erectus*

[a] FI = fragmentation index. FI category 5 is more preserved than FI category 4, after Van Arsdale (this volume). Date and region information: Hublin et al. 2017; Niewoehner 2001; Smithsonian Museum of Natural History 2019; Wolpoff 1999.

[b] KYA = thousand years ago.

[c] MYA = million years ago.

[d] Although we do not think Neandertals are a separate species from *Homo sapiens*, they are labeled as *Homo neanderthalensis* in these tables to make the point about uneven sampling and representation in data.

and an early modern human from Israel; one archaic form each from Greece, Zambia, and Ethiopia; two *H. erectus* and one *H. habilis* from Kenya, and one South African *A. africanus*. There are 11 FI 4 specimens: one Italian Neandertal; four early moderns from Israel, Morocco, and Tanzania; two Indonesian and one Kenyan *H. erectus*; two *H. habilis* from Kenya and Tanzania, and another *A. africanus* from South Africa. We could sort this sample at least three ways by geographic area, time, and putative species, each of which points to the serious inadequacy of this sample (Tables 11.1–11.3). Van Arsdale asks significant questions about the fragmentary fossil record (Chapter 9): "Which set of fossils is more important? Which has more evolutionary information? Which is more likely to influence how we understand the

Table 11.2 Hominin fossils with fragmentation Index 4 or 5, from Van Arsdale (this volume, Table 9.1), sorted by date range

FI[a]	Specimen name	Geographic area	Date range	Species name
4	STS 71	South Africa	2.8–2.4 MYA[b]	*Australopithecus africanus*
5	STS 5	South Africa	2.5–2.1 MYA	*Australopithecus africanus*
4	KNM-ER 1470	Kenya	1.9 MYA	*Homo rudolfensis*
5	KNM-ER 1813	Kenya	1.9 MYA	*Homo habilis*
4	OH-24	Tanzania	1.8 MYA	*Homo habilis*
5	KNM-ER 3733	Kenya	1.78 MYA	*Homo erectus*
4	KNM-ER 3883	Kenya	1.6 MYA	*Homo erectus*
5	KNM-WT 15000	Kenya	1.6 MYA	*Homo erectus*
4	Sangiran 17	Indonesia	1.3–1.0 MYA	*Homo erectus*
4	Sangiran 2	Indonesia	>1 MYA	*Homo erectus*
5	Bodo	Ethiopia	600 KYA[c]	*Homo heidelbergensis*
5	Petralona	Greece	350–150 KYA	*Homo heidelbergensis*
5	Kabwe	Zambia	300–125 KYA	*Homo heidelbergensis*
4	Jebel Irhoud 1	Morocco	300 KYA	*Homo sapiens*
4	Saccopastore	Italy	130–100 KYA	*Homo neanderthalensis*[d]
5	Skhul 5	Israel	120–80 KYA	*Homo sapiens*
4	Laetoli 18	Tanzania	120 KYA	*Homo sapiens*
4	Qafzeh 6	Israel	100 KYA	*Homo sapiens*
4	Qafzeh 9	Israel	100 KYA	*Homo sapiens*
5	Amud	Israel	41 KYA	*Homo neanderthalensis*[d]

[a] FI = fragmentation index. FI category 5 is more preserved than FI category 4, after Van Arsdale (this volume). Date and region information: Hublin et al. 2017; Niewoehner 2001; Smithsonian Museum of Natural History 2019; Wolpoff 1999.
[b] MYA = million years ago.
[c] KYA = thousand years ago.
[d] Although we do not think Neandertals are a separate species from *Homo sapiens*, they are labeled as *Homo neanderthalensis* in these tables to make the point about uneven sampling and representation in data.

trajectory of human evolution? How will the significance of these fossils change as preferred methods of analysis change within the discipline?" Obviously, limiting ourselves to this data subset is not scientifically tenable. However, bias in specimen choice or methodology has the potential to influence our views, a topic often debated in paleobiology (Flannery Sutherland et al. 2019). We should be aware of this potential in thinking not only of what analyses to perform, but also when reviewing manuscripts with small sample sizes.

Melanie Beasley and Margaret Schoeninger (Chapter 10) explore the evidence available to reconstruct paleoenvironments using stable isotopes, and ask what

Table 11.3 Hominin fossils with fragmentation Index 4 or 5, from Van Arsdale (this volume, Table 9.1), sorted by species name

FI[a]	Specimen name	Geographic area	Date range	Species name
4	STS 71	South Africa	2.8–2.4 MYA[b]	*Australopithecus africanus*
5	STS 5	South Africa	2.5–2.1 MYA	*Australopithecus africanus*
5	KNM-ER 1813	Kenya	1.9 MYA	*Homo habilis*
4	OH-24	Tanzania	1.8 MYA	*Homo habilis*
4	KNM-ER 1470	Kenya	1.9 MYA	*Homo rudolfensis*
5	KNM-ER 3733	Kenya	1.78 MYA	*Homo erectus*
4	KNM-ER 3883	Kenya	1.6 MYA	*Homo erectus*
5	KNM-WT 15000	Kenya	1.6 MYA	*Homo erectus*
4	Sangiran 17	Indonesia	1.3–1.0 MYA	*Homo erectus*
4	Sangiran 2	Indonesia	>1 MYA	*Homo erectus*
5	Bodo	Ethiopia	600 KYA[c]	*Homo heidelbergensis*
5	Petralona	Greece	350–150 KYA	*Homo heidelbergensis*
5	Kabwe	Zambia	300–125 KYA	*Homo heidelbergensis*
4	Saccopastore	Italy	130–100 KYA	*Homo neanderthalensis*[d]
5	Amud	Israel	41 KYA	*Homo neanderthalensis*
4	Jebel Irhoud 1	Morocco	300 KYA	*Homo sapiens*
5	Skhul 5	Israel	120–80 KYA	*Homo sapiens*
4	Laetoli 18	Tanzania	120 KYA	*Homo sapiens*
4	Qafzeh 6	Israel	100 KYA	*Homo sapiens*
4	Qafzeh 9	Israel	100 KYA	*Homo sapiens*

[a] FI = fragmentation index. FI category 5 is more preserved than FI category 4, after Van Arsdale (this volume). Date and region information: Hublin et al. 2017; Niewoehner 2001; Smithsonian Museum of Natural History 2019; Wolpoff 1999.
[b] MYA = million years ago.
[c] KYA = thousand years ago.
[d] Although we do not think Neandertals are a separate species from *Homo sapiens*, they are labeled as *Homo neanderthalensis* in these tables to make the point about uneven sampling and representation in data.

characterizes a mosaic environment. Chimpanzees, they point out, can use a subset of possible ecological niches available to them, so hair δ^{13}C samples may not match their generalized ecological habitat (Schoeninger et al. 2016). Enamel sources for δ^{13}C values differed from expectations based upon environmental precipitation data. They note that a species uses its environment differently for different behaviors: "[what] if early hominins procured food resources in particular microhabitats but ranged broadly throughout an environment for mating and sleeping? Would that change how we interpret the δ^{13}C values of pedogenic carbonates of a region compared to the δ^{13}C values of tooth enamel from fossil species occupying that region?" (Chapter 10). This means that what evidence we use to reconstruct paleoenvironments can capture different activity elements. Clearly, it is extremely important to focus on the finer-scaled, local resolution of habitat and feeding environments. If biological isotopes alone are used to reconstruct hominin paleoenvironments, we might mischaracterize how our behaviorally flexible, adaptable hominin ancestors used their environments.

Biological Anthropologists as Social Justice Advocates

In December 2018 the American Association of Physical Anthropologists announced the results of their non-binding membership survey about changing the association's name (Aiello 2018). The majority of voters indicated they preferred the replacement of "biological" in place of "physical." Why does the word "biological" matter? Fuentes (2010:4) argues that the word "physical" is "prioritizing the descriptive and structural rather than the dynamic and evolutionary." Caspari (2018) notes that physical anthropology grew, in part, from race science that focused on the essential physical and behavioral traits through which we could study human differences. Nelson (Chapter 5) points out that Hrdlička (1918) felt one of the central aims of the discipline was to establish a system of body measurements so that quantitative assessments of the human body could help us understand human differences. The politically charged beginning of the subfield is carried into the present a century later with the discussion of our field's name. In any enterprise, including scientific ones, words signal both the role of the subject participants in the research and the attitude of the researcher toward the subject. So we hope that the upcoming name change, should it occur, will signal the field's movement away from our essentialist past. We have a long road ahead, however, in that public consumption of genetic information often gets reduced to essentialist explanations.

The persistence of the race concept, despite the strong messaging from biological anthropology that the human species does not group biologically into racial categories, belies the increased racialization in society through political, social, and economic lenses (Caspari 2018; Sussman 2014; Véran 2012). Why are we not getting through? What is the meaning of race in the post-genomic era? A definition of race in law is not well defined, in America or elsewhere, and genetic research can be impacted by colonial views on racial mixing (de Souza and Santos 2014; Lowe 2009). This is true of the general public (Phillips et al. 2007), and is particularly important in this era of exploding interest in commercial genetic tests and issues of identity. As anthropologists, what is our obligation in engaging with the public? Do we consider that books like *A Troublesome Inheritance* (Wade 2014), which argues that human variation can be understood by hereditarian racialist notions, or Pinker's *Enlightenment Now!* (2018) that eugenics are old news, no longer important to monitor? No, this is our job to counter (Fuentes 2014; Kissel, this volume; Marks 2009; Roseman 2014).

Race is one area where we can analyze this interplay that highlights the peculiar differences of self-reflective species studies. For example, miscegenation laws and behaviors that have affected who one can marry can impact patterns of variation as seen in European American and African American admixture (Chapter 8). But how we study race matters. Causes and patterns of human biological variation are complex, and are studied in many varied ways (see papers in Edgar and Hunley 2009).

Heather Edgar (2009) uses dental morphological traits to study African Americans and their ancestral populations. She identified geographic and temporal patterns of admixture that correlate with historical and social events, such as the African Diaspora and the Great Migration. With Corey Ragsdale, she studied cultural effects on biological distance among pre-European contact Mexican and US Southwestern Hispanic populations (Ragsdale and Edgar 2014). Cultural identity affects admixture patterns within the Hispanic community as well (Willermet and Edgar 2009). Patterns of admixture can differ by group due to cultural effects; for instance, Lopes Maciel and collegues (2011) found preferential inclusion of indigenous women in African descent groups in the Brazilian Amazon. Studying population substructure can reveal cultural factors that affect mate choice (Bortolini et al. 1999) and health (Gravlee 2009).

Biological anthropology has skirted the reflexive storm that shook cultural anthropology. Fewer biological anthropologists than cultural anthropologists took seriously the social and political position that we (should) occupy. However, that questioning can no longer be denied nor delayed. In some ways we have made strides, but the history of the field of biological anthropology is not separable from its colonial history related to race (Nelson, Chapter 5) or gender (Khorasani and Lee, Chapter 1). The call for action and self-reflection is an urgent one. Research products of biological anthropology are appropriated by non-experts and translated for public consumption, sometimes without context, in popular science books (Kissel, Chapter 3) or in museum dioramas (Khorasani and Lee, Chapter 1).

In these times, the authority of scientists to speak on their expertise is sometimes met with public skepticism (Funk 2017). Science is in need of advocacy, and since 2017 there have been hundreds of annual Marches for Science held all over the USA and abroad (see www.marchforscience.com). Scientists in general, and biological anthropologists in particular, are realizing that public advocacy is an increasingly essential part of keeping our fields dynamic, relevant, and funded. Here are just a few from-the-headlines topics to which biological anthropologists can meaningfully contribute, in alphabetical order: addiction (Dingel et al. 2015); aging (Agarwal 2019; Edes and Crews 2017); breastfeeding (Stuart-Macadem 1995; see papers in Tomori et al. 2017); epidemics (DeWitte 2016; Lock and Nguyen 2018; Pálfi et al. 2015); epigenetics (Jackson et al. 2013); forensic identification in migrant contexts (Latham and O'Daniel 2018; Ross et al. 2016); genetic testing (Lock and Nguyen 2018); gut microbiome (Amato 2016; Warinner and Lewis 2015); health and nutrition (Dufour and Piperata 2018; Kuzawa 2010; Mohsena et al. 2015); human–wildlife interactions (Parathian et al. 2018); inequality and public health policy (Gravlee et al. 2009; Hicks and Leonard 2014; Kuzawa 2014); migration effects (Houldcroft et al. 2017; Mascie-Taylor and Kryzanowska 2017); postmortem child abuse (Buckley and Whittle 2008); psychoneuroimmunology (Shattuck 2018); reproduction and women's health (Myers and Johns in press; Stone 2016). This list is neither exhaustive nor representative of the entirety of research on these topics. The point is that we anthropologists have a lot we can discuss in the public forum. We should not wait to be asked to do so.

Through both osteobiography (Stodder and Palkovich 2012) and the related practice of forensic biohistory (the osteobiography of known individuals [Stojanowski and Duncan 2017]), we can stimulate the public's scientific interest and appetite for narrative toward understanding the past. Public engagement is taking new forms: the Wenner-Gren Foundation's online publication *Sapiens* that launched in 2016 uses a robust multimedia presence – photo essays, videos, blogs, podcasts – to further their aim to "transform how the public understands anthropology" (Sapiens 2019). A check of the American Anthropological Association websites in February 2019 lists nearly two dozen podcasts for anyone to enjoy, and at least as many webinars. A number of biological anthropologists appear in these venues. There is no similar public outreach presence on the American Association of Physical Anthropologists website. Julie Lesnik is launching www.octopusandape.com, designed to make biological science accessible through short, entertaining video clips.

Conclusion

We cannot help but agree that much of the discussion about hegemony in biological anthropology comes from the still-present effects of our colonial past (Athreya and Ackermann in press; Glantz, Chapter 2; Sussman 2014), still lingering as "west is best" (Glantz, Chapter 2; Kissel, Chapter 3). The Man the Hunter model uses foragers from colonized societies for ethnographic analogy (Athreya and Ackermann in press; Khorasani and Lee, Chapter 1). Disability was originally envisioned as a determination about whether an individual can productively work (Stodder and Byrnes, Chapter 6). Research must be published in English (Glantz, Chapter 2). And so on.

Cultural bias is inevitable, as we are humans, and we study humans. We recognize that what we are proposing may be a big lift. But many hands make the lift easier. Our hope is that an increased reflexivity of our discipline will result in deeper, richer research that moves the field further. The contributors to this volume provide examples of how to do that work. By critically examining our familiar thinking, we uphold the highest standards of science. By creatively evaluating our evidence and analytical techniques, and opening our field to new perspectives, we avoid the hegemonic pitfalls (as best as they can be avoided!). And by recognizing that our research questions, and results, do not speak to the public by themselves, we can engage with people in a meaningful way. After all, isn't that what "broader impacts" are really about? We add our voices to the rising clamor; we can do better.

References

Agarwal SC (2019) Understanding bone aging, loss, and osteoporosis in the past. In Katzenberg MA and Grauer AL, editors. *Biological Anthropology of the Human Skeleton*, 3rd edition. Wiley. Pp. 385–414.

Aiello LC (2016) Reintegrating anthropology: from inside out. *Current Anthropology* 57(S13):S1–S2.

Aiello LC (2018) Results of the non-binding name change survey. American Association of Physical Anthropologists website. www.physanth.org/news/results-non-binding-name-change-survey.

Amato KR (2016) Incorporating the gut microbiota into models of human and non-human primate ecology and evolution. *Yearbook of Physical Anthropology* 159(S61):196–215.

Athreya S and Ackermann RR (in press) Colonialism and narratives of human origins in Asia and Africa. In Matthews J and Porr M, editors. *Interrogating Human Origins: Decolonisation and the Deep Past*. Routledge.

Bortolini MCW, Silva-Junior A, De Guerra DC, et al. (1999) African-derived South American populations: a history of symmetrical and asymmetrical matings according to sex revealed by bi- and uni-parental genetic markers. *American Journal of Human Biology* 11(4):551–563.

Buckley HR and Whittle K (2008) Identifying child abuse in skeletonized subadult remains. In Oxenham M, editor. *Forensic Approaches to Death, Disaster and Abuse*. Australian Academic Press. Pp. 123–132.

Calcagno JM (2003) Keeping biological anthropology in anthropology, and anthropology in biology. *American Anthropologist* 105(1):6–15.

Caspari R (2018) Race, then and now: 1918 revisited. *American Journal of Physical Anthropology* (Special Issue: Centennial Anniversary Issue of AJPA) 165(4):924–938.

de Souza VS and Santos RV (2014) The emergence of human population genetics and narratives about the formation of the Brazilian nation (1950–1960). *Studies in History and Philosophy of Biology and Biomedical Sciences* 47(A):97–107.

DeWitte SN (2016) The anthropology of plague: insights from bioarchaeological analyses of epidemic cemeteries. *The Medieval Globe* 1(1), Article 6. http://scholarworks.wmich.edu/tmg/vol1/iss1/6.

Dingel MJ, Ostergren J, McCormick JB, Hammer R, and Koenig BA (2015) The media and behavioral genetics: alternatives coexisting with addiction genetics. *Science, Technology, and Human Values* 40(4):459–486.

Dufour DL and Piperata BA (2018) Reflections on nutrition in biological anthropology. *American Journal of Physical Anthropology* (Special Centennial Issue of AJPA) 165(4):855–864.

Edes AN and Crews DE (2017) Allostatic load and biological anthropology. *Yearbook of Physical Anthropology* 162(S63):44–70.

Edgar HJH (2009) Biohistorical approaches to "race" in the United States: biological distances among African Americans, European Americans, and their ancestors. *American Journal of Physical Anthropology* 139(1):58–67.

Edgar HJH and Hunley KL, editors (2009) Race reconciled: how biological anthropologists view human variation. *American Journal of Physical Anthropology* (Special Issue) 139(1):1–107.

Ellison PT (2017) The evolution of physical anthropology. *American Journal of Physical Anthropology* (Special Issue: Centennial Anniversary Issue of AJPA) 165(4):615–625.

Feresin E (2009) Lighter sentence for murderer with "bad genes." *Nature*. DOI:10.1038/news.2009.1050.

Flannery Sutherland JT, Moon BC, Stubbs TL, and Benton MJ (2019) Does exceptional preservation distort our view of disparity in the fossil record? *Proceedings of the Royal Society B: Biological Sciences* 286(1897):20190091.

Fuentes A (2010) The new biological anthropology: bringing Washburn's new physical anthropology into 2010 and beyond – the 2008 AAPA luncheon lecture. *Yearbook of Physical Anthropology* 53:2–12.

Fuentes A (2012) Proposal 2: humans as niche constructors, as primates and with primates – synergies for anthropology in the Anthropocene. *The Cambridge Journal of Anthropology* 30 (2):141–144.

Fuentes A (2014) The troublesome ignorance of Nicholas Wade. *Huffington Post*, July 19. www.huffingtonpost.com/agustin-fuentes/the-troublesome-ignorance-of-nicholas-wade_b_5344248.html.

Fuentes A and Weissner P (2016) Reintegrating anthropology: from inside out. *Current Anthropology* 57(S13):S3–S12.

Funk C (2017) Mixed messages about public trust in science. *Issues in Science and Technology* 34(1). www.issues.org.

Gifford-Gonzalez D (1993) You can hide, but you can't run: representations of women's work in illustrations of Palaeolithic life. *Visual Anthropology Review* 9(1):23–41.

Goodley D (2014) *Disability Studies: Theorising Disablism and Ableism*. Routledge.

Gravlee CC (2009) How race becomes biology: embodiment of social inequality. *American Journal of Physical Anthropology* 139(1):47–57.

Gravlee CC, Non AL, and Mulligan CJ (2009) Genetic ancestry, social classification, and racial inequality in blood pressure in southeastern Puerto Rico. *American Journal of Public Health* 95 (12):2191–2197.

Hicks K and Leonard WR (2014) Developmental systems and inequality: linking evolutionary and political-economic theory in biological anthropology. *Current Anthropology* 55(5):523–550.

Houldcroft CJ, Ramond J-B, Rifkin RF, and Underdown SJ (2017) Migrating microbes: what pathogens can tell us about population movements and human evolution. *Annals of Human Biology* 44(5):397–407.

Hrdlička A (1918) Physical anthropology: its scope and aims; its history and present status in America. *American Journal of Physical Anthropology* 1(2):133–182.

Hublin J-J, Abdelouahed B-N, Bailey SE, et al. (2017) New fossils from Jebel Irhoud, Morocco and the pan-African origin of *Homo sapiens*. *Nature* 546(7657):289–292.

Jackson FL, Niculescu MD, and Jackson RT (2013) Conceptual shifts needed to understand the dynamic interactions of genes, environment, epigenetics, social processes, and behavioral choices. *American Journal of Public Health* 103(S1):S33–S42.

Kuzawa CW (2010) Beyond feast–famine: brain evolution, human life history, and the metabolic syndrome. In Muehlenbein M, editor. *Human Evolutionary Biology*. Cambridge University Press. Pp. 518–527.

Kuzawa CW (2014) Why evolutionary biology is crucial for effective public health policy. *Current Anthropology* 55(5):542–543.

Latham KE and O'Daniel AJ, editors (2018) *Sociopolitics of Migrant Death and Repatriation: Perspectives from Forensic Science*. Springer.

Lock M and Nguyen V-K (2018) *An Anthropology of Biomedicine*, 2nd edition. Wiley.

Lopes Maciel LG, Ribiero Rodrigues EM, Carneiro Dos Santos NP, et al. (2011) Afro-derived Amazonian populations: inferring continental ancestry and population substructure. *Human Biology* 83(5):627–636.

Lowe WQ (2009) Understanding race: the evolution of the meaning of race in American law and the impact of DNA technology on its meaning in the future. *Albany Law Review* 72 (4):1113–1143.

Marks J (2009) *Why I Am Not a Scientist: Anthropology and Modern Knowledge*. University of California Press.

Mascie-Taylor CGN and Kryzanowska M (2017) Biological aspects of human migration and mobility. *Annals of Human Biology* 44(5):427–440.

Mohsena M, Goto R, Mascie-Taylor CGN (2015) Regional variation in maternal and childhood undernutrition in Bangladesh: evidence from demographic and health surveys. *World Health Organization South-East Asia Journal of Public Health* 4(2):139–149.

Myers S and Johns SE (in press) A life history perspective on maternal emotional investments during infancy. *Human Nature*.

Niewoehner WA (2001) Behavioral inferences from the Skhul/Qafzeh early modern human hand remains. *Proceedings of the National Academy of Sciences* 98(6):2979–2984.

Pálfi G, Dutour O, Perrin P, Sola C, and Zink A (2015) Tuberculosis in evolution. *Tuberculosis* 95: S1–S3.

Parathian HE, McLennan MR, Hill CM, Frazão-Moreira A, and Hockings KJ (2018) Breaking through disciplinary barriers: human–wildlife interactions and multispecies ethnography. *International Journal of Primatology* 39(5):749–775.

Phillips EM, Odunlami AO, and Bonham VL (2007) Mixed race: understanding difference in the genome era. *Social Forces* 86(2):795–820.

Pinker S (2011) *The Better Angels of Our Nature: Why Violence Has Declined*. Viking.

Pinker S (2018) *Enlightenment Now: The Case for Reason, Science, Humanism, and Progress*. Viking.

Ragsdale CR and Edgar HJH (2014) Cultural effects on phenetic distances among Postclassic Mexican and Southwest United States population. *International Journal of Osteoarchaeology* 26 (1):53–67.

Roseman CC (2014) Troublesome reflection: racism as the blind spot in the scientific critique of race. *Human Biology* 86(3):233–240.

Ross AH, Juarez CA, and Urbanová P (2016) Complexity of assessing migrant death place of origin. In Pilloud MA and Hefner JT, editors. *Biological Distance Analysis: Forensic and Bioarchaeological Perspectives*. Academic Press. Pp. 265–284.

Sapiens (2019) www.sapiens.org.

Schoeninger MJ, Most CA, Moore JJ, and Somerville AD (2016) Environmental variables across *Pan troglodytes* study sites correspond with the carbon, but not the nitrogen, stable isotope ratios of chimpanzee hair. *American Journal of Primatology* 78(10):1055–1069.

Shattuck EC (2018) Ecological context and human variation: applying the principles of biological anthropology to psychoneuroimmunology. In Yan Q, editor. *Psychoneuroimmunology*. Springer. Pp. 55–76.

Smithsonian Museum of Natural History (2019) What does it mean to be human? The 3D fossil collection. http://humanorigins.si.edu/evidence/3d-collection/fossil.

Stodder ALW and Palkovich AM, editors (2012) *The Bioarchaeology of Individuals*. University Press of Florida.

Stojanowski CM and Duncan WN, editors (2017) *Studies in Forensic Biohistory: Anthropological Perspectives*. Cambridge University Press.

Stone PK (2016) Biocultural perspectives on maternal mortality and obstetrical death from the past to the present. *Yearbook of Physical Anthropology* 159(S61):150–171.

Stuart-Macadem P (1995) Biocultural perspectives on breastfeeding. In Stuart-Macadem P and Dettwyler KA, editors. *Breastfeeding: Biocultural Perspectives*. Aldine de Gruyter. Pp. 1–37.

Sussman RW (2014) *The Myth of Race: The Troubling Persistence of an Unscientific Idea*. Harvard University Press.

Tomori C, Palmquist AEL, and Quinn EA, editors (2017) *Breastfeeding: New Anthropological Approaches*. Taylor and Francis.

Véran J-F (2012) Old bones, new powers. *Current Anthropology* 53(S5):S246–S255.

Wade N (2014) *A Troublesome Inheritance: Genes, Race and Human History*. Penguin Books.

Warinner C and Lewis Jr CM (2015) Microbiome and health in past and present human populations. *American Anthropologist* 117(4):740–741.

Weissner P (2016) The rift between science and humanism: what's data got to do with it? *Current Anthropology* 57(S13):S154–S166.

Willermet CM and Edgar HJH (2009) Dental morphology and ancestry in Albuquerque, NM Hispanics. *HOMO: Journal of Comparative Human Biology* 60(3):207–224.

Wolpoff MH (1999) *Paleoanthropology*. McGraw-Hill.

Zadeh LA (2015) Fuzzy logic: a personal perspective. *Fuzzy Sets and Systems* 281(2015):4–20.

Index